Questions, Beards, and Big Ideas

A Very Brief History of Human Ideas

Michael Polley

ISBN: 978-1-326-44683-3

PublishNation, London
www.publishnation.co.uk

"All are lunatics, but he who can analyze his delusion is called a philosopher"

Ambrose Bierce (1842-1914)
American Satirist

1

Time Changes Nothing but the Size of Your Underpants

"Humour is reason gone mad"
Groucho Marx (1890-1977)

Unless you have a ghost town quietly sitting where your brain should be, you will likely know that two plus two equals four. Those who paid a little more attention at school may also be able to explain the ins and outs of linear equations or the wide variety of life on our planet in terms of evolutionary processes. Those whose brains approach watermelon-sized proportions could likely also explain the workings of say the internal combustion engine, and at last count there are apparently even two or three people alive today with foreheads so large that they can even explain the magical workings of the universe (although no one else can actually understand their ideas so we can't be sure that they're not just making it all up anyway). Science and mathematics it seems provides the answers to all such things and more, our understanding limited only by our desire to learn and our grey-matter posting an IQ high enough to make sense of it.

But it seems there are also some questions that (at the time of writing at least) not even those with brains so large that they can be measured on a planetary scale are able to provide answers to, "is there really a God?", "do we have a soul?", "are we here for a reason, and if so, just what happens if we finally fulfill that reason?". These are what educated-types like to call *philosophical questions*, they are questions that we feel are important enough to ask (as a species we've been asking them ever since evolutionary advantage afforded us the luxury of spare time enough to think about such things) but where rather disappointingly all that clever science and mathematics stuff is seemingly of no use at all. There are it seems no definitive text-book, or "ask the brainy kid at the front of the class" answers to such questions, and so somewhat disappointingly we are each left to come to our own conclusions as to how to explain or answer them. Such is *philosophy*.

Maybe it's the very fact that many such philosophical questions seemingly have no clear black and white "you can't argue with that kind of logic" answers, or that the people who do try to provide answers to such questions (those we loosely term as *philosophers*) don't wear lab-coats, mix things in test-tubes, or scribble indecipherable formulae on chalkboards (all universally recognized signs that we should believe what these particular boffins are telling us), but today more than ever we see various misconceptions around just what philosophy is, and what those who label themselves as practitioners of its "dark arts" actually do all day.

Some of these common misconceptions surrounding the noble art of philosophy are that it's just one endless round of debate about meaningless ideas which have no logical conclusion or benefit to the rest of us happily sat here in the "real world". Or even that most of today's philosophers are themselves just smug pipe-smoking intellectuals who laze around all day stroking their amply bearded chins contemplating such meaningless thoughts and ideas. While philosophical thought itself is often seen as either just a collection of clever one-liners that are probably more appropriately scribbled on the walls of public toilets ("don't squat with your spurs on", "if at first you don't succeed, then sky-diving likely isn't for you", etc), or that trying to grasp its complex and often conflicting theories can be as challenging as trying to nail jelly to the ceiling. In short, philosophy is often seen as about as interesting and constructive as other people's shopping lists.

Naturally this view irritates the rather sensitive academic philosopher-types of the world (they are of course only human too) who rather see themselves as pioneers, challenging the way we see and think about the world around us, the way we are expected to behave, the way we perceive knowledge and how we use that knowledge to construct our logical views of the world. They will tell you they are at the cutting edge of knowledge, thought, logic, and ideas, radical thinkers who are here to save us all from intellectual mediocrity and blind belief in all we are told. They are travellers on a Starship Enterprise for the mind, boldly going where our minds have never gone before.

But a quick survey amongst those whose T.V's are noticeably larger than their bookcases will generally confirm that the perception of philosophers as just pseudo-intellectual types with impressively large beards and ill-fitting knitted sweaters, and philosophy itself as being just about as boring and painful as listening to someone describe the details of their gall-bladder operation is, it seems, a hard one to shake.

Of course the reality is we all think, we all ask ourselves questions, "do I really have to go to work today?", "how did my overdraft get so big?", "do these jeans make me look fat?". These are the questions we ask to help get us through our day, they have clear answers, or force us to make decisions and judgement calls (although clearly we don't always choose the correct ones, which is why we have divorce lawyers and therapists), and we ask them so we can function alongside everyone else on the daily merry-go-round of modern life without having to look too foolish, being arrested, or being forced to live in solitude in a cave high up on a mountain somewhere surrounded by joss-sticks.

But then there are also those pesky little questions that as a species we humans can clearly still eat, drink, work, sleep, poop, and just about survive without knowing the answers too, but as humans born with seemingly inquisitive minds and (varying degrees of) intellectual ability, it seems we still find ourselves asking despite having no expectation that we or anyone else can possibly find answers to them. These are the "big" questions, "Why am I here?", "Is there life after death?", "Why do pairs of socks go into a washing-machine but only single socks emerge?".

We "humans" have been asking ourselves these "big" questions ever since our brains grew large enough to operate in something other than just simple evolutionary "where's my next meal coming from" survival mode, after all it's one of the things that distinguishes us from say your goldfish, or your neighbor's cat, it's what those

3

clever bods in the white lab-coats tell us is part of what makes us "human". These are *philosophical questions*, and are the questions that philosophers over the last 3,000 years or so have dedicated significant chunks of their lives to tackling head on (while at the same time also hopefully ensuring we do indeed stay one step ahead of the goldfish and your neighbor's cat), if rather disappointingly not necessarily answering.

The first philosophers (traditionally thought to be the early Greeks but with some conflicting evidence now that the rather inscrutable peoples of China and India had already been quietly "philosophizing" for some several hundred years before the Greeks even stumbled across the magical combination of logic, sandals and beards) were thinkers who spent their waking hours daring to challenge the established explanations to such questions, explanations that the religious thought and mysticism of the day had up to that point in time provided, and that had gone seemingly unquestioned for centuries (Demitrius down the road forgot to make an offering to the Gods last week, and so obviously that's why it rained a plague of locusts yesterday). These early thinkers instead chose to apply their own reasoning and logic to search for more rational explanations for the world they saw around them and their role in it (and presumably help figure out the real reason why there was a plague of locusts yesterday before everyone runs off to stone poor Demitrius to death).

Thus, philosophy is not just about asking the question, it's really a way of thinking, debating, constructing a logical and coherent argument around a question and not just accepting what you are told. It's really about the "process of philosophizing". Indeed, many philosophical questions may well have no right or wrong answer (easy for students, tough for examiners), and philosophers themselves will often come to differing conclusions (tough for students, easy for examiners). But although sometimes not empirically provable by science and its army of lab-coat wearing eggheads, they are conclusions arrived at not by simply accepting the beliefs handed down or forced upon them by either religion, society, or their know-it-all neighbour, but rather by the philosopher's own reasoning and logic.

4

So then let's quickly recap, philosophy it seems is the art of questioning the world around us and our role in within it, all in the knowledge that there may well be no right or wrong answer, and with no expectation that whatever our conclusions may be anybody actually needs to agree with them anyway (sporting a sizable beard, wearing 1970's fashion, and smoking a pipe may also help but is by no means seen as mandatory).

Seems easy enough then, and will likely have university Under-Graduates queuing up for the next available Philosophy course down at their local seat of higher education in a vague expectation of only having to turn up for a few days each term to deliver some "thoughts" on some "important" questions, participate in a few quick debates, and then promptly line up to receive their Bachelor of Arts degree along with their membership to the Philosopher's Union. Sounds ideal, and it seems that philosophy then could easily make "boffins" of us all in no time, watermelon-sized brain or not.

But philosophers are not merely the great illusionists of the academic world, being all smoke (pipe or otherwise) and mirrors, or clever mental tricks that are ultimately meaningless outside of study halls and coffee houses. Philosophy is relevant not only in the domain of the lazy under-graduate, or the pseudo-intellectuals and new-age hippies who have "switched-on" their inner-child and are now happily skipping through flowered meadows gazing in awe at the wonder around them and asking "what's the meaning of it all?". Philosophy is not a hobby to simply occupy your time when there's nothing on the TV, or while waiting for the next big lottery draw.

Actually (and you may want to make sure your sitting down for this as it may come as something of a shock to many), philosophy, and importantly the skills that philosophy teaches, is decidedly useful. There are in fact some very clear benefits of philosophy to each and every one of us, benefits that can apply to our everyday lives and not just on those rare occasions when we pick up our thinking-pipe, settle into our favourite comfy chair and decide to gently stroke our chins for a few hours as we consider up-sizing our underpants.

The people who we trust to know about these things tell us that the study and understanding of philosophy is now recognized as developing in those willing enough to invest the time such essential skills as critical thinking, logical thought, problem solving, and helps broaden the mind by enabling a better understanding and appreciation for both your own views and those of others. It also encourages intellectual tolerance and imagination, something hopefully we can all agree would benefit us all particularly in this age of racism, religious intolerance, Boy-bands, and people who stubbornly still choose to wear spandex.

Thus it's not just for the sake of a "jolly good wheeze" that our top educators now inflict Philosophy-101 upon most medical, law, and science-based students of under-graduate courses. The skills it instils are seen as a vital ingredient in the armour of our future brain surgeons, law-makers and wannabe Stephen Hawking's. Even sharp-suited businessmen are now learning to apply similar techniques to improve negotiation skills and to help make more appropriate business decisions that are not only just about improving balance sheets, reducing the age of their next wife, or increasing the size of their next car, but are also decision that are ethically sound. Philosophy, or more accurately an understanding of how to think philosophically, does not have to be all about asking the big questions, it's not just "thinking about thinking", it can be about broadening your mind, improving your life-skills, and simply just becoming a better person.

Thus (and now prepare yourself for the second big shocker), we don't all need to have the intellect of a chess Grand-master, sit on multiple Government "think-tanks", or be able to comfortably converse in the language of universal string theories or quantum mechanics to be a philosopher. You can have an IQ on a par with a well-trained dog, maybe the closest you have come to a brain-storm is a light drizzle, or maybe your sole purpose in life may even simply to be to serve as a warning to others, but philosophy can still offer something that you can positively apply to your own personal and working life, and if you are so inclined even your spiritual well-being too.

So then, it all seems quite easy, we all just need to stop and think about things for a few minutes, rationally, logically, and with an open-mind, and in no time at all we will all be thinking as logically

6

as Mr. Spock, found solutions to all our problems, have opened our eyes to how best we ought to live our lives, determined just who we are and why we are here, and just for good measure located all those missing socks. Well, hmmm, not quite, history is unfortunately littered with philosophers who have seemingly had their own proverbial philosophical light-bulb switched-on and subsequently proposed philosophies that in the cold light of day make about as much sense as a tea-pot made out of chocolate.

Take for instance the idea of *Presentism*, first purported by *Heraclitus* in 500 B.C., which would have us believe that the only things that really exist are those that are happening right now, right this minute, and thus there is in fact no future and no past. Under this view we should all stop worrying about what we did or what we may do at some point in the future, we need only focus on what we are doing right now, nothing else matters. Seemingly then we could then all just run around doing whatever we like as there can be no consequences of our actions in a non-existent future, and no one will know what we did anyway in a non-existent past.

Or how about the idea of *ethical egoism* introduced to the world in 1874 by the philosopher *Henry Sidgwick* and which proudly declares that we all just ought to do only what is in our own best self-interest. A philosophy that effectively states that anything we do can be considered as morally right if it is done to maximize that own self-interest, regardless of how it may affect anyone or anything else. It all sounds like a philosophy we could all happily buy into (history is littered with the names of those who have already tried to live by such a "it's all about me" moral code), but I'm guessing if more widely adopted, anarchy and chaos would quickly replace Mr. Sidgwick's philosophical vision.

And then there is the somewhat confusing theory of *Solipsism*, a philosophical theory first introduced by the early Greek philosopher *Gorgias* around 400 B.C. which states that every individual cannot be sure of anything at all other than that they themselves exist, and so by extension that they are the only thing that does actually exist. In other words, *solipsism* expresses the idea that you should believe that you are the only real thing in the world, and everything and everyone else is possibly just a mere illusion and thus not to be trusted. Clearly

7

the ultimate theory for the egomaniac but one likely to lead to a somewhat lonely and isolated existence.

Clearly then it seems that even philosophers could benefit from something of a built-in, shock-proof crap detector the same as the rest of us, and similarly not all philosophers are bearded peaceful tree-hugging gurus whose every sage-like utterance helps lead us all gently down a path to ultimate wisdom, quite from it. Philosophers themselves can also sometimes be as "eccentric" as some of the theories they have proposed. For every *Socrates, Aristotle,* or *Emmanuel Kant,* there are many others who fell somewhat short of philosophical greatness. Many a great man was first thought to be insane before he went on to change the world, but of course most never did go on to change the world, and thus proved themselves to just be insane and merely legends in their own lunchtime, and in this respect philosophy is no different.

The ancient Greek philosopher *Diogenes* apparently chose to live in a small barrel, urinated on people who annoyed him, defecated in public, and thus clearly was, at least in some part, a few bricks short of an amphitheatre. *Rene Descartes,* who gave us possibly philosophy's most famous one-liner, "I think, therefore I am", and who put reason above any other source of knowledge, something that later became known in more light-hearted philosophical circles as "putting the Descartes before the source" (even philosophers it seems can have a sense of humour) was an over-sensitive recluse who strangely preferred to sit and do his thinking in a large bread oven (presumably it was either off, or at least set to low, at the time). *Karl Marx* came from a wealthy background but chose to live like a pauper and was seen as merely arrogant on a good day but decidedly belligerent the rest of the time, while *Georg Hegel* (considered to be a philosophical giant by those who measure such things) was a man almost as complex as algebra and quite honestly just way out there in his own "Hegelian" world, but in his defence maybe this was just in response to the fact that in the real world he was German.

However, the purpose of this book is not to act simply as an historical account of philosophers and their ideas (eccentric or otherwise), nor is the intention for it to find its place on the reading list of 1st year philosophy students, or in any way be a work of academic reference. It assumes that when your General Studies teacher offered the sage-like instruction to "take notes from Chapter 3" so he could pop out for a quick cigarette, you likely preferred to test the rather bold claim emblazoned on your "shatterproof" ruler, and thus know little or nothing of philosophy or its history.

The book's only purpose is to try and inspire a little "philosophical navel-gazing" that the reader may then apply to their own day to day lives, and maybe along the way rekindle a little of that sense of wonder in the world around us, and maybe reignite a little of their own "inner philosopher".

Most introductory books on philosophy (and this one it seems turns out to be no exception) rather strangely will usually start by first trying to answer the question "just what is philosophy?", as if the author expects that the reader may well have picked up the book by mistake expecting maybe an oddly titled murder mystery. Maybe this approach has consigned many such books straight to the alternative role as a rather high-brow door-stop after just a handful of pages, although understanding that philosophy is all about asking questions maybe this is not such a strange place to start after all.

Strangely, trying to answer the question "what is philosophy?" has itself grown into its own complete field of study, known as *meta-philosophy*, all leading to the rather peculiar situation in that such "meta-philosophers" are probably the only people in the world whose chosen profession is actually all about trying to understand just what their profession is.

Now, simply outlining a brief history of philosophy clearly is not in itself philosophy (nor does it automatically make the reader a fully paid-up member of the philosopher's union), but strangely philosophy is often taught by reviewing its history, primarily because philosophical methods of reasoning do not unfortunately breakdown into simple step by step skills and directions that are easily taught through practice and memorizing facts. Unfortunately, philosophy is not just ask question A, follow steps 1 through 9, stand up, touch your toes, then spin around three times and your clear and definitive answer will miraculously pop out fully formed on the other side. Although we can't be certain, it's a fairly safe bet that the truth behind life, the universe, and everything, will not be a simple number or an object such as 47 or a banana.

Philosophy, or more appropriately the art of "philosophizing", is best learnt through example and experience, and thus by studying the great philosophers of the past we can hopefully learn a little something from their presumably lofty example.

Of course you can't become a great philosopher by just reading what others have previously thought or done, just in the same way as reading a biography of JFK, memorizing a few clever one-liners by Groucho Marx, or watching Spiderman movies, will not automatically make you either a politician who gets to date movie stars, a comedian, or a web-spinning superhero. But by studying the philosophers of the past who have presumably already spilled a great deal of philosophical ink over these things already, we hopefully find a source of techniques, arguments, and opinions that we can conveniently tap into, learn by their example, and since we see rows of books dedicated to their works in our local libraries and book stores, we have to presume they are something worth investing at least a little of our time in.

Philosophy then is not a body of knowledge or a list of facts that need to be learnt, (you can't look up whether God exists, or if there is life after death in any encyclopaedia), it is a technique, a skill, one that hopefully allows the budding philosopher to approach problem solving with an open mind, and allows him (or her) to see and understand the world in different ways. Ways that hopefully allows them to live and act a little better (a little less Jack the Ripper and a little more Dalai Lama), respect a little more the opinions and perspectives of others, and ultimately help them to achieve their goals.

As for answering those "big" questions, maybe some yet to be born Einstein-like prodigy with a large enough forehead and a beard approaching fire-side rug proportions will stumble upon the undisputable answer to life, the universe and everything, all in some glorious "eureka" moment. Hopefully it will be some simple obvious truth that explains the meaning of it all in a way we can all understand, maybe it will in fact turn out to be 47, or even a banana. Maybe the answer is already out there scrawled on the walls of a public toilet somewhere just waiting for someone to recognize its significance, or maybe, as many believe, the dolphins already know the meaning of it all but don't know how to (or simply don't want to) tell us humans.

In the end we've all made decisions that probably would have benefited from just a little more thought (that Mohawk haircut, that "joke" tattoo, that ill-advised remark made to your boss at the Staff Christmas party), and we can certainly all do with a little extra help to safely navigate through our daily lives. However, I'm certainly not suggesting that what follows will provide any answers or "light-bulb" moments for anyone, but hopefully the following brief, maybe even sometimes factually dubious sprint through philosophy's varied history, may offer some insight into what some presumably rather clever bods have "thought" before, and thus maybe encourage just a little more "thought" amongst the rest of us who may not all have such lofty philosophical goals or intellect, but nonetheless still have questions, problems to solve, decisions to make, and socks to find, that all still need answers and direction all the same.

At the end of the day if some ancient Greek with a long beard and sandals, or some 17th century renaissance-man who believes we're all just an illusion, or even some angst-ridden pipe-smoking intellectual wearing a sweater his Mom knitted for him can possibly help provide some direction, sure I'll take it.

2

It's All Just Hot Air

"The most difficult thing in life is to know yourself"
Thales (c. 624-546 B.C.)

Brainy bods, who we assume have something other than tumbleweed blowing between their ears, reliably inform us that the history of philosophy in the Western world began with some rather clever Greeks sometime around 600 B.C. Now this certainly doesn't mean that up to that point in time the great civilizations that had gone before such as the Egyptians or the Sumerians were in any way less intelligent or just didn't bother to question the world around them (the pyramids on their own would seem to indicate that at least some Egyptians possessed something of an above average intellect). However those early Greek thinkers did something that those who had previously sat scratching their heads over the "big" questions had (as far as we know) seemingly not bothered themselves with.

It is in the writings of those early Greeks that we start to see demonstrated a focus on reasoned argument for their theories rather than the rigid assertions of earlier "great" minds that were clearly influenced by their religious and mythological beliefs. It is this rejection of religious and mythological explanations for the world around them for theories based purely on reasoned thinking and logic that marked these early Greeks as the first true "philosophers".

Actually, pretty much from the time of Fred Flintstone right up until the point when those early Greeks started to stroke their chins in philosophical thought, it seems that the good people of the world had sought answers to just about all their questions regarding "life, the universe and everything" in tales of mystical serpents and monsters, feuding Gods, galactic-sized heroes and villains, and countless other legends, religions and myths, all of which had about as much basis in truth as a politician's election pledge. In fact a quick headcount at any Sunday church service or Mosque at daily morning prayers will indicate that such beliefs to some extent still continue to this day.

Such supernatural explanations were handed down from generation to generation, and conveniently provided people with neatly packaged (if somewhat dubious) explanations for all the natural phenomena, creative forces and events that they saw as beyond their control such as lightning, earthquakes, the beginning of the universe, how the world was formed, the creation of man, how good and evil came to be, and why sandals were apparently the only acceptable footwear for the grown men of the day.

In this respect the Greeks were no different to every other civilization up to that time, (or indeed many of the civilizations that followed), the names (and the number) of the Gods may have been different and the myths surrounding those Gods may have varied, but ultimately they all offered conveniently packaged mythological and religious explanations for the world people saw around them. It was these mythological explanations that those early Greek philosophers started to see as maybe just a little too heavy on the "myth" and not enough on the "logical" and so feeling they were probably not to be trusted as true explanations they sought their own rational answers.

Now the ancient Greeks were not a people to shy away from excess and their religious beliefs were no exception. Not content with just one or two Gods they worshipped at least twelve such lofty individuals led by Chairman of the Board, Zeus, all of whom had apparently setup home on Mt. Olympus (in a kind of commune for immortals). These "Premier league" deities were joined by seemingly hundreds of other minor Gods (it seems there was no facet of Greek life that was not "protected" by at least one God, there were Gods for food, wine, sex, day, night, and even of all things pottery), and the myths and legends that surrounded these Gods played an integral part of their society, domestic affairs, and civic organization.

The Gods were thought to be immortal (a basic requirement for a God it seems, although the myths surrounding them often demonstrated that they too were not immune from that rather more human characteristic of bickering and fighting amongst themselves) and most importantly to our story they apparently controlled all the natural and social forces that the determined people lives. They wielded their power it seems either on a whim (presumably on a slow day atop Mt. Olympus), because someone or something had upset them, or presumably simply just because, as Gods, they could.

Greeks also worshipped Oracles (fellow mortals apparently endowed with mystical super-powers but who rather inconveniently were generally only to be found sat alone and aloof on top of a remote and inaccessible mountain somewhere), who offered those lucky enough to be granted an audience some supposedly sage-like guidance and advise on all aspects of life. Such Oracles held the power to foresee a person's fate, and were also seen as a means to seek the will of the Gods, (a kind of well connected fortune-teller) and as such Oracles often controlled many decisions around peace, war, crime and punishment, as Greeks sought the direction of the Gods through their divine "hotline". If you were planning to go to war it would make sense to first see what your Gods felt about the idea first.

Gradually though, out of this mythological picture of the world guided by Gods and Oracles a small number of free-thinking Greeks decided to put their sizable brains to good use and started to question the mythological explanations of how the natural world and its forces were created and controlled. They started to look for their own answers, ones based on experience and reason, one based on "natural" rather than "supernatural" explanations. Not unsurprisingly then, these early Greek philosophers are sometimes referred to as the *natural philosophers.*

The first of these *natural philosophers* that we are aware of is *Thales*, who was born around 624 B.C. and who lived in the Greek colony of Miletus on the coast of what is today Turkey. In all honesty we don't know much more than that about Thales for sure, but he was still being referenced over two centuries later by none other than *Aristotle* and so we should at least respect his reputation.

Thales apparently marvelled at how the world around him was in a constant state of change. Plants grew from seeds that flowered which then eventually withered and died, mountains grew and were eroded, and chickens emerged from eggs (apparently the question around which of these actually came first was not one that had yet crossed the minds of these first philosophers) tried to fly but settled for just laying more eggs then died and ended up in Greek cooking pots, all in a seemingly endless state of transformation.

But in the face of all this constant transformation *Thales* believed that there must be a single basic substance that was at the root of all this change, a "something" that all things came from and returned to. Thales was looking for a rational explanation for the change he saw around him, for the physical world he experienced, thunder, the seasons, the cycles of life, eggs to chickens to Greek kebabs, but he wanted to do so without having to resort to the ancient myths and religious beliefs that for him just didn't stand up to any rational examination.

This idea that everything in the universe can be reduced to a single substance is what the bright-sparks of today call *monism*, and in searching for this fundamental material *Thales* not unreasonably deduced that it must be something out of which everything else can be formed, it must be essential to all life, and to be capable of change it must also be capable of motion. For *Thales* this line of reasoning led him to the conclusion that it was only water that seemed to tick all the right boxes, it was clearly necessary for all forms of life, the rivers and oceans showed it was capable of motion, while its ability to exist as solid, liquid and vapour showed it was more than capable of change. Thus for *Thales*, water seemed the only logical candidate to be this fundamental substance of the universe, and thus he concluded that at the very basic level everything in the universe was therefore fundamentally just water in varying stages of transformation.

Now today *Thales'* conclusion may seem a little naïve (although in fairness we are reliably informed by the clever science-bods that the human body along with most other animals and plant-life is actually made up of around 60% water, a fact which itself then raises the interesting question of why then don't we all just evaporate on a hot summers day?), but it's not necessarily *Thales'* conclusion that is important to our story, it is his first known use of deductive reasoning to find rational answers to such fundamental questions that should start to excite our own inner philosopher. Indeed with this first step *Thales* appears to be responsible for the key shift in the way academics started to view the world. Philosophical thought, and indeed all future scientific thought, can probably be traced back to this key moment in history some 2,600 years ago somewhere on the coast of Turkey.

Students of *Thales*, collectively known today as the *Milesian philosophers*, followed his lead, but for some their own deductive reasoning led them to somewhat differing conclusions as to the explanation for the constant transformation of the world they saw around them. *Anaximander* who was born around 610 B.C. believed that rather than water, the single basic substance from which everything evolved had to be something somewhat more "infinite and eternal" which clearly could not be something as ordinary or mundane as any known substance such as water. Although he clearly would have had difficulty explaining to his fellow philosophers exactly just what this unknown "infinite and eternal" substance was, he was clearly very excited about it, excited enough to give it a name, *apeiron* (the infinite or indefinite).

While *Anaximenes*, born around 580 B.C. also searched for this basic substance of the universe but his own reasoning led him to believe that it must be air, believing as he did that water itself was just condensed air, and so when presumably condensed even more air would presumably and quite miraculously go on to become earth, rock, plants, and every other object, species, and "thing" in the universe.

These *Milesian philosophers,* although disagreeing as to exactly "what" this universal single substance was, were all *monists*, all believing in the existence of a single basic substance that was the fundamental source of all things. Now however crazy and naive their conclusions seem to be to us today we must remember they had no scientific instruments with which to measure or test their theories, no handy-dandy calculators or microscopes, they had little understanding of the laws of physics, or really anything other than their ample beards, their sandals, and their own intellect and deductive reasoning with which to both question and seek answers to the world around them.

Thus, despite some rather dubious conclusions, with these first *natural philosophers* we see both philosophy itself and the initial fledgling steps of what was to later become the natural sciences (physic, biology, chemistry) were now firmly out of the their Greek starting blocks. Philosophy's history had officially begun, albeit seemingly driven by water, air, or something apparently "infinite and eternal" that they could not quite put their finger on.

3

Nothing Comes From Nothing

"One cannot step twice in the same river"
Heraclitus (c. 540-480 B.C.)

There are three basic things you need to know about the early Greeks. Firstly, they loved a good beard, secondly they loved their sports particularly wrestling, and for reasons best known to themselves wrestling naked, and most importantly they loved to debate about everything (fortunately the idea of "naked debating" never really caught on otherwise philosophy itself may have taken a whole different path).

Thus, for those early Greek philosophers their new found approach of sustained chin-stroking and logical thinking to help unravel the mysteries of the universe was clearly never going to be just plain sailing with just the odd little difference of opinion over air and water to deal with. Not unsurprisingly then around 500 B.C. two philosophers arrived on the scene whose own reasoning about the nature of the universe around them seemed to lead them to fundamentally very different and contradictory conclusions.

Parmenides was from the Greek colony of Elea in Southern Italy, and who presumably through an extended period of quiet contemplation and navel gazing had quite logically come to the conclusion that if something "exists" it cannot also "not exist" and vice-versa (obvious really). With some further slightly more advanced navel gazing he concluded that by extension then a state of "nothing" (where everything does "not exist") cannot therefore also "exist".

Not wanting to stop there *Parmenides* then took this logical line of thinking a step further by deducing that if "nothing" cannot then "exist" clearly then "something" cannot come from "nothing", and so to *Parmenides* everything that does "exist" always must have existed (confusing I know, but hang in there). Further, he concluded that everything that "exists" must exist in a permanent form, which itself clearly cannot change either as something that is permanent cannot change into something else without first ceasing to be permanent.

And so out of this little mind-twisting voyage of logical progressions *Parmenides* finally concluded that logically fundamental change is therefore impossible. *Parmenides* had (via what seems a rather confusing and convoluted path) arrived at the somewhat controversial conclusion that everything that is real must be permanent and unchanging, as clearly nothing can come from nothing given that a state of nothing cannot exist in the first place.

Now this clearly gave *Parmenides* a bit of a problem as he could see with his own eyes that the world around him was very clearly in a state of constant change (chickens, eggs, etc), but he could not reconcile what his senses were telling him (that everything changed), with what his navel-gazing and logical reasoning had told him (that nothing can change). Clearly there was a rather glaring flaw somewhere here, this contradiction between the senses and reason likely gave poor *Parmenides* more sleepless nights than Lady Macbeth until eventually we see him make what was probably mankind's first philosophical leap of faith. Eventually forced (likely due to his need to eventually get a good night's sleep) to choose between what his senses were telling him and what his reason told him, *Parmenides* chose reason (something that today's bearded intellectuals call *rationalism*).

But then around the same time, and in stark contrast to our sleep deprived *rationalist Parmenides,* we find another Greek, *Heraclitus* (he of the dubious notion of *presentism*), who believed that it is actually constant change that is the basic characteristic of the universe. Clearly he could not have been more at odds with the ideas of *Parmenides* if he tried.

Heraclitus had come to his conclusions by taking a somewhat different slant on nature and the world around him. Where other early philosophers had looked for scientific explanations for the universe through a single universal substance such as water or air,

Heraclitus envisaged the universe as driven not by any such fundamental substance but rather by a *process*.

Heraclitus saw the universe as governed by what he called *logos* (which to those of us not versed in ancient Greek we and can take to mean *"reason"*), and it is *logos* which provide a kind of cosmic law by which all things come into being and are held in balance, and thus create a unity, a "oneness" in the universe.

Heraclitus believed that this universal balance was actually a balancing of opposites, hot and cold, war and peace, love and hate, spandex and fashion, and that such balancing of opposites naturally results in a state of constant tension between the two opposites, and because of this tension everything must always be in a state of change. To *Heraclitus* then the universe is a place of constant struggle and tension between opposing forces striving to maintain a form of balance (not unlike the dynamic that we would see behind the closed doors of any family home) and one which naturally results in a state of constant change. *Heraclitus* famously used the example of stepping into a river stating "one cannot step twice in the same river", meaning that when you step into the waters a second time the water in the river has already moved on, it has to all intents and purposes changed.

And thus, *Heraclitus* saw the universe not as fixed an unchanging but rather as in a state of constant flux, and thus rather inconveniently at complete odds with *Parmenides*, with one seemingly ignoring his senses and trusting only his reason and the other seeing a universal "balancing act" based only on what his senses were telling him, and thus resulting in a rather confusing state of affairs for the good philosophers of the time.

Subsequent thinkers tried to inject something of a reconciliatory approach to the current philosophical thinking by proposing ideas that seemed to some extent at least to try and reconcile these conflicting views. Primary amongst these was *Empedocles* from Sicily who around 450 B.C. proposed that it was not one single substance that was the source of all things but rather four substances, earth, air, fire, and water, and it is the infinite combination of these fixed elements in varying proportions which results in our universe. In this way we see that the universe is fixed and unchanging through four basic substances, and as these elements come together to form say an elephant, they then separate and disperse again when the poor elephant dies, and once separated they then go on to help form something else (possibly similar, say your mother-in-law), and it is in this constant coming together and separating of the four elements that we also witness the constantly changing world around us.

It seemed like a compromise worthy of any United Nations negotiator and one that would presumably satisfy all, however, even *Empedocles'* valiant attempt still seemed somewhat unsatisfactory to many. For a start it was not easy to see how a creature as complex as a living, breathing, 2 tonne mammal with an unfeasibly large nose and ears (elephant or mother-in-law) could possibly be constructed of just fire, water, earth and air. Presumably the arguments and confusion over the nature of the universe remained until around 390 B.C. when we see another presumably rather smart *natural philosopher* named *Democritus* arrive on the scene and attempt to enlighten the ancient Greek world with his own ideas on the matter.

For his part *Democritus* also believed that the universe was indeed made of just one fundamental substance, but rather than try to attribute any known substance such as water or fire as the "key" substance of the universe which as we have already seen clearly was never going to hold up to any real scrutiny, he suggested that everything was actually made of tiny, indivisible particles which themselves were eternal and unchangeable, and which he named *atoms* from the Greek meaning "un-cuttable".

Now unlike fire or water which were substances that people could at least get their heads around, these atoms proposed by *Democritus* were distinctly unfamiliar. If they did exist at all the technology of the day still had a thousand years or so of major advances to go before anyone might be able to prove their existence let alone be able to see them, but nonetheless *Democritus* saw his tiny atoms as the only logical and reasoned explanation and so set about trying to convince his fellow Ancient Greeks of the validity of his theory.

For his theory to hold true *Democritus* believed his atoms (his building blocks of the universe) should not themselves be able to be broken down into any smaller fractions (otherwise everything would rather inconveniently just dissolve away), and since it had already been established (logically at least) by our friend *Parmenides* that nothing can come from nothing these atoms must also be eternal, and furthermore there must also be an infinite number of them to enable them to build something as vast as the universe and all it holds (including a 2 tonne elephant-cum-Mother-in-law).

However *Democritus* also declared that the number of different combinations that these atoms could arrange themselves into was actually finite, which conveniently helped explain why we see generation after generation of elephants and crocodiles, but never random instances of say *"Crocophants"*, which is good as the last think we need is 2 tonne killing machines just randomly appearing in our lakes and rivers. But although infinite in number these atoms themselves were also not all the same (else everything in the universe would all just look the same, boring, and not ideal), thus according to *Democritus* some were round, some flat, some jagged, some smooth, some rough, and every combination in between.

Democritus further claimed that an empty space (a void) separated these atoms which allowed them to flow freely around the universe where they would collide with each other and join together and due to their variety eventually combine to form all the wondrous and varied things we see around us, trees, planets, stars, mountains, books, elephants, you, and me, even your mother-in-law. *Democritus* also believed that as things die they do not just decay, rather the atoms were just released back into the void ready to recombine as something new, in a kind of perpetual process of birth, death and rebirth.

Under such a theory every atom in your own body would thus have presumably already spent time forming part of say a tree, a T-Rex, or a pot-plant, and would continue to help form any number of the huge variety of things we see in the universe long after your death (if true, that chair your sitting on may well contain a few atoms of one of your long departed ancestors, so think carefully before you consider passing wind on the upholstery). In such a way we can see how the world around us is constantly "changing" as the "unchangeable" atoms constantly move and form new objects.

Democritus' atom theory is known to today's boffins as *atomism* and offered the first complete view of the universe and its mechanics outside of any God-like or supernatural intervention, and has since proved to be remarkably close to the atomic theories developed some 2,000 years or so later by some overly brainy-types with large foreheads and lab-coats. Quite a feat for someone who had no access to any scientific instrumentation and merely the power of his own reason with which to come up with such a theory long before scientists such as John Dalton, Max Planck or Albert Einstein would indeed prove the existence of such *atoms* with the help of some rather clever technology, chalk-boards, and much interim scientific progress.

However, while these *natural philosophers* padded around various parts of Greece agonizing over the nature of the universe and why there was a plague of locusts last week, another slightly more shady (but no less important) group of bearded Greek individuals were forming amongst the cobbled streets of Athens, and who were collectively known as *Sophists* being named after the Greek word *sophia* meaning "wisdom" and thus denoting individuals perceived as wise and informed (not least it seems by themselves).

By the time the world had edged towards around 450 B.C. Athens had evolved into the cultural and political centre of the Greek world which was now organized into city-states that were highly ordered with a mature democracy, established legal system, and courts of law ready and waiting to settle legal disputes or to dish out appropriate punishments to citizens who chose to forget, ignore, or flaunt the laws of the day.

Anyone that appeared in court was expected to plead their own case and so being able to build and articulate your own defence or argument in support of a dispute quite understandably became something of an essential skill in Athens. Thus Greeks put great stock in mastering the arts of oratory and rhetoric, and as such teachers and philosophers from all over Greece who understood the law, were able to build persuasive arguments, could lecture in rhetoric, or could merely argue the hind legs off a donkey, all flocked to Athens in their droves to earn a living as advisors to the good (or in the case of those forced to appear in court, presumably not so good) citizens of Athens.

While as we have seen the *natural philosophers* spent many sleepless nights agonizing over the natural world, its changing or constant state, and whether water, fire, air, or some small little units of "something" were responsible for all we see around us, the *sophists* saw this as something of a pointless exercise (probably because there was no money in it), and so they focused purely on what they saw as the very practical (and far more lucrative) issues of man and his place in society, the lines between right and wrong, human behaviour, and applying such thinking to their chosen day-job.

Now many *natural philosophers* of the time saw the *Sophists* as nothing more than rhetoricians whose aim in an argument was not the noble goal of seeking the truth but rather merely to win the argument (and so get paid), and thus history has collectively painted them as philosophical mercenaries interested more in gold coin than the truth (the parallels with modern-day lawyers is hard to miss). However, this may be a slightly harsh view, firstly everyone has to pay the rent, and secondly (and more importantly) many so-called *sophists* did provide significant insights and steps towards our understanding in the field of *ethics*. One such *sophist* was *Protagoras*.

Protagoras lectured in law and rhetoric in Athens while also "double-hatting" as the chief advisor to the rulers of the city-state, but he also recognized many of the true philosophical implications of what he taught. He saw that by definition every argument or dispute has two sides, with both sides strongly believing the validity of their case (no real shock there), and that often such disagreements are settled not by the ultimate validity of one case over the other but rather by the skills and persuasiveness of one individual over the other.

Protagoras thus began to form the view that belief itself is subjective and relative to the individual (what is seen as true for one man may not be true for another) and the merit of the truth is based purely upon the individuals own needs and circumstances. What you or I may believe is a day cold enough to put fingers and toes at risk an Eskimo may believe to be positively balmy, both beliefs although

24

seemingly contradictory are in fact true when taken in the context of the individual.

This led *Protagoras* to famously declare that "man is the measure of all things", and by which he means that belief is subjective and relative, something is right or wrong, ethical or criminal, only because an individual (or a society as a whole) deems it to be. Of course just because a conveniently passing Eskimo happens to convince you it is indeed "a positively balmy day" it doesn't mean that you still won't lose your fingers and toes (and likely other slightly more delicate appendages) if you subsequently decide to stroll around in just your beach-wear. But, in this way *Protagoras* ultimately rejected the existence or validity of any absolute definitions of truth, justice, moral values, or ethical behaviour, which could be deemed as applicable to all. What is morally right or just for one person may well be just plain wrong for another.

This belief (or rather the teaching of this belief) that there can be no absolute or universal norms for right or wrong (and thus clearly there can be no ethical or moral laws that could be applied to everyone) clearly made *Protagoras* something of a thorn in the side of the Greek hierarchy whose role it was to uphold the established legal and democratic system of the day. Ultimately *Protagoras* was tried for impiety and his books publically burned (probably the ultimate humiliation for a philosopher), although we must assume that regardless of whatever "absolute" truth he was ultimately found guilty of he continued to argue his own "relative" innocence even as his books burned. Regardless of how history paints the *Sophists* (somewhere between Shylock and Henry Kissinger) they did succeed (whether intentionally or not) in bringing the world of human behaviour and ethics into the realms of philosophical discussion.

Now *Protagoras* and the *Sophists* (coincidentally not a bad name for an early Greek Jazz band), may have rejected the existence of any absolute definitions for ethical behaviour or what is right or wrong, but the world was about to be introduced to someone who would take a somewhat different view, someone who would have a profound influence on Western thinking, and who history would go on to paint as one of the giants of philosophy. The good people of Athens were about to be introduced to *Socrates*.

4

I Know Nothing.... honestly

"The unexamined life is not worth living"
Socrates (c. 470-399 B.C.)

Socrates we are told was a classical Greek philosopher who lived in the 5th century B.C. and whose contributions to the study of ethics and moral philosophy have seen him crowned by many of today's pipe-smoking intellectuals (who presumably know a thing or two about these things) as one of the founders of Western philosophy and leading figurehead of many of its central themes. His influence is seen by those same intellectuals as so great that all philosophers before *Socrates* are known collectively as *pre-Socratic*, in fact the name *Socrates* has become almost universally synonymous with the wise and enlightened. His skills as a rhetorician were supposedly so masterly that he could give half-time pep-talks to two competing teams so compelling that both sides would go on to win. Even the philosophical philistines of the world whose best guess would probably be that *Friedrich Nietzsche* was a German soccer player, will still likely know the name *Socrates*.

However, there is a small issue with *Socrates*, something the academic-bods call the "Socratic problem", and the problem is a somewhat fundamental one. The problem with *Socrates* is that no one really knows whether he actually existed or not. There seems to be no proof that *Socrates* ever wrote down anything of his philosophy or established any school, and whatever it is we do know of him, either about his life or his work, we know only from the writing of his "students", and even those writings are written in a somewhat "artistic" style rather than as straightforward historical accounts, and so call into question whether their tales of *Socrates* and his teachings are indeed fact or they are merely using a fictional character (one they seemingly collectively agreed to name "Socrates") as a means to explain their own philosophies and so rather embarrassingly rendering *Socrates*, deemed to be probably one of the greatest philosophers of all time, as a mere artistic gimmick.

However given that these accounts of *Socrates* and his teachings are by such notable and respected ancient Greek citizens as *Plato, Aristotle, Xenophon*, and *Aristophanes* (2 philosophers, an historian, and a playwright, all of whom we know for sure did indeed grace our rocky planet) he is generally assumed to be something more than just a philosophical invention, and so (despite the lack of any real evidence) he should be rightly counted amongst the living population of early Greece.

So then assuming the premise that *Socrates* did indeed grace Athens for much of the 5th century B.C. we can start to pull together a picture of the man himself and his life. From portraits and busts it seems fairly clear that *Socrates* was not the best looking man around town with indications being that he was short and round with bulging eyes, and with a nose that looked like it was put together by Picasso, (certainly not the looks generally expected of your average classical Greek hero).

Through the writings of his contemporaries *Socrates* is believed to have been born in Athens around 469 B.C. the son of a stonemason and a midwife, who went on to distinguish himself in the Athenian military before returning to Athens where he studied *natural philosophy* like most Greek thinkers before him, and paid the bills by becoming involved in Athenian politics. However, on the death of his stonemason father (who it turns out must have been quite adept at his chosen craft) he was suddenly financially independent and thus free to follow his true interests which were around the nature of justice, ethics, morality, and knowledge.

From this point on *Socrates* seems to have spent his life wandering around the cobbled streets of Athens randomly involving himself in philosophical discussions with its good citizens. Now most of what we know about *Socrates* and his philosophy comes to us from the writings of *Plato*, a pupil of his who himself also went on to become something of a legend in the world of philosophy, and which records many of these philosophical discussions *Socrates*

27

supposedly had with the Athenians of the day. Now again we cannot be sure whether *Plato* is truly recounting the words and discussions of *Socrates,* or if it is actually his own philosophy that he is putting into the mouth of *Socrates* in such dialogues, but it is the portrait of *Socrates* and the teachings it communicates that *Plato* paints that is important in terms of Western philosophy rather than any proof of either his or the dialogues actual existence. It is thanks to these works, these dialogues, which include the *Apology, Phaedo,* and the *Symposium,* that the ideas, thoughts and methods of *Socrates* have survived at all.

Interestingly, what we see in theses dialogues of *Socrates* is that he was not actually trying to directly teach anyone anything (something of a first for a philosopher), he was not seeking answers or explanations for himself (another first), rather he seems to use these dialogues to try to help others see the weaknesses in their own arguments, opinions, and knowledge, helping them to evaluate and reassess them, and thus help lead them to find answers, and clearer understanding and insight for themselves.

Socrates was not interested in winning arguments or helping others to win their arguments (not a *sophist* then), he demanded no payment for his services (further evidence of his "anti-sophist" leanings, although as we have seen thanks to his father he was not short of a drachma or two anyway), he simply sought to help others gain their own insight to the answers they sought, for he believed that true understanding can only come from within, it cannot be simply taught by someone else. *Socrates* then saw himself not as a teacher but as a guide (a kind of Greek philosophical "Sat-Nav") helping others to find their way and thus helping them to "teach themselves" in a kind of DIY-philosophy approach for early Greeks.

Socrates sought to examine the basic ideas and logic we apply ourselves, and in doing so look to help others to gain a better understanding of what is good and evil, right and wrong, and what is ethical and moral behaviour. *Socrates* believed that only in the examination of our own lives can we each hope to understand philosophical truths, and that the answers to these truths lay in our own innate reason, he only looked to help guide that reasoning.

Now this approach clearly means that an individual seeking philosophical enlightenment would have to put in some effort themselves and use their own reasoning to come to their own conclusions (*Socrates* was not just going to provide the answers on a conveniently printed handout for any passer-by who appeared interested), but it is this understanding of who we are, what we are, and how we should live that *Socrates* believed to be the real task of philosophy, and he felt it his duty to help others to achieve that understanding. *Socrates* apparently likened his role to that of his midwife mother, except he helped others to give "birth" to ideas rather than screaming newborn Greeks demanding their first pair of sandals.

And it is *Socrates* techniques, his approach to asking questions, driving a conversation as a means to ultimately guide someone to this understanding which was his true gift to philosophy. Today this method of dialogue between opposing views is known to the world as the *Socratic Method*. *Socrates* would generally start such dialogues from a position of knowing nothing about the subject or problem to be solved (or more accurately pretend to know nothing, itself known today as *Socratic irony*), and then merely ask simple questions to help tease out and understand a person's underlying beliefs, the extent of their knowledge, and examine the validity of such beliefs such that weaknesses would be exposed and hypothesis eliminated and new ones proposed. All this teasing and feigned ignorance hopefully lead participants to the answer being sought, or at the very least a better more rounded understanding of the point at hand.

In this way people were forced to face their own ignorance or misunderstandings around the meaning of essential concepts that we use every day to formulate our view of the world and how we should behave in it. But as you can imagine this very public method of ruthlessly questioning people's beliefs about themselves, sometimes even openly humiliating them as the weaknesses in their arguments and beliefs are exposed, did not often earn *Socrates* too many friends or brownie-points amongst the Athenian elite.

As a rule people don't generally like to be made to look a fool or be exposed as being not quite as bright as they tried to portray, (especially by a short, fat, ugly man who pretends to know nothing) but *Socrates* was nothing if not committed to his task, to him peace of mind was not to be found in living comfortably within the moral codes of society or chasing high office or even material wealth, it could only be achieved as a result of "doing the right thing" something that for him can only be determined by rigorous self-examination by the individual themselves.

Socrates believed that we only do wrong because we don't know or understand any better, and thus the right insight would lead to the right action and thus to a more "virtuous" man (or woman). For *Socrates*, the understanding between what is right and what is wrong was to be found as a result of someone's own reasoning, not as set down by others or by society.

Thus *Socrates* believed that there was only one real "good" and that was knowledge, while the only true "evil" was ignorance, and thus it is our level of understanding (our knowledge) that creates who we are, good, evil, or somewhere in between one and the other. For *Socrates* it was an imperative that we all constantly examine our lives to search for truth and understanding, and it is this constant effort of examination, this gaining of "self-knowledge" that is the ultimate goal in life and to *Socrates* the very reason why we exist.

For *Socrates* then, it seems no one actually "wants" to do evil things or intentionally act the bad guy or scoundrel, they merely do so purely as a result of their own ignorance. Now from this premise we must assume that poor old Attila the Hun, Vlad the Impaler, and Jack the Ripper, must have merely been the victims of their own poor education as clearly a more "knowledgeable" Attila, Vlad, or Jack, would have "known" that rape, murder, dismemberment, and pillaging, are all clearly not the behaviours of a positive role model, and thus performing such acts would thus be against their better judgement (against their conscience), and in the knowledge that it's only through a clear conscience that we will achieve real happiness why would anyone (even the most deranged of serial killers) perform evil acts if it would clearly lead to their own unhappiness.

In short our deeds in life are a result of our varying individual degrees of knowledge or ignorance, these were absolute and fundamental truths for *Socrates* that applied to everyone, and not relative to individuals as *Protagoras* had earlier argued. Clearly then by following such a train of thought if Attila, Vlad, or Jack, had spent a little less time sharpening their knives and a bit more time in self-reflection, the world likely would have been a happier (and clearly are far safer) place.

Now as honourable as *Socrates'* motives were in helping others to examine their own beliefs he must have finally publically humiliated one powerful Athenian too many as he was ultimately arrested and charged with corrupting the minds of the youth and not believing in the "Gods of the state" and so found guilty he was duly sentenced (rather harshly by today's judicial standards I would suspect) to death, a sentence to be carried out by forcing him to drink a cup of poison hemlock.

Plato recorded the speech *Socrates* delivered at his trial in his work *The Apology,* and in it we see that *Socrates* could well have avoided death had he agreed to leave Athens and effectively just kept his mouth shut, and by all accounts even once sentenced he still had the opportunity to escape via a plan hatched by his friends. However it seems *Socrates* preferred to stay true to his conscience, his belief that the truth and pursuit of self-knowledge was worth far more than his own life. So with what was likely a rousing final speech to his friends *Socrates* drank the hemlock and in doing so promptly became the first and likely most famous martyr in the history of philosophy.

Much of the "legend" of *Socrates* is centered on the story of his death, and in choosing to accept death rather than compromise his beliefs and stop bugging the general public, he set the philosophical commitment bar pretty high, with likely only Jesus of Nazareth (a.k.a. the son of God, J.C.) trumping *Socrates* in history's "dying for the cause" stakes. Ugly then, but ultimately very important.

5

The Ideal Cat

"Ignorance is the root of all evil"
Plato (c. 427-347 B.C.)

Now as we've previously stated much of what we know about *Socrates* is thanks to the work of one of his pupils, *Plato*, who published accounts of his teachings and was still only in his late twenties when *Socrates* chose the hemlock option over just agreeing to keep his lips buttoned in public places, and thus becoming philosophy's martyr-in-chief. But *Plato* is remembered today for much more than just his recordings of Socrates' dialogues, he was an outstanding philosopher in his own right and one whose influence is present still, even amongst today's modern chin-stroking thinkers.

 Plato was born of noble birth around 427 B.C. and named *Aristocles*, only acquiring the nickname *Plato* (meaning "broad" in Greek) apparently due to something of an unfortunately "above average" sized forehead. Rather than enter the world of politics as would have been expected of him, he instead became a pupil of *Socrates* and was seemingly driven by the same beliefs that in an ever changing world there were eternal and absolute truths for not only the nature and substance of the universe but also for morals and society, what was right or wrong, and that by using our own reason we are all capable (even Attila the Hun) of reaching an understanding of these truths and living by them.

 The fact that society had condemned *Socrates* to death for merely seeking to guide the good people of Athens towards these universal truths only provided *Plato* with further evidence of the conflict that exists between the world in which we live and the "ideal" world of truth and understanding. Thus suitably disillusioned with Athens and the way it had treated the man he saw as its most noble citizen, he

32

promptly packed his bags and left town. *Plato* then spent the next 15 years or so travelling throughout Egypt and Italy immersing himself in pyramids, pasta, mathematics and philosophy, and only eventually returning to Athens (likely fed up with pasta and craving a good Greek salad) to found his own school which he named after the Greek hero *Academus* and known as the *Academy*, which not unsurprisingly is where today we get our word "academic" which we freely apply to those brainy types amongst us whose IQ is generally higher than the collective IQ's of an average rugby team.

Plato eventually came to believe that like his predecessors, *Democritus* with his atoms and *Empedocles* with his cosmic mixture of fire, water, earth, and air, that there was indeed a certain "something" that was eternal and constant and that out of which our ever changing universe was built. But rather than that "something" being a mere physical substance, he saw rather a world where everything (whether a physical object or a moral concept) was made based on an "ideal" form (a kind of mold) for each and everything we see and know. According to *Plato* we are all somehow aware of these "forms" in our minds, they are eternal and immutable, abstract and spiritual, but rather unfortunately do not conveniently exist in our own physical world, and so we can't see them, touch them, smell them, or trip over them, and yet these forms are the "ideal" mold by which everything should indeed be created, trees, mountains, birds, your neighbour's cat, cerebrally challenged rugby teams, and moral codes. *Plato* called these molds, "ideas".

Plato believed that there was actually a world of "ideas" that exists totally separately from our own physical world, and it is in this world that the mold (the "idea") of the perfect tree, the perfect mountain, the perfect set of moral codes, and the perfect cat to sit on your neighbour's lap all happily exist. *Plato* concluded that this world of "ideas" sits behind our physical world and that we cannot perceive this strange but seemingly perfect world through our senses rather it can only be perceived through reason.

And just in case we weren't confused enough already, he proposed that it is in fact this *world of ideas* that is the one true reality while the world of our senses, the material world, is merely an illusion full of physical objects and moral concepts each merely modelled upon its "ideal" forms. This rather mind-bending view is known today as *Plato's theory of ideas*.

Now at first glance this *theory of ideas* sounds at best confusing and in all honesty just a little like *Plato* had likely spent most of his 15 year sabbatical absorbing whatever "happy pills" the "beautiful people" of the fourth century B.C. were gleefully tripping on rather than travelling around Egypt and Italy absorbing any actual knowledge and ideas. But although clearly the idea of an alternate reality consisting purely of "ideal" forms may seem to be one more suited to those powered by pharmaceuticals rather than any logical reasoning, we should consider that *Plato* very likely was not expecting us mere mortals to take the concept of a world of ideas so literally. For example, let's consider for a moment your neighbour's cat.

Now your neighbour's cat may be old and mangy, it may be blind in one eye, it may even be missing its tail or even a leg, but we would all still recognize it as a cat, admittedly a fairly ugly cat, but still a cat. No matter how disfigured, old, or smelly, no one outside of the most cerebrally challenged would believe it to be a horse or a dog, we just know it is a cat. Similarly for every other cat in the world, no matter how different from one another, no matter how strange looking, or how varied, we all recognize them as cats. But how do we know this, how do we all just somehow know that these are all cats and that some are not for instance say a peculiar looking, and rather small breed of horse?

Well we think we know because in our minds we believe we cleverly understand what a cat should look and behave like. We believe that over time we've seen enough furry creatures that we've been reliably informed are indeed cats such that in our heads we have formed a picture as to what a cat should look like. This picture in your head is very likely not that of your neighbour's cat, but it is such that you believe you are able to understand that the mangy, smelly, 3-legged creature that pees in your backyard is in fact a cat. Maybe what you in fact have in your head is what over time your senses have told you is the "form" of a cat, and one by which you can compare your neighbour's furry creature and conclude that it is indeed feline in nature.

34

But *Plato* believed that our senses merely give us an imperfect view of the world, maybe we will see a long procession of "imperfect" cats throughout our lifetime and even enough to create an "opinion" on what a cat should be (surely if you see enough cats you will eventually understand what a cat should look like), but our senses can never have "true knowledge" of what the perfect cat is (the "idea" of a cat, the cat in the *world of ideas*), we can only come to know this through reason.

If I stop and ask 100 random strangers in the street to describe the "perfect" cat I will likely get 100 different answers, and more importantly if I then ask them what is the perfect "idea" of justice or moral behaviour, I will most certainly get 100 different answers (or more likely 100 different variations of suitable expletives explaining that I should just kindly move on). This is because we use our senses to form "opinions" based purely upon our own individual sensory experiences on what we believe these things should be, and thus we all have different "opinions" on what is right or wrong, what is morally acceptable, or whether your neighbour's furry creature is indeed a cat or a rather strange looking small horse.

However if I then ask the same 100 people what is two plus two, they will (hopefully) all without hesitation reply four, this is because they are now all using reason, and as such they have "true knowledge" of what two plus two should be. Two plus two equals four, and barring some hugely embarrassing admission by the world's mathematicians, will do so for all time, it is unchanging, and we know this only through reason. In the same way we know that the angles of a circle add up to 360 degrees because reason tells us this, yet we may never see such a "perfect" circle (the "idea" circle) in the real world (the world of our senses), it exists only in the *world of ideas* and thus we can only come to know of it through reason.

Thus, according to *Plato*, if we want to truly know the "idea" of the perfect society, the perfect moral code, what is truly right from wrong, the perfect circle, or even the perfect cat, we can only look for it in the *world of ideas* and only find it through reason.

Plato believed that we each do indeed have access to this world of "ideas" where we see the perfect and unchanging "form" for everything that exists both physical (including your neighbour's cat), and abstract concepts such as good and evil, or even how we should behave. So how do we all tap in to this *world of ideas* so we can all presumably start to understand the ever changing world around us and all start to live a little less like Attila the Hun and a little more like the Dalai Lama?

Well, the good news is that according to *Plato* we are all born with this *world of ideas* already firmly within us, it is innate, but in a cruel twist of fate we seemingly just don't realize it and we certainly don't recognize it (clearly an inconvenience), but why?

Well for *Plato* he sees man as divided into two very distinct parts, the body and the soul. Our body, our physical incarnation, possesses our senses through which we experience the material world, while our soul possesses our reason and only through reason (thus our soul) can we perceive this *world of ideas*. *Plato* further states that although our bodies are ever changing and unfortunately for us all eventually die (just like everything other living thing in the material world), our soul is eternal and indeed existed in the *world of ideas* long before it conveniently aligned itself to our physical bodies, and in fact according to *Plato* it will return to that mysterious world after our death.

The problem for all of us mere mortals forced it seems to live in the imperfect physical world, is that our bodies unfortunately don't have a direct line to all the wondrous truths and perfect forms that our soul has access to in the *world of ideas*. According to *Plato* it seems we can only tap into our soul and the wonders it holds through the use of reason, and that (unfortunately for our generally lazy species) requires effort. *Plato* believed that because it requires effort many of us just prefer to remain believing in the material world along with all the imperfect concepts and views that are formed there purely through our senses, it's easier and much less work. But by doing so we are denying ourselves access to a world that is potentially far more beautiful, a world full of "ideals" and "truths".

For *Plato* it is the role of the philosopher to use reason to discover this *world of ideas*, a world supposedly found deep in our "souls" (accessed via the telephone hot-line of reason), and to help others to similarly awaken (or more accurately "connect" to) their soul.

Within *Plato's* dialogue, titled *the Republic*, he illustrates this *world of ideas* with what has become known as his "Allegory of the Cave". In it *Plato* asks the reader to imagine a dark cave in which a number of people have been imprisoned since birth (their crimes seemingly unspecified), and in a further act of cruelty they have their hands and feet chained and sat such that they can only ever see the back wall of the cave. Behind them at the mouth of the cave is a high wall along which people walk holding up various objects, and as there is also a fire behind the wall these objects subsequently cast shadows on the back wall of the cave. Consequently, these shadows are all the prisoners ever see and are all they know of the world, and thus they have no concept of the actual objects themselves.

Then one day in a brave bid for freedom one of the prisoners manages to free himself from his chains (presumably he was some kind of early Greek Houdini-type), turns around, and steps outside of the cave. Suddenly he sees not the shadows but the actual objects themselves, he sees real colours and clear shapes, and he sees the true beauty of the real animals and objects that before were just grey shadows on the back wall of the cave.

The freed prisoner now has a choice to make. Having spent a lifetime happily living in a world of shadows (well, as happy as a prisoner can be living in a cave chained to a chair) he may now be too dazzled and confused by the brightness and wonder of this new colourful world and may choose to simply go back to the wall of shadows and the comfort and safety of the only reality he has ever known. Or, he may be so delighted and overcome with joy that he simply skips off into the countryside outside the cave to enjoy his new found world of color and beauty for himself. Or now, understanding that the world he and his fellow prisoners have previously lived in is merely a world of poor reflections of the "real" world he now sees outside of the cave, he may choose to return to the cave to help convince the other prisoners that there is a better more beautiful world outside of the shadows they see.

In the *Republic*, the freed prisoner does indeed return to the cave to try to enlighten his fellow prisoners, but unfortunately for the well-meaning escapee, they don't believe him, they reject his attempts to try and "open their eyes" and in a clear reference to the fate of his teacher *Socrates*, they promptly kill him, although it's not made entirely clear how they achieve this given that their hands and feet are still chained (clearly story-line continuity was not of great concern for early Greek storytellers and playwrights).

Now although clearly not having the happiest of endings, *Plato* uses the "Allegory of the Cave" to try to illustrate the philosopher's path from the "shadows" of the material world, (the world of the senses), to the "light" of the *world of ideas* (the world of reason) and that often we choose to stay in the illusionary world we have always known as this is where we feel most comfortable and safe rather than committing to the effort it takes to follow reason and open ourselves up to what will reveal itself to be a far more wondrous and beautiful world.

Later in the *Republic*, *Plato* expands on his ideas going as far as to state that he believes it is only philosophers who should rule any "ideal" state (so called Philosopher Kings), as only philosophical thinkers can start to understand the true nature of the world, the *world of ideas*, and thus the truth of moral values, justice, right and wrong, even your neighbour's cat.

Plato's theories may have been a little hard for your average Ancient Greek to grasp but his teachings and philosophy were to go on to influence philosophical thought for many centuries. His ideas were to be found in the future philosophies of mediaeval Islamic and Christian thinkers, and his belief that reason, rather than observation, was the only way to acquire knowledge remained influential right through to the 17th century.

6

The Potential to Be a Chicken

"The gods too are fond of a joke or two"
Aristotle (384-322 B.C.)

As philosophy's reigning "top-dog" of the day, *Plato* naturally would have attracted many willing students to his *Academy*, all keen to learn from the great man himself, and all likely just as keen to support and expand his "other worldly" vision for the ever changing world they experienced around them, and sat at the front of class and always first to hand in his homework was one *Aristotle* (384-322 B.C.).

However, although likely top of the school's honour-roll, *Aristotle* was of a very different temperament to his teacher. Both were brilliant and clearly shared a mutual respect for each other, but where *Plato* was a poet, intuitive, and dealt in abstract concepts, *Aristotle* was scholarly, methodical, precise, and more concerned with the natural world around him. *Plato* grew up in world of nobles and politics, while *Aristotle* was the son of a physician and thus a scientist. Where *Plato* was seemingly trendy, hip and exciting (a kind of new-age, poetic genius), *Aristotle* was dry and methodical (more akin to a stuffy academic) but no less a genius.

And it was these differences that were to lead *Aristotle* to ultimately start to question his teacher's theories and ultimately propose new theories of his own, theories that were equally remarkable (if less abstract and sexy) and ones that would also go on to have a lasting effect on philosophical thinking for the next 2,000 years.

Aristotle was born in Macedonia in 384 B.C. and was sent to *Plato's* Academy at the age of 17 when *Plato* himself was already turning 60 years old and had already devised his great *Theory of*

Forms. Aristotle was to stay at the Academy for the next 20 years or so both as a student and a teacher. However, on the death of *Plato* he was surprisingly passed over as *Plato's* successor and presumably in a philosophical huff he promptly left the *Academy* and set off for the Island of Ionia where he spent the next several years indulging his passion for studying wildlife.

It is this study of the characteristics of plants and animals that led *Aristotle* to believe that in such observations he could clearly observe and define what it was that distinguished each plant and animal from every other plant and animal, what today science bods happily declare as defining a "species".

Aristotle thus started to believe that rather than having to revert to a recognition of eternal and perfect "forms" in some strange and mysterious "alternate world" to understand what it was for instance to be a cat (the mysterious *world of Forms* as defined by his now long departed teacher), we actually only had to observe in the natural world around us what it was that makes a cat distinct from say your mother-in-law or any other overly furry creature that appears to laze around the house all day doing nothing.

Thus where *Plato* believed that everything in the material world is just an imperfect version of some "other worldly ideal", the understanding of which could only be found *"outside"* of the natural world and only through reason, *Aristotle* came to the remarkable conclusion that the essential essence of each and everything in the natural world is actually inherent in every instance of that thing. For *Aristotle* then, everything that makes a cat a cat, those characteristics unique to all cats (the "ideal" form of a cat) is actually *"inside"* every single cat no matter how old, mangy, deformed or weird looking any individual cat may seem to be to us.

Like *Plato, Aristotle* believed that we are born with no innate ideas, we arrive in this world a blank book with minds as empty as a turkey farm on Boxing Day. But unlike *Plato* who believed we only come to know the true perfect forms of animals, plants, justice, virtue, right and wrong, by using reason to "remember" what our "soul" apparently already knew from its previous existence in the *world of Forms, Aristotle* sees us slowly building up our views and refining our understanding of such perfect forms by observing them in the material world around us.

Thus for *Aristotle*, when we are born we have absolutely no idea of right or wrong, what a circle is, or even what a cat is, but as we encounter examples of these things through our senses, we learn to recognize the qualities and characteristics that make such things what they are, and thus slowly over time we hopefully build our understanding of what right and wrong truly are, what makes a perfect circle, and indeed what a cat actually is.

However, *Aristotle* was not so naïve as to deny the power of reason all together, indeed he believed that although we are each born with our minds as hollow as a bass drum, we are nevertheless born with the power of reason all set and ready to go "out of the box" the day we are born. But *Aristotle* saw reason merely as our way to organize and make order out of what our senses tell us, and it is reason that helps us to "categorize" all the sensory information we gather from say all our cat experiences into our understanding of what the form (the species) of a cat truly is.

Aristotle still firmly believed that it is the power of reason that defines us as human (cats, horses, plants and rocks, clearly do not possess such powers, else they'd all be flying rockets to the moon, solving quadratic equations, and debating the meaning of it all) but unlike *Plato, Aristotle* sees that reason needs input from our senses to come to any meaningful conclusions.

Thus *Aristotle* did not necessarily disagree with his former mentor in that eternal and universal forms exist, but where *Plato* saw these forms existing only "*outside*" of our material world, Aristotle on the other hand saw them as existing "*inside*" everything in the material world. While *Plato* believed we could only arrive at an understanding of these forms and universal truths through reason, *Aristotle* saw our senses as key to our understanding.

In believing that the "form" of anything resides "inside" the thing itself, *Aristotle* proposes that everything in our ever changing world is a unity between its actual physical form (what he calls its *substance)*, and its specific characteristics, what defines it (what he calls its *form)*. The *substance* of your neighbour's cat unfortunately may be old, mangy, one-eyed, and with only three legs, but its *form*

41

still remains that of a sleek, nimble, 4-legged furry mammal, a hunter of small animals that strolls around the house like it pays the mortgage.

Now your neighbour's cat clearly has never, and very likely will never, fulfill all its potential "*form*", but although failing miserably in this case nature certainly nonetheless tried. As such *Aristotle* sees everything in our material world as *substance* striving to become its *potential*, its true *form*, and in this way he rather conveniently solves the problem of why everything in our world is in a constant state of change.

For *Aristotle* change is merely the constant transformation of *substance* striving to achieve its *form*. For *Aristotle* then change is not a bad thing at all, it does not as *Plato* believed show how imperfect our material world is, rather change is part of the natural course of things, it's necessary for things to fulfill their *potential* (whether they get there or not is of course another matter), and in fact for *Aristotle* change actually has a purpose.

Let's take the example of a chicken egg, it has the *substance* of an egg but also the *potential* to become a chicken, (or maybe end up on your breakfast plate), and it will strive to constantly change to achieve this *potential* (its *form*), to become a chicken. We must note however that the egg cannot strive to become say a duck, an owl, or a donkey, its *potential* is limited to its *form* (that of a chicken), and thus something's *form* defines not just its potential but also its limitations. No matter how much we may want to humans will never be able to fly like a bird, (although the surface of our planet is littered with the indentations of those who still tried), it's just not a characteristic of our species, we have zero *potential* to get ourselves airborne under our own steam.

Aristotle's concept of *form* then is clearly not just a matter of defining the unique "physical" characteristics of everything in our world, it also speaks to what it does, and how it does or does not behave (birds fly, humans don't). *Aristotle* thus went on to expand his ideas to consider the "reason" for a thing's existence, and he does this through what he calls the "*four causes*". Firstly *Aristotle* saw a *material* cause which he sees as defining just what something is made of (in the case of us humans that would be skin, bone, muscle, organs, and varying degrees of fat). He then saw a *formal* cause defining the shape or physical characteristics of something (for you and me that would be a body with four long appendages sticking out each corner with a largish head stuck on top), then an *efficient* cause being how a thing is brought into being (I presume your mother has explained how this bit works), and lastly what *Aristotle* called the *final* cause which is the purpose or function of something (the jury it seems is still out on this one for us humans it seems), and it is this *final* cause that particularly interested *Aristotle*.

Aristotle's notion that change was a natural part of all living creatures preceded that of a certain *Charles Darwin* by more than 1,500 years. But where *Aristotle* saw that change as purposeful, that all creatures strived to the ultimate goal of fulfilling their *potential*, *Darwin* would eventually go on to prove that although living things do indeed change over time they actually do so randomly and thus without purpose, and that it is only subsequent natural selection, survival of the fittest, that determines if a change is "good" and thus works towards the evolution of any particular species.

However, back in the 4th century B.C. *Aristotle* remained obsessed with the idea that everything has its own purpose (*final* cause). The purpose of an eye is to see, of a bird is to fly, of your mother-in-law is to nag, and that of a bullet is to remind us we are all indeed mortal. But *Aristotle* wanted to expand his ideas of final cause into the world of ethics, he wanted to understand what is a "good" life, how we should we live and behave. To this end *Aristotle* states that if we know the purpose of something then we should naturally then understand what is a good or bad version of that thing, for instance a good eye allows you to see while a bad eye will have you constantly bumping into walls.

As a human being, in *Aristotle's* eyes, a "good" life is thus one where we fulfill our purpose (our *final cause*). For *Aristotle* this meant the pursuit of virtue and wisdom, and we only get to understand virtue and gain wisdom by using our senses to observe such "good" behaviours in others and using our reason to help categorize what our senses show us such that we may apply such "good" behaviours and wisdom in our own lives. Indeed for *Aristotle* we can only be truly happy as human beings if we are fulfilling our purpose, if we use all our capabilities in the pursuit and application of virtue and wisdom.

According to *Aristotle* our purpose then is to live life well, and for him this meant the use of such virtues as living honestly and with courage while at the same time showing moderation emotionally, intellectually and physically. For *Aristotle* this was the way to true happiness. Indeed *Aristotle* actively promotes avoiding extremes, something he calls the *Golden mean*, the idea that too much or too little of anything is bad, and that everything that is good thus lies somewhere in the middle ground (the "mean") between the two extremes.

He saw happiness in the shape of three distinct forms, a life of pleasure and enjoyment, one as a free and responsible citizen, and one a life as a philosopher, a thinker. For *Aristotle* all three must be present and in balance for us to live a happy and harmonious life. Too much emphasis or extreme behaviour in any particular area will lead to an imbalance and out of such imbalances ultimately comes forth Attila the Hun and Jack the Ripper.

Aristotle's studies also took him in many other different directions. He even founded the first biological classification for all living things, devising a hierarchal system that forms the basis for taxonomy (the name clever science bods use for the field of science that encompasses the description, identification, and classification of organisms by specific characteristics) still in use today, first dividing the natural world into living and non-living things (clearly a pretty obvious place to start), then dividing living things between plants and animals, and gradually subdividing into ever more precise categories.

What makes his classification so important is that this was not just some random hierarchy for living things that he just threw together on a whim one slow Sunday afternoon, but that he uses his idea of *forms* to distinguish between species, and how they should be classified into which category. For instance to classify a specimen in the "fish" category *Aristotle* first identified what it is that makes a fish a fish (its *form, such as* breathes through gills, lives in water, dies on land)*, and only placed specimens into this category if it met what he had defined as the "*form*" of a fish. In this manner Aristotle built up a classification of all living things from the simplest organisms to humans, and did so in a way that further supported his theories around *substance, form* and the nature of change.

Aristotle also went one step further drawing a distinction between what he called *essential* and *accidental* properties. *Essential* properties are those things without which a thing would not be what it is (its *form*), for instance gills in the case of a fish, while *accidental* properties are those that determine "how" a thing is but not "what" it is, for instance the colour of a fish or the shape of its head.

As an example let's consider that man-eating, streamlined killing machine of the sea, the shark. To be a shark it must have the *essential* property of being able to swim. Take away its ability to swim and it would effectively no longer be a shark (more of a sleek killing-machine that merely bobs in the water), but take away say its teeth (an *accidental* property) and it will still be shark, just not so scary looking and likely very hungry.

This classification for living things went on to dominate Western thinking throughout the Middle Ages where it rather conveniently formed the basis of the Christian *scala naturae* (the "Ladder of Nature") which depicted an evolutionary ladder from plants, to insects, to animals to humans and ultimately to God. A theory which supported by *Aristotle's* ideas of everything being born with a purpose, was used to support the Church in its teachings of God being the *formal cause* of everything, that man was superior to all other living creatures on Earth and whose *purpose* was to serve God being the "prime mover", and thus the cause and purpose of all movement in nature.

In *Aristotle* we find the first all-encompassing "one-world" philosophy, and one that has its feet firmly planted on the ground of both the material world and science (at least science as the ancient Greeks understood it). The sheer scope of *Aristotle's* work ensured his place in the history of both philosophy and science, and cemented his place as the poster-child and guru of future armchair philosopher's and scholars alike. He was an astronomer, a meteorologist, a physicist, a geologist, a biologist, a botanist, a psychologist, he also studied anatomy, zoology, politics, economic, literature, theology, and was the first logician of any note. Many of his ideas would remain unchallenged for almost 1,500 years, and if all that wasn't enough by all account he was a bit of a snappy dresser too.

But *Aristotle's* work was not without fault, his astronomy was flawed, his ethics supported the use of slaves, he considered women as inferior to men, and his views became so central to church teachings of the Middle Ages that any contrary theories were actively discouraged for centuries and thus effectively becoming an obstacle to scientific progress. But taken as a whole *Aristotle's* work amounted to nothing less than a virtual encyclopaedia of Greek knowledge and a revolution in both philosophy and science.

7

Just Suck It Up

"We have two ears and one mouth, clearly we should listen more than we speak"
Zeno of Citium (c. 336-265 B.C.)

In the summer of 356 B.C. the eldest son of Philip II, the then king of Macedonia, was born and duly named Alexander by his presumably doting regal parents. As the first born son, Alexander was naturally groomed for succession and thus accorded the best education money (or royal orders) could buy, which would naturally have included private tuition by the leading intellectuals of the time. History reliably informs us that one such tutor was our multi-talented friend *Aristotle*, who as we have seen already had his hands full busying himself laying down nothing less than the foundations for the future of Western philosophy and science. However, clearly not wanting to find himself on the wrong side of his king's good books, it seems that *Aristotle* still managed to find enough free-time in his busy schedule to educate the young Alexander in the finer arts of philosophy and science.

With the unfortunate assassination of his father (assassination appears to have been the all too common solution to disputes amongst the ruling classes of the day) the young Alexander suddenly found himself the ruler of Macedonia at the tender age of 22, and with an ever growing army in tow (matched only in size it seems by his ego and ambitions for world domination) he spent the next 10 years of his life trampling all over Europe, Asia Minor, India, and North Africa, conquering all in his path.

By the time of his death in 323 B.C. at the age of only 32, (which rather disappointingly seems to have been from a brief illness rather than any heroic mortal injury sustained in the heat of battle)

Alexander had led his army over 12,000 miles, had remained undefeated in battle, and had brought the empires of Southern Europe, Persia, Egypt, and even as far east as parts of India and the Himalayas, all under his (and thus Greek) control, and in light of his exploits had by that time also now acquired the additional title of "the Great" appended to his name, which is how history now remembers him.

But the imperial achievements of Alexander the Great as stunning as they may be are not what is of interest to us here in the context of our brief history of human ideas. Rather it is more the consequences of Alexander's globe-trotting military exploits that we need to get excited about, as in the wake of his conquests great swathes of the globe were now under the control of Greek speaking rulers, and were thus introduced to Greek culture, trade, language, kebabs, cheap package-holidays, and most importantly to our story, Greek philosophy.

This period in European history (the period from Alexander's death and the subsequent decline of the kingdoms he helped form, to the shift of power to a region of Europe with a somewhat more Italian flavor as Rome began its own chapter in the history books around the 1st century B.C.) is known to history boffins as the *Hellenistic age*. It was out of this period of Greek globalization and eventual decline that we see the rise of what historians rather unimaginatively call the *Hellenistic philosophers.*

The *Hellenistic* period sees people becoming less and less idealistic, and by that we mean that rather than concerning themselves as *Plato* and *Aristotle* had done with discovering cosmic truths the good people of the time were now far more concerned with how to cope with the ups and downs of day to day life in their new "global" world. Rather than asking "what is reality?" people now were beginning to ask "How the hell do we cope with reality?".

This shift was in no small part due to the gradual and eventual rise of the ever practical Roman Empire. Romans had little time for other-worldly philosophies, they were far more concerned with watching lions feast on Christians, building walls high enough to keep out warriors in skirts, and creating order and civil obedience, and thus their philosophical pursuits focused more on how best to live rather than worrying about where we all came from in the first place.

Thus the *Hellenistic* period saw the rise of several philosophical schools of thought each providing their own unique insight into how the good citizens of the Greco-Roman Empires should conduct themselves and cope with the daily challenges of life, first under increasingly warring factions as the *Hellenistic* empire gradually went the same way as its founder Alexander, and then under varying degrees of despotic Roman Emperors.

Of these new philosophical schools of thought one of the more extreme were the *cynics*. Founded by *Antisthenes*, a former pupil of *Socrates*, in Athens around 400 B.C. the *cynics* believed that true happiness and virtue could never be found in wealth, power, material goods, worrying about their own or even other people's problems, or even concerning yourself with good health. No, for followers of *Antisthenes* true virtue and happiness could only be found in pursuing a simple life, free of the external restrictions imposed by society and the internal struggle caused by desire, emotion, and fear, and thus living totally in harmony with nature, a kind of "back to basics", "get in touch with your roots" philosophy.

The *cynic's* most famous (or infamous) practitioner was *Diogenes of Sinope* (c. 404-323 B.C.) who clearly embraced his calling wholeheartedly and with a stubborn blind determination that would not be seen again until the Spanish Inquisitions or Robert Falcon Scott's desire to plant a British flag at the South Pole, took its teachings to an extreme by rejecting all material possessions and living life in as natural a state as possible, and thus presumably a life in perfect harmony with nature. To this end he reputedly lived in a barrel on the streets of Athens, wore nothing but discarded rags (on the days he actually chose to dress at all), scrounged for scraps of food, and ignored all forms of social etiquette and custom. He lived a life governed only by reason and natural impulses (he reputedly urinated wherever or whenever the need took him often much to the discomfort and embarrassment of many passing citizens of Athens). In the words of *Diogenes* "he has the most who is most content with the least", and in living out his philosophy to such an extreme he was either completely mad or the happiest man that ever lived, or as is

49

most likely just a little of both. Regardless of either the validity of *cynicism* as a philosophy or the ultimate state of mind of its most famous advocate, to this day *Diogenes* is more often remembered as a prime example of what happens when philosophy goes completely mad.

By the 19th century emphasis on the negative aspects of *Diogenes* bold experiment has led to the modern understanding of *cynicism* to mean a general distrust of others and their motives, a lack of faith or hope, and general disillusionment, unfortunately not quite what *Diogenes* had in mind as he sat bare naked in his barrel in the middle of Athens quietly smiling to himself.

Emerging from the notion of virtue residing in simplicity and the borderline madness of *Diogenes* came *Zeno of Citium* (336-265 B.C.) who founded the school of philosophy known as *stoicism* which preached that nature is the only one reality and that to find true happiness in this world we must simply accept the things over which we have no control while at the same time controlling our "destructive" emotions and desires. *Stoics* taught that we should all live in conformity to nature, but nature as viewed by reason not emotion or feelings, indeed, we may well view *stoics* as to some extent preaching indifference or apathy, as to them love, anger, fear, desire, are all pointless and even dangerous and destructive, we must simply just accept all that we cannot control.

To the *stoics* all natural processes such as sickness, pain, death, earthquakes, your moaning mother-in-law, or your foot being run over by a passing chariot, all are just part of your destiny, they cannot be controlled or changed, they are all part of nature's unbreakable law where everything happens through necessity and thus there is little point in either complaining or fighting against it. We must just suck it up and accept nature's cruelty and injustice, while at the same time enjoying her benefits as and when they come.

For the *stoics*, bad things will always happen (usually just when you think everything is going fine), but we should just accept them and move on and not let them get to us, good things will also happen and we should simply enjoy them when they come but not pursue them. You may lose your right arm in battle but just stick a band-aid on it and learn to fight left-handed, your boss at the Salt-mine may reward you with a bonus of Skoda's latest model chariot, enjoy its functional practicalities but don't envy the guy next to you who was given the solid gold Rolls Royce model.

Despite this resignation to our destiny the *stoics* still believed that man possessed the power of reason and free-will, but they asserted we must use such reason and free-will to chose to accept all those things over which we have no control, and learn to temper those that we can such as greed and desire. We can't control what happens to us but we can control our attitude and how we deal with such events. It was only through this acceptance that an individual would lead a truly virtuous life, achieve true happiness, and live in harmony with nature and everything it decides to throw at us either good or bad.

Stoicism went on to find many willing followers amongst Romans who found its "life is tough so just suck it up and get on with it" approach fitted rather well with their down to earth, uncompromising way of life, driven by their preoccupation with order, strength, and ethics both personal and political, particularly in the somewhat troubling times many Romans found themselves living in under the rule of some increasingly despotic Emperors.

Roughly at the same time as *Zeno* was preaching his message of dogged *stoicism*, the Ionian Island of Elis saw the birth of one *Pyrrho* (c. 365-275 B.C.). *Pyrrho* served in many of Alexander's military campaigns where he was presumably exposed to and influenced by Asian culture and their concept of inner peace and tranquility, so much so that on his return (presumably fed up with the warrior life of pillage, rape, and plunder) he felt compelled to form his own philosophical school that became known as *Scepticism*.

Pyrrho was the first to put *doubt* at the centre of their philosophy. Building on the thinking of *Socrates* who made it his mission to wander the streets of Athens happily pointing out to its many citizens that people are often wrong in their beliefs around what is, or is not true, *Pyrrho* build a whole philosophy around doubting just about everything we think we believe we know, and what this then tells us about how we should act.

Like *Socrates* and his pupil *Plato, Pyrrho* believed that we cannot trust anything our senses tell us and similarly we cannot rely on anything anybody else has to say either as their senses are

51

presumably just as fallible as our own. For *Pyrrho* any evidence for a belief that comes from our senses is inherently unreliable, but this does not mean it is necessarily wrong, but equally we cannot know for sure it is right. These *sceptics,* as they became known, believe that for every assertion a completely contradictory assertion can be made with similar justification. What people see or hear or smell may well be completely different to what you see, hear, or smell, and thus we can't truly hold anything or anyone to be true, we can only know how they appear to us.

Clearly you would have thought this would create a bit of a problem for *Pyrrho* and his followers, how can you live (or even know you exist) in a world where you don't believe or trust anything your senses tell you or even anything anyone else you?

But for *Pyrrho* such suspension of belief was the only true way to a tranquil mind. *Scepticism* was not just about going around happily criticizing and disbelieving everyone and everything you see, it was more about accepting that many things happen that are beyond our control and we should just accept this fact. We should all just accept that nothing in life can be taken for certain, and thus we should just throw out any expectations we may have about how things should be or even how we want them to be, and just let them be. In this way we will never be disappointed with our place in the world or what it throws at us.

In theory then *scepticism* allows us to detach ourselves from the pains, anxieties, and disappointments of life and achieve a level of serenity and tranquility. The problem is that with such a "I don't believe a word you say" approach, you will very quickly find yourself with no one friends to share your new found happiness with.

Scepticism can be seen as a rather extreme philosophy (actually it's hard to imagine something more extreme than living a life disbelieving everyone and everything), and as such it not unsurprisingly didn't gain the popularity the *stoics* would go on to find particularly in Rome, but its central premise of doubt would go on to play an important and influential role in modern thinking, particularly in the fields of modern science and the logic based philosophies. The first modern scientists took nothing for granted, they questioned every finding, every theory, doubt was thus also a central theme of their work, and although unlike the followers of *Pyrrho* who effectively point blank accepted nothing as true, scientists took *scepticism* as a very practical tool to progress and ultimately prove (or unfortunately disprove) their theories by questioning (doubting) their validity and thus forcing further and deeper analysis ultimately leading to (hopefully) an empirical and unquestioned scientific proof.

The most appealing (on paper at least) of the new *Hellenistic* philosophies was the brainchild of *Epicurus* (c. 341-270 B.C.) a native of the Aegean island of Samos and who was a follower of the philosophies of *Democritus,* he of the tiny, unchanging, and indivisible particles that he believed were responsible for making up everything in the Universe, and which became known for ever more as *atoms.*

Like the *Stoics* and the *Cynics, Epicurus* believed that the one true goal of life was to find peace of mind and thus freedom from all anxiety and pain, both physical and mental. But unlike the *Stoics* and *Cynics* whose preached a philosophy based on enduring such pain, *Epicurus* sought rather to avoid pain and anxiety all together and thus emphasised a life in pursuit of sensory enjoyment, preaching that "the highest good is pleasure and the greatest evil is pain".

Epicurus' philosophy not unsurprisingly became known as *Epicureanism* and on the face of it any philosophy that positively encourages its followers to spend their lives wholly dedicated to the pursuit of sensual pleasure would appear to be one that would have people queuing to sign-up on the dotted line. I for one would much rather spend my days happily ignoring any and all mental pain that may be brought my way by the vagaries of fate and destiny by fully embracing a life of sex, and drugs, and rock'n'roll (it certainly seems a far more appealing option than having to manfully grin and bare my destiny as proposed by the likes of the *Stoics).*

Indeed, the word "epicurean" is now used in our modern vernacular to describe someone who lives their life purely in a single minded pursuit of sensual pleasure and self-indulgence regardless of its affect on anyone or anything else (Keith Richards and Ozzy Osbourne have likely been called many things in their lives but epicurean may probably be one of the most apt).

But although *Epicurus* and his followers were not adverse to enjoying the pleasures of the sensual world (even philosophers are human), what they were really interested in was finding peace of mind (something shared by all the *Hellenistic* philosophies) by avoiding mental pain, and as *Epicurus* was quick to point out (probably much to the dismay of the queue of potential "party-people" lined up outside of his front-door) even the sensual pleasures can often cause mental pain in the long run (consider the pain of that morning after hangover, or the uncomfortable indigestion suffered by that one extra slice of pie too many) and so must also be tempered to ensure long term peace of mind. As such, *Epicurus* preached that any short-term pleasure must first be weighed against any possible longer-term pain that may be caused as a consequence. Thus the pursuit of happiness must be undertaken bearing in mind what we saw *Aristotle* call "the Golden Mean", meaning self-control, and moderation.

While mental pain in our modern world may mean having to pay the mortgage, a miserable boss, a desire for a Porsche but only the budget for a Skoda, in the time of *Epicurus* the main cause of mental pain was an unhealthy fear in the power of the God's over man's destiny, along with an equally unhealthy fear of death brought on by the expected consequences any such wrath of the Gods may mean to them in the "afterlife".

To counteract this (to "avoid" such fear) *Epicurus* taught that in fact the Gods paid no attention at all to what people may or may not do (they had far more important things to concern themselves with such as the latest squabble happening on Mt Olympus) and as such we had nothing to fear from either the Gods or even death itself.

To support his claim that death was nothing for us to fear *Epicurus* returned to his early days as a student and the teachings of *Democritus* and his atoms. *Epicurus* argued that the Universe and everything in it consists merely of atoms or empty space and as such we are all just the fortunate result of random atoms that have conveniently stuck themselves together into our human form, and which will all just disperse back into the empty space on our death and thus go on to collide again with other atoms to form yet another of the Universe's wondrous forms.

Thus death itself should be nothing for us to fear, there is no after-life, no purgatory, no punishment from the God's waiting for us once we die, we merely dissolve back into the void, even our soul (which *Epicurus* conveniently also saw as being formed from such atoms). *Epicurus* was probably the first philosopher to openly state that man does not have an immortal soul, a cornerstone of most religions and which no doubt made him less than popular in the religious circles of the day.

What's more, *Epicurus* preached that death itself cannot hurt because at the point of death we simply just won't exist anymore, there is no more "you" to feel pain either mental or physical, merely a bunch of atoms coming apart, you would already have ceased to exist so why worry about death or whether the Gods may punish you in some after-life for your actions of Earth, rather simply just enjoy the life you have without the fear of either death or the Gods (a kind of "licence to thrill" with only the "earthly" consequences of your actions to worry about).

Unconcerned about death and any after-life the *Epicureans* now felt free to enjoy life, but they weren't finished there, they also saw many social customs as impediments to true peace of mind and so they preached against such social conventions as marriage, believing they inhibited the true pursuit of one's own happiness given that you now had to take on the additional responsibility of being concerned (or at least giving the pretence of being concerned) about the happiness of someone else. Even politics and trade were actively frowned upon as they encouraged the pursuit of goals and wealth, which also inevitably caused a degree of mental stress, which all in turn interfered with the one true goal of finding peace of mind.

In fact it appears that *Epicureans* much rather preferred to live a life of quite seclusion away from the world of pain-giving temptations or concerns around what the Gods may or may not be planning for them, and as such they gathered with other like-minded "seekers of happiness" in what we would probably refer to today as "communes", a safe harbour where they could all collectively huddle together in a kind of group effort towards their own individual piece of tranquility. Prime amongst these "communes", more correctly known as philosophical schools, was *The Garden* which was found by *Epicurus* himself around 300 B.C., and for a brief period at least *The Garden* was more popular than either *Plato's* school, *The Academy,* or *Aristotle's* own *Lyceum,* probably because the focus was very much on the pursuit of happiness rather than study, clearly a much more appealing school curriculum for any budding student of philosophy.

Although *Epicurus* and his "party-time" philosophy has now been largely ignored for centuries, he would no doubt be suitably enthused (and thus likely a little closer to his own peace of mind) to know that the central core of his philosophy pops up firmly enshrined in the words of the United States' Declaration of Independence, "life, liberty, and the pursuit of happiness". It maybe that indirectly *Epicurus* ultimately became one of the most influential philosophers in history after all (in the West at least).

8

Meanwhile Back in the East...

*"What you know, you know; what you don't know, you don't know.
This is true wisdom"*
Confucius (c. 551-479 B.C.)

Around the same time that *Socrates* was being served his hemlock and soda and dutifully dying for the cause, and *Plato* stumbled around searching for the entrance to his cave, far away on the other side of world the inscrutable peoples of India and China had been quietly formulating their own philosophical ideas, happily ignorant of any such great Western thinkers or thought.

From around 1,000 B.C. China had lived under the rule of the Zhou Dynasty which had imposed a political and social system based upon aristocratic families acting as lords and masters of individual domains, a system unfortunately remarkably similar to what we would now call "feudalism". Not unsurprisingly then as various states grew in ambition and backbone the system eventually started to break down into a long and bloody competition for bragging rights and power between rival states in what is still recognized today as one the darkest periods of Chinese history, known to Eastern historians as the Warring States period (c. 475-221 B.C.).

However, this time of significant political upheaval also led to the rise of a collection of philosophies that were less concerned about understanding the nature of the universe and its workings (generally seen by the great eastern minds of the time as unfathomable, and thus a pointless waste of time), than with the rather more pressing needs of how best to address the current social and political issues, how to organize a just society, defining how everyone should behave within that society, and what constitutes a "good life". If your homeland is falling apart under bloody civil wars I guess it's understandable that your focus is more around how best to try and fix it rather than worrying about if the universe is made of water, air, atoms, or noodles.

Obviously a philosophical reaction was not the only response to the ongoing political upheaval (it wasn't known as the "Warring States" period for no reason), however the philosophical schools that came out of this period provided the world with some of its most popular schools of thought, giving rise to philosophies that are still followed by millions across the world even today. Thus, we see the seeds of Chinese philosophy growing out of practical needs, politics, ethical and moral concerns, rather than any burning need to understand the nature of the cosmos in rational terms which had acted as the initial catalyst for the sandal-clad thinkers living in the somewhat safer and politically more stable confines on the other side of the world in sunny Athens.

It was during this period that we see the rapid rise in China of what has become known as the *Hundred Schools of Thought* as many (presumably one hundred) philosophies were proposed by the good and great of the time in response to the prevailing political turmoil. So despite most of the population being embroiled in endless battles, slaughter, and general mayhem, this period is still considered to also be the golden age of Chinese philosophy, and it is out of this period we see the emergence of the major philosophies that were to dominate Chinese thinking and culture for the next 2,000 years, *Confucianism, Daoism, Mohism,* and *Legalism.*

Of all the great Chinese philosophers probably the most mysterious is *Lao Tzu (c. 6th century B.C.).* Indeed, much like his contemporary *Socrates* in the west, historians can't actually be sure that he actually existed at all, and so he has become an almost mythical figure in Chinese history. But, whether he existed or not, it is the "historical figure" of *Lao Tzu* who history has attributed with authoring one of the most important books in Chinese history, the *Dao De Jing* (loosely translated as "The Way and its Power" for those whose knowledge of the Chinese language is limited to the menu items at their local Chinese takeaway). It was one of the first attempts to propose a theory of just rule based solely upon individual virtue which could be achieved only by following *Dao* (the Way of the Universe), and is the basis of the philosophy known to the world as *Daoism*.

Lao Tzu's philosophy was based on a means of achieving wisdom by tuning the inner mind to the rhythms of nature, the Way of the Universe, what he called the *Dao*. However, to understand this idea of *Dao* we have to first understand how Chinese of the time viewed their world. For them, all change was cyclical, continually moving from one state to another, day to night, peace to war, flood to drought, feast to famine, and back again.

However, these continually changing states were not viewed as opposites (as those living on the western side of the planet would), but rather as related states, one giving rise to the other, together making up a whole. It is this process of change, the constant flow from one state back to the other, that creates and maintains the harmonious balance of the universe (the *Dao)*, and thus the process of change is seen as just a natural expression of the *Dao*.

Lau Tzu's philosophy basically rests on the belief that if all things (elephants, insects, fish, men, women, and even mother-in-laws) act in accordance with the *Dao* then all things will remain in harmony and thus the universe will be as it should be (peace, love and understanding around every corner), and thus any man who lives in such accordance with the *Dao* will himself live a well-balanced, virtuous, happy life.

But *Lao Tzu* recognized that there was also a problem here particularly in respect of the Universe's perennial problem child (namely man), for man is also born with desire, a desire for wealth and power (a bigger more shiny wok, name-brand flip-flops), a desire to seek something better for himself. In addition, man is also born with free-will that enables him to chase such desires, and it is this dangerous double-act of desire and free-will that can easily make us stray from what *Lao Tzu* saw as our natural path, the path of *Dao*, and thus disturbing not just our own natural balance but ultimately that of the universe as a whole.

Exerting your own will then against the natural order of the universe disrupts the overall harmony and thus leads to imbalance in the *Dao* resulting not only in unhappiness, conflict, and stress for yourself (a bad enough state of affairs for sure), but also for society, the world, and ultimately the universe as a whole, which are all now also put out of balance (all because you want a bigger ox and cart, or that bigger and more shiny wok).

However, the good news, at least as far as *Lao Tzu* saw it, is that the answer for all us wealth seeking, power crazy, overly ambitious, free-will junkies, is simple. To live a happy, harmonious, virtuous, well-balanced life, one full of wisdom, love, and unlimited group-hugs, all we have to do is just simply live a life in accordance with the *Dao*, in accordance to the rhythms of the universe. Simple then, well, unfortunately not quite.

Following the "Way of the universe" is not as simple as you would first think. Firstly, according *to Lao Tzu*, the *Dao* itself is not something that us mere mortals can possibly understand. It seems you could dedicate the next twenty years of your life sat in all manner of complex yoga positions, surrounded by joss-sticks, and philosophizing about the *Dao,* but in the end it seems you'd still be no closer to understanding it than the day you started. The answer seems to be that we have to stop scratching our heads, put down our joss-sticks and thinking pipes, stop wasting twenty years of your life, and just accept the fact that the *Dao* does indeed exists.

It also seems that the only way to live in accordance with the *Dao* is by what *Lao Tzu* calls practicing *wu-wei*, literally "non-action". This idea of achieving peace, love, inner-harmony, and wisdom, simply by "non-action" sounds ideal, and will likely have couch-potatoes all over the world straining to put down their TV remotes and potato chips just long enough to sign on the dotted line. Unfortunately however, by "non-action" *Lao Tzu* did not mean "do nothing" (back on with the TV's for now then), for him "non-action" means not acting against the *Dao*, it means acting in accordance with your nature, acting without desire, ambition, and selfishness, it means acting with simplicity, compassion, and humility. Instead of trying to "control" everything, we should all just act naturally avoiding all unnecessary effort and behave only in accordance with nature, just "let things happen", for as *Lao Tzu* tells us, to be wise is to realize one's unity with nature.

To the *Daoist* even social structures, social conventions, government, politics, (or the need for a bigger ox and cart, or a more shiny wok), are all obstacles to human happiness, which according to *Daoist* teachings depends solely on man's own individual freedom to express the nature within themselves. If we all accept and act only according to the way of the universe, we, society, the world, the universe, will all remain in harmony, happy and content without the need for any such social structures or order.

This may sound like preaching just one giant hippy-fest, but today, almost 3,000 years on from *Lao Tzu's* first teaching his *"wu-wei"* approach to life, there are still over 200 million people in the world today all happily leading a life of such "non-action" and trying to live by his *Daoist* teachings.

However, someone was soon to come along who didn't necessarily buy into this eastern "get in touch with my inner feelings" hippie-type ideology, and who would evolve his own philosophy, one which was to be very much based on society, social structure, social conduct and conventions, and one which preached harmony of the state over any inner harmony of the individual.

Confucius (551-479 B.C.) was born in Qufu, in the Chinese state of Lu (roughly in the north eastern corner of modern day China for those not versed in China's geographical regions), originally his given name was Kong Qiu later earning the title Kong Fuzi (Master Kong), and it was this title that westerners (who likely were too lazy to learn how to pronounce his name properly) later Latinized to become *Confucius*.

Confucius had become part of a quickly growing new breed of scholar in China who earned their position not through any patronage or inheritance but through merit, and who acted as civil servants and advisors to the imperial courts of the day. Although part of this new growing class of self-made men (kind of ancient Chinese Yuppies), as a "good citizen" *Confucius* still retained a healthy respect for the past and its emphasis on ritual, ancestor worship, and respect for parents, elders, and superiors, and it was in his synthesis of these old ideals with the new movement of a merit-driven hierarchy that he produced his own unique philosophy.

The core of *Confucianism* rests in the belief that virtue is not something that is heaven sent only to the select few, nor something reserved merely for the rich and powerful (it can't be bought, sold, or found inside a fortune cookie), it is something that can be taught and taught to anyone (you, me, even politicians and lawyers). *Confucius* preached that once one has learned to live such a virtuous life (become what he calls a *junzi*, a "gentleman" or "superior man"), they will also then understand their natural place in the social hierarchy (*Confucius* still believed in a rigid class system, from ruler to peasant farmer) and will then act in that role with their new found virtue and benevolence to help achieve a just and stable society for all (if you are a lowly peasant farmer, rejoice in the fact and be the best damned peasant farmer you can be for the good of all).

Confucius actively promoted ruling and acting by example rather than by fear or self-interest, preaching that when sincerity and virtue become apparent they are made manifest in the world which can then be seen by others who are then themselves transformed by it, thus inspiring others to follow a similarly virtuous life (effectively the philosophical equivalent of a common cold, once you get it you will very likely pass it on to others). In this way *Confucius* preached that the "virtuous man" can transform society.

To define the various means by which an individual can indeed transform themselves into such a virtuous benefit to society, a *junzi*, *Confucius* used traditional Chinese values to outline his ethical concepts and practices, prime amongst these are loyalty, filial piety (in simple English meaning respect for parent, elders, ancestors, and one's superiors), adherence to rituals, and reciprocity (basically that old religious and philosophical staple of "do unto other as you would have done to yourself").

In loyalty *Confucius* stressed a strict hierarchy in respect of significance, (to *Confucius* loyalty was not something to be equally shared amongst all) first and foremost was a subject's loyalty to their ruler, but such loyalty should not mean subservience to authority, to *Confucius* loyalty must work both ways and that rulers must also show benevolence to their subjects. A similar relationship is then held between a father and his son, then husband and wife, elder to younger brother, friend to friend, and then finally (last and in this case very much least) to strangers. To *Confucius* political loyalty was to be held above all others, then loyalty to the family and then finally to others. Loyalty and love are thus graded and has a very clear hierarchy in the world of Mr. Kong Fuzi.

This hierarchy also reflects *Confucius'* thinking that each person must clearly know their position in society and reinforces the idea of loyalty and respect from inferior to superior (to be a good Confucian it seems you must know your place in this world, accept that place, and strive to do your best in that role for the good of society as a whole). Knowing your place also relates to the idea of "filial piety" which is also central to *Confucian* thinking and in general terms means taking care of one's parents, behaving yourself in a way that upholds the family name, showing love, respect and support, and displaying courtesy. Such filial piety naturally extends up through the hierarchy, culminating in unquestioning love and respect for the ruler. Social harmony thus results in part from everyone knowing their place in the natural pecking order of things, playing their part within it, while all the time demonstrating the prerequisite degree of loyalty and respect.

Confucius also extended this notion of loyalty and respect into an insistence on ritual. However, in the eyes of *Confucius* such rituals were not limited to simply ceremonies for ancestor worship or formal ceremonies such as funerals or weddings. It seemingly also included almost the entire web of interaction in the daily lives of the individual, ranging from the etiquette of how to receive guests, using correct and formal names, tea drinking, mourning, even to everyday gestures of politeness such as bowing. Such concern for rituals and proper etiquette in everyday life fell short of stating what sock you had to put on first, or on what side of your head you should comb your hair (but only just), but nevertheless *Confucius* saw adherence to rituals and etiquette as vital to help bind an individual to his community and society as a whole, and could also be seen as an outward sign of one's inner virtue (despite the fact that this meant that everyone now looked and acted exactly the same, leaving little room for self-expression or individualism)

Reciprocity or self-reflection is also a key *Confucian* value and is seen as a means to govern our actions towards others. The "golden rule" of many moral and ethical philosophies (and many religions) is "do unto others as you would wish done to yourself", however, in this respect *Confucius* preaches this rule as a negative "not to do unto others as you would not wish done to yourself" (if you don't want someone to steal your wok or covet your wife, then don't steal their wok or wife first). In this subtle difference *Confucius* preaches restraint rather than action, and thus implying modesty and humility, which he also sees as a form of loyalty to oneself.

Confucius' philosophy can be seen as very much a guide book for ethical and social conduct that has at its root the goal of an harmonious society ruled by a just and virtuous ruler. This clearly is in stark contrast to the philosophy of the *Daoists* who preached that society was in many ways harmful to an individual's goal which was one of seeking to find harmony within themselves as an individual. *Daoists* were reclusive individuals who downplayed rituals, political loyalty, and a person's role in society, rather stressing that wisdom was to be found by tuning one's "inner person" to the rhythms of nature, seeking harmony within oneself. *Confucius* on the other hand sought the same wisdom and virtue but much more in the context of seeking harmony within society as a whole, and in relation to others.

Ultimately, *Confucius* found few takers for his ethical and social vision at Court and so likely somewhat miffed (but obviously in a loyal, sincere, and self-reflective way) he decided to pack his bags and spend the rest of his life travelling throughout China teaching his philosophy to anyone prepared to listen. Although he did eventually find many pupils and disciples for his teachings, it was not really until the formation of the Han dynasty (206 B.C. - 220 A.D.) some 250 years after his death that *Confucianism* gained any real prominence when it was formally adopted as the official state ideology.

However, even outside of the Hippie-styling's of the *Daoists*, many other scholars of the time were also not convinced by *Confucius*' vision for world order. One such objector was *Mo Tzu* (c. 470-391 B.C.), sometimes referred to as *Mozi* or even *Micius*, a scholar born around the same time that *Confucius* was taking his final ritualistic bow, and who seemingly felt so strongly about his objections to *Confucian* teachings that he decided to found his own rival school of philosophy, one that became known as *Mohism*.

Mo Tzu looked to escape what he saw as the *Confucian* over-attachment to the state, family, and clan structures, and instead taught a view of what he called "universal love", a love where everyone cared for everyone else equally rather than in some graded form of degrees of love as argued by Confucians. *Mo Tzu* believed that if everyone loved one another equally regardless of their rank, status, sexual orientation, physical appearance, or Chinese slipper size, then that shared mutual love would bring benefit to all. Now we can view *Mo Tzu's* philosophy as preaching something of a flower-power, communal love-fest for willing Chinese hippies of the Warring States period, but there was more to his philosophy than merely preaching collective group hugs.

Mo Tzu believed that in treating all others as we would wish to be treated ourselves, we will receive similar treatments in return. Such universal caring when applied by rulers avoids unrest, conflicts, and war, and when applied by everyone it leads to a more harmonious, happy, and thus more productive society. It would also lead to opportunity for all based upon talent rather than background and so placed no emphasis on individuals "knowing their place" as the Confucians preached.

In *Mo Tzu's* world, actions are deemed to have moral worth based on how the action contributed to the whole (the state) in terms of social order, stability, and benefit, thus promoting his idea of universal love with the aim of mutual benefit to all. *Mo Tzu* also emphasised self-reflection rather than obedience to ritual, believing that reflecting on one's successes and failures was the only way one would find true self-knowledge, not through chanting, lighting joss-sticks, praying for dearly departed, bowing to precisely the correct angle, drinking your tea with your little pinky-finger raised, or any other form of what he saw as mere blind conformity to rituals.

Mohism, along with *Daoism* and *Confucianism*, were to that point the three most widely adopted philosophies to emerge from the chaos of the Warring States period. But then just as these schools of thought were getting into their stride a philosophical disaster was about to strike. Strangely, it was a philosophical disaster born out of the peace that was to finally settle over China as the country eventually fell under the control of the Qin dynasty bringing the

Warring States period to a close, the very peace and stability that each philosophy in their own unique way had looked to foster.

The Warring States period was effectively a power struggle between seven rival states (the Yan, Zhao, Qi, Chu, Han, Wei, and Qin states, for those with a budding interest in Chinese history), each trying to defeat the others in an attempt to unify the country under their own control. Power and control ebbed and flowed as battles were won and lost, and political manoeuvrings succeeded and failed, but effectively little progress was made by any state for almost 100 years. It looked like this Warring States period of Chinese history was in for the long haul but then around the middle of the fourth century B.C. the State of Qin discovered and then unleashed a secret weapon.

Their secret weapon was in the form of a statesman by the name of *Shang Yang* (390-338 B.C.), an uncompromising and very stern looking individual (if surviving statues of him are to be believed), and who under the favouritism of the Qin king became Chief Advisor to the state, and immediately set about changing Qin from the rather peripheral state it was at the time to one of unrivaled military power with a strong, efficient (and notably ruthless) centralized political base. *Shang Yang* achieved this remarkable feat by implementing his ideology of extreme reforms all underpinned by a philosophy that effectively amounted to a policy of setting strict laws, and delivering harsh punishments for anyone who disobeyed those laws, a philosophical school of thought that was to become known as *Legalism.*

However, despite his single-handed efforts to successfully drag the Qin state to the top of the Warring States league tables, *Shang Yang* was deeply despised by the Qin nobility who's power and lands he had ruthlessly devolved to a far more centralized administration. So much so that on the death of his one key ally and supporter, the then Qin king, he fell foul of the next ruler who promptly charged him with inciting rebellion and, in a manner that would have under different circumstances appealed to *Shang Yang's* ideology of harsh and swift punishment, sentenced him to a rather unpleasant death. If the history books are to be believed it appears that *Shang Yang's* head and limbs were each tied to separate chariots which were then encouraged to gallop off in five different directions, taking various parts of the previous Chief Advisor with them.

Unlike other philosophies of the time there was no real organized school of *legalism*, it rather grew out of the reforms of the different states and political manoeuvrings of various leaders, slowly building upon each other to the point where *Shang Yang* merely implemented such ideologies but with the added twist of doing so in a far more draconian and ruthless fashion. *Shang Yang* believed totally in the rule of law and considered loyalty to the state to be above that of the family or clan, (in reality not too dissimilar to the teachings of Confucius), however, he promoted not just the rule of law but an absolute adherence to that rule of law regardless of who you were or what your circumstances were.

Han Fei (280-233 B.C.) a philosopher and scholar (famed as much for his habitual stammering as his philosophical works) did go on to further synthesize the ideas of *Shang Yang* and other earlier *legalist* scholars into a formal school of thought, and one which took as its basis the assumption that all people are naturally evil and thus always acted in a way to avoid punishment while trying to achieve gain. As such the law must severely punish unwanted actions while at the same time reward those who follow it. The philosophy also emphasised that the emperor (the head of state) held total authority and as such his decisions must always command unflinching respect and obedience from his people. The state very clearly came first, with individuals having no civil rights or personal freedom outside of that which would strengthen the ruler (*Lao Tzu* would have been turning in his grave).

Han Fei's interpretation of *Legalism* stressed that the ruler would be able to achieve the ultimate ends of *Legalist* philosophy (one of firm and total control over the state), by the use of three concepts to govern his subjects. Firstly by ensuring that both the law is clearly written and made public and that everyone regardless of rank, power, sex, hairstyle, or size of their wok, were equal before that law. Secondly the ruler should employ tactics and craft to ensure that others cannot take control of the state, and finally recognize that it is the position of ruler and not the ruler himself that holds the power (respect the role not the man).

67

As such, the now highly structured and ruthlessly ruled centralized kingdom of Qin with its strong political base and lean, mean, "take no prisoners" military fighting machine which *Shang Yang's* reforms and *legalist* agenda had created, now quickly went on to conquer the other six states and to eventually gain control over all China. Thus by 221 B.C. the first imperial dynasty of China, the Qin dynasty (221-206 B.C.), had been born under its founding emperor Qin Shi Huang. And it's at that point that the philosophical wheels started to fall off the noble philosophies of *Confucius, Lao Tze* and *Mo Tzu*.

Qin Shi Huang was (not surprisingly) keen to consolidate his power and cement *legalism* as the dynasty's one true philosophy and so in something of a "sledgehammer to crack a nut" approach he promptly ordered the burning of any and all books that held even the slightest whiff of advocating viewpoints that challenged either *legalism* or the state. And not content with just eradicating other schools of thought the emperor also decreed that any scholar who refused to submit their work for burning was themselves to be executed by being buried alive. This of course caused something of a problem for the other rather more peace-loving rival schools of thought and their scholars, and understandably their schools rather lost their popularity (publically at least), with *Mohism* it seems suffering particularly during this period (*Mo Tzu's* idea of equal love and respect for all was never going to cut any truck with the "ruler is all powerful" approach of the *Legalists*).

Partly due to this forced suppression of all other schools of thought, along with the strictness of the laws and ruthless severity of the punishments for those who disobeyed them, the Qin dynasty did not last long. After the death of its first emperor in 210 B.C. a popular revolt (which should have come as no surprise to anyone) broke out and the now weakened empire fell to a rebel leader who promptly brought the curtain down on a rather short-lived Qin dynasty to form an imperial dynasty of his own. The Han dynasty (206 B.C. - 220 A.D.) went on to span over four centuries and is considered a golden age of Chinese history.

But most importantly to our little story, with the fall of the somewhat brutal Qin dynasty *legalism* quickly became demonized and as such disappeared from the philosophical map almost as quickly as it had appeared. The earlier philosophies of *Confucius, Mo Tzu* and *Lao Tze* were now once again accepted (although the popularity of *Mohism* never really did recover from the beating it took under the Qin rulers), and although the Han court did ultimately give exclusive patronage to *Confucianism*, China it seems had once again found its philosophical bearings, and so the nation was now free once again to go on and invent gunpowder, paper, the compass, take-away food, cheap Kung Fu movies, and fake handbags.

9

From Under the Bodhi Tree

"Happy is he who has overcome his ego"
Siddhartha Gautama (c. 563-483 B.C.)

We are reliably informed by the clever bods who study these things that the oldest form of recorded philosophy (and we do have to use the term "philosophy" very loosely here) comes from India. These ancient texts are known as the *Vedas* and give or take a day or two date back to around 1,500 B.C. and are really a combination of poetry, mythology, and cosmology, which form a loose collection of "philosophies" bound up under the general heading of *Hinduism.*

Hinduism itself is today seen as a "philosophy-come-religion" that is populated by a central trinity of gods, *Brahma* (the creator), *Vishnu* (whose job is to maintain the Universe), and *Shiva* (the god of destruction). Three gods who themselves can apparently take on many other forms and manifestations, serve different functions, and confusingly can go by many different names (*Vishnu* alone seems to have at least 1,000 alternative manifestations and names). However, even more confusingly, these are all just the faces of one God, a God who presides over absolute reality that is made of one substance, a substance known as *Brahman,* (something that clearly would have added to the confusion of poor old *Thales* and his students back in Athens) which itself exists in the infinite number of manifestations that create the universe we all know and love.

Unfortunately, knowledge of *Brahman* (the One) it seems cannot be understood simply through reason, simple reflection, or even just plain straight forward spiritual belief, no, it apparently also requires something of an all-encompassing mystical experience to understand its true nature. Hence we see the numerous *Hindu* practices and exercises (such as body-contortioning *yoga*) all geared towards the goal of that pre-requisite "mystical" experience of *Brahman*, the true reality.

The idea that there are many gods who are actually just different manifestations of the same one God, along with the rather bewildering concept of an absolute reality (*Brahman*) that is completely independent of, and unknown to us mere mortals, can leave many as confused as a hungry baby in a topless bar. Thus, it was out of this melting pot of mysticism and mythology that we see step forward one *Siddhartha Gautama* (563 - 486 B.C.), more familiar to us as *the Buddha* (the *Enlightened one*), and who chosen mission it seems was to provide the good people of India a far more straightforward and somewhat less mystical philosophy.

Siddhartha Gautama would go on to gift the world the philosophy we now know as *Buddhism* which offered the likely spiritually confused Indian populace of the day a far simpler personal philosophy, one which importantly preached equality, free from any mysticism or gods, and one which itself would go on to influence millions of people around the world.

Siddhartha Gautama was born into a privileged family sometime around 560 B.C. somewhere in modern-day Nepal, and as such we can safely assume he spent much of his younger life indulging himself in the various luxuries and pleasures that were thus afforded him. However, it appears that at some point the young *Gautama* seems to have become somewhat dissatisfied with his lifestyle and he began to feel that his 6th century "lives of the rich and famous" lifestyle was not enough on its own to bring him true happiness (although we can assume that likely he had given the tires a good kick).

Young *Gautama* became acutely aware of all the suffering he saw in the world around him, suffering caused by sickness, death, jealousy, poverty, and also a recognition that even the pleasures he had so happily enjoyed himself only gave temporary relief from such suffering. *Gautama* (not unsurprisingly) also found that adopting a life of extreme abstinence and frugality (effectively steering clear of any sensual or aesthetic pleasures) also brought him no nearer to either achieving or understanding any true happiness (although fair

71

play to him for trying, particularly given his lifestyle up to that point).

And so, in search of a way to find true happiness *Gautama* packed his bags, put on his Tibetan coat, turned his back on his previous life, and set off south in the general direction of India to find the true meaning of happiness and hopefully a way of attaining it. However, rather than looking for the answer in any religious or divine revelation, *Gautama* sought answers through reason, and thus his quest was a philosophical one, one designed to discover truths, truths that would be available to all through the power of that reason.

The first step in *Gautama's* reasoning was to draw the conclusion that suffering is universal (seemingly no one escapes at least some level of pain), it is an integral part of our existence and is caused by the frustrations of our desires and expectations, our need for self-preservation, our pride and ambitions, what he called our *"attachments"*. Even our health, our family and friends, can all be seen as a form of *attachment*, we become mentally and emotionally attached to them and so when things change (illness, death, an argument with a neighbor over an inappropriate lawn ornament) we feel pain.

Gautama saw that we can often satisfy our desires and ambitions in the short-term (as he clearly had done in his youth), but these were only temporary, and *Gautama* did not see this as the way to any true happiness, it was the *attachments* themselves that were the problem. In many ways we can see life as a constant cycle of frustration and boredom, when we don't have what we want we are frustrated, and when we do have what we want we become bored and desire new distractions.

Gautama's next (and actually quite obvious) logical step was to conclude that if we just get rid of any and all such *attachments* this should then naturally prevent such suffering and so open up the door to true happiness, simple really. But to do this, first he had to find the root cause of such *attachments* (just where was all this greed, ambition, desire, coming from?), and for *Gautama* the root cause was our own *ego*. It is our *ego*, our belief in our "self" as an independent being, which drives our desires, our selfishness, self-centeredness, our need for gratification. According to *Gautama*, if we let go of what drives these things, our *ego*, stop seeing ourselves as unique, special, as independent from everything else in the universe, then we can free ourselves from all such *attachments* and so finally be truly happy.

But then *Gautama* was faced with a problem. Our desires and ambitions, our emotional and mental *attachments* (and thus our *ego*), are all part of who we are, part of our nature and to some extent what makes us human. Clearly we all need our *ego* to have half a chance of surviving in our world fuelled by such ambition and desires, so then how to explain our *ego* in a way that it makes "logical" sense for us to actually want to let go of it?

It seems that after many hours of quiet contemplation and chin-stroking sitting in the shade of a Bodhi tree with his feet up it appears that *Gautama* experienced an "enlightenment" that made it all suddenly very clear to him. He reasoned that in fact nothing exists permanently, there is only perpetual change, everything being the result of some previous action via some all-inclusive giant causal chain linking everyone and everything to each other in a constant cycle of universal change. As such, everything we see, feel, desire, is just a momentary part of an eternal process, and so ultimately impermanent and without substance. Therefore, there cannot be any permanent body, soul, or self, we are all really just a temporary composite of body, feeling, thoughts, and consciousness, and thus true reality amounts to nothing more than just a series of momentary existences.

Gautama thus sees that our vision of ourselves as a permanent unique "self" (as seen and supported by our *egos)* is all just one big illusion. In reality there is no "self" we are all just a constituent part of a simple but much greater whole, but it is our failure to recognize this (our delusion that our *egos* have reality) that is the cause of all our suffering.

Now, clearly *Gautama* wasn't preaching that we should all run around denying our own and everybody else's existence or identity (of course we all still exist), but what he was saying was that by understanding that you are merely part of a much greater whole, transient and insubstantial, you will find the key to letting go of your *attachments* and thus find a release from suffering. In short, you will find true happiness. As a philosophy, *Buddhism* is at its root quite simple, hang on to your *ego* and you will continue to suffer, let go of your *ego* and you will find true happiness.

Gautama formalized his reasoning in the *Buddhist* teachings of the *Four Noble Truths*, namely that suffering is universal (no one is exempt), that desire and *attachments* are the cause of all suffering (whatever it is you desire, eventually you will suffer for it), suffering can be avoided by eliminating desire and *attachments* (take plenty of cold showers, it makes sense in the long run), and that what he called the *"Eightfold Path"* is the means to eliminate all that desire and so overcome the *ego* (the end-game, happiness is achieved).

The *Eightfold Path* as outlined by *Gautama* is effectively a practical guide, a rule book, by which followers can themselves eliminate desire and the illusion of the *ego* and thus achieve enlightenment. In brief, it is the *Buddhist* code of ethics, a guide for leading a good life, and ultimately finding true happiness. The *Eightfold Path* preaches (surprise ,surprise) eight steps to such enlightenment, the steps being right action, right intention, right livelihood, right effort, right concentration, right speech, right understanding, and right mindfulness. By following these eight steps anyone it seems can overcome their *ego* (presumably in much in the same way as alcoholics can free themselves of their addiction to the happy-juice by following the Alcoholics Anonymous slightly longer twelve-step plan), and thus free themselves from the endless cycle of eternal suffering, free themselves from their *ego*.

After experiencing his own "enlightenment moment" under the bodhi tree, *Gautama* devoted the rest of his life travelling throughout India under his new title as the "enlightened one", the *Buddha*, teaching his philosophy and gaining quite a considerable following. The *Buddha's* teaching were subsequently passed down through the generations by word of mouth until they were finally committed to paper in the 1st century A.D.

Buddhism has since exercised a profound influence in shaping many aspects of not just Indian but Eastern society as a whole (and indeed around the world). Although in India it would never dislodge *Brahmanism* from its lofty perch, it was never meant to be a "religious" alternative, but it did however succeed in jolting it out of its increasingly elaborate and complex ritualistic teachings.

In a country that by that time had become dominated by the caste system and its inherent racist evils, *Buddhism* offered the people a simpler ethical code, one based on charity, equality, self-sacrifice, truthfulness, and love. Importantly it laid an emphasis on the fact that man himself could control his own destiny rather than the Gods, and its promotion of social equality and justice found many willing to adopt its teachings.

Thus to some extent *Buddhism* was the right philosophy born at the right time, and once widely accepted across the Indian continent went on to become a world "religion" to over 350 million of today's global citizens looking for spiritual guidance towards their own "happiness".

Buddhism's rise in India can be seen in contrast to the rise of the major philosophical schools that arose in China where we can see philosophy built primarily more out of necessity, out of a need to find solutions to very practical problems (such as the fact that the political system and the country as a whole was falling apart). As such Chinese philosophy can be seen as a very practical school of thought, giving rise to philosophies that were to prove so popular they were even taken up by China's future leaders and ones which shaped the politics of the "Middle Kingdom" for millennia to come. Chinese philosophy was and remains ever practical, was built for everyone from Emperor to farmer, and reflects the same practical approach seen in their views on science and technological discovery.

China has a technological and scientific tradition that dates back long before any in the West, inventing gunpowder, eyeglasses, the compass, paper, chopsticks, and even the mighty Chinese noodle (or as they simply call it in China, the noodle) long before the West had even thought about a knife and fork or numerous different ways to slice, cook, and eat, the mighty potato. But their approach has always been a practical one, addressing real problems, rather than random advances brought about because some eccentric science bod woke up one day with a "good idea". Invention and scientific knowledge for its own sake simply made no sense to the pragmatic Chinese (it was seen as a waste of valuable time, time probably seen as better spent enjoying noodles), and so it is with their approach to philosophy, which had little to do with any idealistic "search for the truth" and much more to do with solving very practical problems.

Interestingly, we can also clearly see that apart from the obvious geographical differences (even the most cerebrally challenged high school student would struggle to miss that one), there are some very distinct differences between the early schools of thought of the East and the West. Primary amongst these differences is that Eastern philosophy was clearly based far more on "collectivism", the concept of finding meaning in our relationship to everyone and everything else around us, our relationship to the larger whole. Eastern philosophy in both India and China was seen as a search for the discovery of the "true" me, a search for meaning "inside" yourself in relation to the universe, and where the stability of the universe, and of society, is deemed more important than any one individuals rights or freedoms.

Western philosophies on the other hand are seen as far more centered around "individualism", the idea that we must try to find meaning first and foremost for ourselves, our own individual relationships with ideal truths and the universe around us. Early Western philosophy is thus seen as a search for meaning "outside" of yourself, and where individual rights and freedoms form the basis for a just society.

The main principles of Eastern philosophies are thus unity, harmony, that life is cyclic and reoccurring, where everything in the universe is connected, and where the truth is revealed to us as we free ourselves from a false "me", a freedom attained only through spiritual meditation. In sharp comparison Western philosophies take a far more linear view of life and the universe where everything has a beginning and an end, and where the truth is revealed to us not by sitting cross-legged on the floor surrounded by incense, joss-sticks, and quietly chanting incantations, but by searching outside yourself through dedicated formal research and analysis.

Thus we see the stereotypes of the practicing Eastern philosopher as the robed sage whose sits silently meditating on top of a mountain surrounded by burning incense with his body effortlessly falling into some impossibly contorted yoga position. While that of the Western philosopher as the pipe-smoking bearded academic whose head is constantly buried in lengthy volumes of dusty books and papers. Simply put, the difference is the focus on the "I" in the West and on the "we" in the East.

Such differences have even permeated right through into the social and political cultures we see today both in the East and West, and is most strikingly obvious in the way each conducts business. In the East business in conducted in a way so as to avoid direct confrontation, emphasises moral conduct and saving face, humility and respect are encouraged, and where harmony across the collective whole is considered paramount. While in the West the individual feels free to do whatever it takes to get the job done, regardless of who he needs to shout at, embarrass, or argue with along the way. From a business perspective neither is particularly right or wrong, both get the job done, the issue is when East and West try to do business together, when the "time is money, snooze you lose" American meets the inscrutable "let's first drink another cup of tea?" Chinese businessman, and both serve as a "practical" example of how philosophy can permeate how we lead our day to day lives.

Thus, on the face of it, it appears that the philosophies of the West and East seem as polar opposite as a beauty pageant contestant and a fully paid-up baggy cardigan, sandal wearing feminist. But despite starting from different perspectives, travelling down philosophically different paths, and having seemingly inflicted differing influences on the cultural make-up of their respective future populations, the two schools of thought still found much common ground in their views around ethics and moral conduct.

Their philosophies may be worded in different languages (literally and philosophically) but the teachings of *Confucius, Lao Tzu, Siddhartha Gautama* , and that of *Socrates, Plato,* and even *Diogenes,* at a basic level all teach that greed, desire, possessions, and power, all corrupt and that if we truly wish to find happiness (regardless whether we expect to find that happiness in this life or in some future life) we should focus our attentions much more on freeing ourselves from such distractions and pain, and look to live in harmony (either individually or collectively) with nature. However, god knows what conversations would have taken place if *Confucius* had actually met *Socrates* or heaven forbid if anyone at all from the East had actually met *Diogenes.*

10

Plato and the Pulpit

"God is not the parent of evils"
St. Augustine of Hippo (354 - 430)

By the 4th century A.D. the mighty Roman Empire that had ruled most of Europe and North Africa for almost 500 years was now effectively on its knees. Corruption, runaway inflation, taxes to make even the most stoic Roman weep, a series of despotic and half mad emperors, topped with the constant threat of strange Germanic hoards with big sticks and designs on the women of the city constantly knocking at the city gates, had all started to take its toll.

Even a last ditch attempt in 330 A.D to save the empire by splitting it in half, creating two separately governed Empires, one based in the west centered in Rome and the other based in the east around the newly formed Eastern capital of Constantinople, merely delayed the inevitable. The Western Empire still fell within 100 years to invading Goths who in 410 A.D. eventually had their Germanic-way with Rome and presumably its female population (they were young, they were male, they'd likely had a few beers, and so the resulting mayhem was a bit of a foregone conclusion, frankly it all got rather ugly), and although the Eastern Empire remained nominally intact right up until the 15 century, it was really only an Empire on paper.

As for philosophy during the several hundred years or so that Rome had been making decisions on the world's behalf, it had not really progressed much more beyond the teachings and philosophies of those early Greeks who had so enthusiastically embraced the magically combination of logic, reason, beards, and sandals some 600 years earlier. In truth, philosophy never really interested the Romans too much, they were much more likely to get excited about military conquests and engineering feats such as building arrow straight roads, viaducts, and huge coliseums where they could watch overly-buffed men fight both each other, hapless Christians, and assorted wild animals in mortal combat.

Rome, particularly around 200 B.C. under the direction of *Seneca*, a statesman and advisor to the then Emperor Nero, had however informally adopted *stoicism* as its preferred philosophical school of thought, but never really progressed its teachings, or indeed that of any other philosophical school, and although the Romans gifted the world many technological, political, and cultural advances, including the bikini, they really paid little or no attention to progressing the work of those early Greek philosophers.

However, while Rome had been slowly sowing the seeds of its own self-destruction, a new religion was starting to gather steam. Christianity had been slowly gaining popularity in and around the Mediterranean and the middle east for quite some time, and had developed out of single individual, namely Jesus of Nazareth, who lived from approximately 5 B.C. to 32 A.D. (although it seems the actual day of his birth is clear to everyone, the actual year apparently remains uncertain) in Palestine, which at the time was still part of the Roman Empire. Jesus was the self-proclaimed son of God, the Messiah, who seemingly died a rather unpleasant death nailed to a cross to save us all from sin, subsequently decided to come back from the dead just for a few days (presumably because he could, and also to give himself the opportunity to tie-up a few unresolved loose-ends), and who apparently is set to return again (the fabled Christian "second coming") at some point to rule over his kingdom on Earth on his Dad's behalf.

As a religion Christianity quickly spread in all directions out of Palestine in the early 1st century A.D., and by the 2nd century Christianity could lay claim to followers in all parts of the Roman Empire. Initially though Romans viewed Christianity as nothing more than an obscure cult and greeted it with open hostility, and although feeding Christians to the lions as a sport may be more of an early example of an urban myth rather than the regular Sunday afternoon entertainment for bored Romans as we are led to believe, it does however give an indication as to the less than lukewarm reception Christians generally received from the good folk of Rome and its Empire.

Rome itself also paid little attention to the new cult, never quite grasping a religion based around someone who was in their eyes simply just a common thief who had already been duly tried and crucified for his misdemeanors along with several other "low-life" back in 32 A.D. Ultimately though, Christianity steadily grew in popularity to the point where by the time the Roman Empire had stumbled on its knees into the 3rd century A.D., the emperor of the day, Constantine, issued an "edict of toleration", effectively accepting Christianity as a legitimate religion of the Empire.

As the Roman Empire slowly imploded and consigned itself into the history books, Europe was plunged into what has become known as the "Dark ages", a period in Europe's history that was to last for about a thousand years and whose name symbolizes the fact that much of the cultural and technological advances of both the Greek and Roman Empires disappeared. Effectively, all that wonderful "civilization" so helpfully introduced by the Romans was packed-away into storage and left to gather dust for the next several hundred years, not to be seen again until the emergence of the Renaissance.

It was a period of seemingly constant war, poverty, stagnant cultural growth, boils, warts, disease and poverty, most of Europe fell back into feudalism, England and France spent almost 100 years fighting a war over something that was probably forgotten after the first five years, and to top it all a plague of biblical proportions swept the continent during the 14th century killing around 200 million people and reducing the population by about a third. It was not the greatest time to be European, particularly a poor European.

But it wasn't all gloom and doom in the middle-ages (the now rather more "politically correct" term for the same period). It was also the time when the various nations of Europe started to establish themselves, each developing their own unique culture, language, folklore and customs. It is also the period when the first universities opened their doors, and it is the period we also romantically associate with kings and queens in their fairytale castles, knights in shining armour riding around the countryside slaying dragons and performing selfless acts of heroism and valor, and folk-heroes such as Robin Hood running around the forest in green tights stealing from the rich and giving to the poor.

And it was also during this period that we see the Christian church rise to power, filling the void left by the collapse of the Roman Empire, effectively becoming a unifying force across the entire European continent, and thus growing to become the single dominant authority across Europe during the period. For the next thousand years it was the Christian Church which would hold sway over all over Europe, it created the rich and powerful great monastic orders all housed in newly built grand monasteries, made pudding-bowl haircuts fashionable and sex a sin, and it was to hold a monopoly on education, thinking, and most importantly philosophy.

Christianity, like its sister religion Judaism which can trace its own roots back to Moses and his 40 year trek leading his people out of Egypt to the promised land (and indeed even further back to around 3,000 B.C. to the Jewish "godfather" Abraham), is based upon a belief in a single all-powerful God, a God who is ultimately good but who nonetheless wields ultimate divine authority. A God who provides God-given divine laws that apply to everyone, everything, everywhere, regardless of who they are, king, slave, rich, poor, handsome, ugly, or mother-in-law. This belief in one single all-powerful God is known as *monotheism*.

Such divine law makes simple business of ethics, basically the rule is that if God says it's wrong, then it's wrong, no ifs, buts, or maybes, end of story. God's word is thus not up for discussion or interpretation, his word is final (God's rules may be restrictive and sometimes overly harsh, but at least they are clear), and Christians should probably give thanks that Moses only came down from Mount Sinai with 10 commandments rather than a more sizable rule-book.

It's no surprise then that Christianity, and indeed Judaism, came to rely very much on the written word to define their doctrines (the Old and New Testaments of the Bible). But this only opened the door to issues of interpretation, particularly when trying to interpret and reconcile these scriptures with even the slightest touch of philosophical reason.

81

Try applying reason and logic to a literal interpretation of the story of Noah's flood for instance (just how big would Noah's Ark had to have been to fit two of every single species onboard, how on earth did they feed them all, how much boarding notice did they have to give to the snails and the sloths, and just what were the sanitary arrangements?) and you will very quickly find your logic on shaky ground. Could reason (philosophy) ever be reconciled to a belief in an all-powerful God and his written divine word? These issues quite naturally came to a head when confronted by Greek philosophy, and although much early Greek philosophy seemed initially at odds with Christianity, the former being primarily based upon logic and reason and the later on faith, the church did however seem to find a friend in *Plato*.

Fortunately, the church found that many of *Plato's* ideas seemed to fit rather well with their doctrines given his belief that man was a dual beast, divided between body and soul, with the soul being more closely identified with goodness and truth, while his *Theory of Forms* and its "ideal world" could easily be interpreted as the Christian Heaven with our physical world merely a poor imitation full of evil. *Plato's* ideas were thus seen by many as complimentary (well almost) to church doctrines, and so opened the door just a little to offer a possible means of reconciling reason and faith.

The first philosopher to try and reconcile religious beliefs with Greek reason was a Jewish thinker named *Philo* (20 B.C.- 40 A.D.) living in Alexandria, the center of Hellenistic culture at the time. *Philo* saw a similarity between what *Plato* had described as "ideal forms", particularly the ideal form of "good", with that of God. To *Philo* these were effectively the same thing.

Philo believed that God, seen as the "ideal" of goodness, is a oneness that underlies all things, and that we can thus come to understand this oneness both through reason and through religious faith. *Philo* saw God as a kind of universal, all seeing, all powerful, mind, through which all other "ideal" forms (*Plato*) can be understood as God's thoughts (religion), and this is where *Philo* got suitably creative recognizing that according to the scriptures man was made in God's image and as such our human mind was also presumably modeled after God's mind, and thus we are also able to understand God's mind (goodness) through our mind, through reason.

However, *Philo* also recognized that as humans we are also constrained by our desires and needs (jealousy, greed, material goods, illness) all of which can distract us from a true understanding, and this is where faith steps in, for faith allows us to achieve a mystical connection with God, something reason alone cannot do.

However, *Philo* also declared that although we can see God as a kind of universal mind, God is also not a mind (philosophy is rarely straightforward), He is something much greater, and that the idea of seeing God as like a mind should only be taken as an approximation of what God actually is, it is an image that helps us to understand God better, to start to understand God through reason. But to truly understand God we need that mystical connection, that vision, that only faith can give us.

In the same way that *Philo* saw reason being able to give us a good approximation of God, goodness, and the oneness that underlies all things, he also saw the words of the Bible also as only approximations of the real truth they pointed to. He thus saw the stories in the Bible as metaphors for the true meaning of God's word, for the "ideal" form of things, and believed that the scriptures should be read not literally, but as allegories to uncover their true meaning, the relationship between the "material" words and their "ideal" meanings.

In this way, *Philo* helped combine the reasoned logic of *Plato* and his "ideal" forms, with that of religion, even at one point going so far as to suggest that it was actually God who had inspired those early Greek philosophers (even though they clearly wouldn't have known it at the time).

This combining of religious doctrine and *Platonic* thinking is known as *Neo-Platonism*, and one of the most important of the *Neo-Platonic* philosophers was an Egyptian thinker named *Plotinus* (205-270). *Plotinus* elaborated on the ideas of *Philo* particularly in respect of the connection between God, the divine oneness, and the world of material things.

Plotinus also saw God as the supreme mind, and for *Plotinus* it was a mind that was constantly engaged in contemplation of itself, as such he saw that the creation itself emerged as a kind of by-product of this contemplation, and thus everything (the creation, ideal forms, and all material things) were effectively the result of God's thinking. This is often called the theory of *emanations*.

In this way, *Plotinus* saw the universe and everything in it as a work of art (a kind of Mona Lisa on a grand cosmic scale), an expression of the divine oneness, the thought of a fully spiritual mind (effectively God thought it and so it came, God's "Field of dreams"). However, unlike *Plato* who saw the material world as a poor version of the ideal world (his allegory of the cave), *Plotinus* saw even the material world as itself spiritual, emanating as it did from the mind of God. Reality then is a kind of work of art that expresses God's thinking, an expression of the divine oneness of which we are thus all a part of. *Plotinus* thus believed that if we can see past our belief in our individuality, our separateness from each other, the difference between ourselves and other things, we can truly experience God, experience the divine oneness of all things.

Plotinus did however still see a hierarchy in God's creation with the Spirit as the highest form of being which emerges directly from His Divine Mind, the Spirit itself illuminates the objects of the Divine Mind's thoughts (effectively *Plato's* forms), while the soul (our human soul) comes from the Spirit and guides life here in the material world which itself is merely the lowest form of the Divine Mind's emanations. Our human souls are thus in some sense divine and provide the link between Spirit and the material world. This mystical connection between God and the material world was a common element of *Neo-Platonism*, and was an important element of both philosophical and religious life throughout the mediaeval period.

Plotinus' theory of *emanations* helped provide the relationship between the divine world and the material world, and thus went a long way towards satisfying both philosophical and religious demands.

Another *Neo-Platonic* philosopher *St. Augustine of Hippo* (354-430) was particularly concerned with what became known as the "problem of evil". Christian philosophers needed to deal with one of the prime arguments against the existence of God, namely, if God exists then why is their evil in the world?

Maybe God is willing to prevent evil, but not able to, but then He cannot be all powerful (omnipotent), or maybe He is able but simply not willing, in which case He is merely malevolent (a distinctly non-God like characteristic). Maybe God is both willing and able to prevent evil, but then why is there evil in the world at all, or even worse, maybe he is neither willing or able, in which case He hardly meets the required standard and is thus clearly not a God at all. Clearly this was a bit of a dilemma for those early Christian philosophers and one that was going to need some sort of rational explanation pretty quickly.

Augustine's solution to this dilemma was a simple one. For *Augustine*, although God created everything that exists, he did not create evil, as evil is not a thing in itself, it is actually a lack of something, a lack of good (you presumably could then similarly argue that there is no ugliness in the world merely a lack of beauty, or no sadness just a lack of chocolate and hugs). But why would there be a "lack of good"?

Augustine saw that God created man as rational beings, but in doing so He also had to give man free-will and freedom of choice, and thus we are able to choose how we behave, choose between good and maybe not quite so good (evil). We thus have the freedom to "choose" to do wrong, and thus the possibility of sin is a necessary feature of free-will.

As rational beings we are able to get closer to God than say your cat or a pair of shoes, but rationality needs freedom of will to evaluate between choices, and so also opens up the possibility for us to choose to be evil (and thus paradoxically actually further away from God than your cat or that pair of shoes). Hence the evil in this world is not of God's making, it is man exercising his free-will in a somewhat less than positive manner. Of course this argument doesn't help at all when we look to explain "natural" evils such as earthquakes, floods, famines, and plagues, which clearly aren't caused because you didn't pay your taxes on time or because you stare at you neighbors wife a little longer than maybe you should.

Critics of *Augustine* argue simply that the world contains just too much evil and suffering to justify any such explanations.

However, perhaps *Augustine's* greatest contribution to western philosophy was his emphasis on one's personal, inner life, and its connection with God and the divine oneness of the universe. His spiritual autobiography, *The Confessions*, remains one of the most important investigations of the "self" in western literature, and as with *Plotinus, Augustine* saw the relationship between God and the human soul as the central concern of religion. As the soul was created out of the mind of God, out of God's divine oneness, *Augustine* saw self-knowledge as the primary way to know God, and it is this focus on the personal, inner spirit, that would slowly start to take center-stage in western thinking.

11

Building the House of Wisdom

"The ink of the scholar is more holy than the blood of a Martyr"
Islamic Prophet Muhammad (570 - 632)

Seemingly unhappy with the current batch of religious options available to them, the good (but presumably spiritually unfulfilled) people of the 7th century Arabian peninsula decided it was time for something of a change. As such they gathered all the leading lights of the day at the local oasis, and having parked their camels and left their curly-toed slippers at the front door, they collectively decided that what they needed was a new religion all of their own, and so they sent a middle-aged merchant out to the mountains near Mecca where he was instructed to wait until he received God's revelations through the medium of a heavenly angel. The duly enlightened merchant returned, documented the revelations in a book declaring it to be the words of the one true God. Hence was born the religion of *Islam*.

Now this may not be exactly how history books, or the followers of *Islam,* will recount the story (primarily as it's not exactly how events unfolded), however what we do know as true is that around the year 570 an Arab named *Muhammad* was born in Mecca (a city now found on world maps in Saudi Arabia), and who did go on to work primarily as a merchant. However, at aged forty, *Muhammad* took it upon himself to retreat to a cave in the mountains near Mecca for several nights (likely in response to a pending mid-life crisis or nagging wife), and it was during this period of quiet retreat and contemplation that he was supposedly visited by the angel Gabriel and received his first revelations from God. Duly enlightened, *Muhammad* returned and started to preach these revelations publically, declaring that from this point forward he was no longer to be considered merely a lowly merchant but now a prophet and a messenger from God.

However, the people of his home town of Mecca were not keen to jump on *Muhammad's* "one God" bandwagon , and so to escape persecution he and what few followers he had gathered up to that point high-tailed it out of town in 622 and headed for Medina, an event that was to go on to mark the beginning of the Islamic calendar. In Medina *Muhammad's* fortunes changed and having united the tribes of the area under his new religion, I*slam*, he gathered a sizable army and in 629 marched back to Mecca and took over the city with little trouble or bloodshed, destroyed all the existing pagan idols and temples he could find, and thus brought Mecca into the Islamic fold. By the time of his death a couple of years later in 632, *Muhammad* had effectively converted most of the Arabian peninsula to *Islam*.

The revelations received by *Muhammad* are recorded in a book that we now know as the *Qur'an*. The *Qur'an* is regarded by *Muslims* as the "word of God" and around which the whole Islamic religion is based. As such, the *Qur'an* is not seen as an earthly inspired book (it's not the thoughts, words, anecdotes, or witty tales of any human being, saint or sinner), but the exact words of God as revealed to *Muhammad* through the angel Gabriel, and thus are regarded as a miracle and so great care has been taken to preserve it without change. In fact, the *Qur'an* is considered so holy that even the letters on the page are deemed sacred. Under *Islam* those who believe and obey the laws as laid down in the *Qur'an* will be rewarded in paradise, whereas those who reject its message will be punished by being forced to listen to Jewish sermons and eating pork sausages all day. *Islam* then, like Judaism and Christianity, is a religion "of the book".

Islam spread rapidly into Asia, across northern Africa and into southern Europe particularly Southern Spain. The new *Islamic* empire rivalled Christian Europe in both size and influence, however unlike the church controlled west, it also actively encouraged philosophical thought recognizing that religious doctrines and rational enquiry could indeed exist side by side.

Thus the uniting of the Arab world under *Islam* proved the catalyst for what became known as the *Islamic Golden Age*, the period in history when the *Muslim* world experienced something of a scientific and cultural flourishing, and is generally recognized to cover the period of time between the 8th and 13th centuries and begins with the formation of the so-called *House of Wisdom* in the then Arabic cultural centre of Baghdad, and ends with the sacking of Baghdad by the Mongol invasion in 1258.

During this *Golden Age,* unlike the European church-controlled scholars of the time, *Muslims* demonstrated a strong interest in assimilating the scientific and philosophical knowledge from Greek, Roman, Chinese, Indian, and Persian civilizations, and so many classic works from the past that might well have been otherwise lost (and in fact were lost to their European counterparts) were saved and translated into Arabic and documented for posterity. As such, Baghdad quickly became something of a global intellectual centre for science, mathematics, medicine, trade, education, and of course philosophy, and the *House of Wisdom*, an intellectual centre for research and education founded in Baghdad around the early 8th century, was where notable scholars and assorted brainy-types from around the world sought to gather to translate this collective knowledge into Arabic, and as a consequence it is where many of the scientific and cultural advances associated with this period were made.

Unfortunately, the Christian Crusades of the 11th and 12th centuries started to put the Islamic world under pressure (nothing can distract you more from your daily routine of translation and invention than an army of sword wielding knights clad in shiny armor and on a holy mission from God, knocking at your door), but the greater threat was to come from the east during the 13th century in the form of the marauding hoards of the Mongol army.

In 1206 *Genghis Khan* (1162-1227) established a powerful dynasty among the Mongols of Central Asia, and in the space of the following twenty years or so Mr. Khan and his travelling Mongol hoards went on to conquer nearly 12 million square miles of territory (more than any other individual in history, including Alexander the Great). In the process *Genghis Khan* cut a somewhat deadly path of rape, pillage, and destruction throughout most of China and Central Asia, with his equally ruthless and ambitious descendants duly following on in the family business and expanding the Mongol Empire further, even as far east as parts of Europe and the Middle East.

By the time *Genghis Khan* was done with his global aspirations it is believed that his deadly trail of destruction was responsible for something in the region of 40 million deaths, and if certain scientific authorities are to be believed his rather enthusiastic approach to rape and pillage might have seen him be personally responsible for hundreds, if not thousands, of offspring around the globe. According to a recent genetic study (admittedly a hotly disputed study) it would seem that as a result of his seemingly prolific contributions to the human gene pool, as many as one in every 200 living men alive today may well carry some genetic footprint that originated from the mighty Mr. Khan, which if true would mean that a full 0.5 percent of today's male population may well be able to claim to be a direct descend to the great Khan himself.

It was in fact one *Hulagu Khan* (1218 - 1265), a grandson of *Genghis Khan*, under whose leadership the Mongols destroyed Baghdad, the then centre of Islamic power and intellectual discovery. The Mongol hoards swept into Baghdad early in 1258, and then (as was their usual practice) began a week long frenzy of looting, rape, pillage, and wholesale destruction. As a consequence, the Grand Library and the *House of Wisdom* containing countless historical documents and books were destroyed. Baghdad was left a ruined and sparsely populated city for several centuries after.

However, despite this inconvenient disruption by the Mongol hoards, the impact of those early Muslim scholars and their preserved Greek texts, along with their advances in astronomy, medicine, and mathematics cannot be underestimated, particularly on future western philosophical thinking. Most Islamic philosophers at the time were what clever-types like to call *polymaths*, meaning that they were usually well educated in numerous fields of study such as science, medicine, mathematics, and astronomy (they were what today we would simply call "egg-heads"). Primary amongst such philosopher egg-heads was *Ibn Sina*, or *Avicenna* as he was to become known in West for reasons best known to those early Europeans.

Avicenna (980 - 1037), who is recognized today as the most important philosopher to emerge from the *Islamic* world during this period, was something of a child prodigy, quickly surpassing his teachers in many subjects such as philosophy and medicine. He was to spend most of his life in the service of various princes both as a physician and a political advisor while spending most of his spare time writing texts on such diverse subjects as medicine, the mechanics of solids, and philosophy. But, despite his obvious brilliance *Avicenna* clearly managed to still upset someone as it is believed that he died under somewhat suspicious circumstances when his medications for colic were apparently intentionally tampered with.

Avicenna was a keen follower of *Aristotle*, but was also influenced by *Plato* and his ideas of *dualism*, the idea that the body and mind (the soul) are two distinct things that actually exist independently. In an attempt to logically prove his dualist ideas, *Avicenna* developed a "thought experiment" where he attempts to demonstrate that the mind (the self) exists because it is able to know that it exists, and that it is indeed distinct from the body.

In what became known as *Avicenna's Flying Man* experiment, he asks us to imagine we are blindfolded and floating in the air with our limbs separated from each other, and thus effectively deprived of all senses (imagine you're a blindfolded, naked, astronaut on a space-walk and you'll get the idea). *Avicenna* argues that despite being entirely without physical sensation, we will still be aware that we exist, that we have a "self", but a "self" that is clearly without any physical substance. Thus it follows that this "self" we perceive is clearly distinct from anything physical, and thus is proof that the existence of our "self" (our mind) is clearly distinct from our body.

Today, scientists and philosophers mostly reject the idea of any mind-body *dualism* given our modern-day understanding of the human brain, our minds and its thoughts are seen as simply just the activity of the brain, although there is still some discussion around the distinctions between the physical brain (the grey matter that presumably does all the work) and the thoughts and reason that result

91

from its activity. However, what *Avicenna's Flying Man* experiment does still show us is that regardless of our physical incarnation, we do all each have a "self", an "I", an "ego" that exists within us, regardless of whether it is entirely independent of our physical body or not.

Avicenna's Neo-Platonic take on the world remained the dominant philosophy of *Islam* for much of the 11th and 12th centuries, but it was not without its critics. *Ibn Rushd*, known to the West as *Averroes* (presumably by the same western scholars who also struggled with *Avicenna's* Arabic name), rather advocated Aristotle's far more empirical and rational approach. *Averroes* (1126 - 1198) was born in Cordoba, at that time part of Islamic Spain, and like all good *Islamic* polymaths he trained in law, science, medicine, and philosophy, but spent all his spare time both translating and writing commentaries on the works of Aristotle, works that would in themselves go on to have a significant influence on later Christian philosophy of mediaeval Europe.

Averroes key philosophical contribution however was his attempts to reconcile religion (specifically the *Qur'an*) and philosophy. The core of his reasoning was that the *Qur'an*, rather than providing an entirely accurate account of the universe, it rather presents a poetic, metaphorical truth, one that can be interpreted with philosophical reasoning. However, in a somewhat elitist slant, *Averroes* states that only educated scholars are capable of such interpretations, and everyone else (those who presumably don't have the prerequisite brain the size of a watermelon) are consigned to accept the teachings of religion (the *Qur'an*) purely on face value, and thus to read it as a literal truth.

Under *Averroes'* reasoning, whenever logic or reason indicates that a literal interpretation of the *Qur'an* is clearly false, these educated elite should ignore the words in their literal sense (presumably leaving such literal interpretation to the uneducated peasants) and rather look to "interpret" the text as a poetic truth, a truth based on reason, and thus providing an interpretation that allows philosophical reasoning and religion to remain wholly compatible.

Effectively, *Averroes* was proposing a kind of two-tiered religious interpretation of the *Qur'an*, one for those with something other than tumbleweed between their ears, and being an interpretative view that reconciled with Aristotelian thinking, and the other for all the rest of us, a straight literal interpretation that only requires us to take the teachings of the *Qur'an* at face value.

Not surprisingly, such "interpretations" of the *Qur'an* based upon *Aristotelian* philosophy (no matter how "poetic") was rather frowned upon by religious leaders and fellow *Muslims* alike, not least because the *Qur'an* is seen as the exact words of God as revealed to his prophet Muhammad, and as such should not be doubted or reinterpreted. However, to this day the idea of treating religious scriptures as merely allegories, a way to interpret text to discover real meaning, is an important bridge for "educated believers" who see it as a way to reconcile their faith with the logic and reason of today's scientific facts.

Despite the *Islamic* world's huge advances in fields such as astronomy, medicine, mathematics, and of course in philosophical thought, European church-controlled scholars remained either mostly ignorant of such advances or suspicious of such "pagan" thought. However, the Christian Crusades of the 11th and 12th centuries and the subsequent conquests of *Islamic* Spain and Jerusalem, greatly increased contact between the two cultures and as a consequence European scholars started to gain access to many ancient texts, associated *Islamic* thought, along with many of the scientific advances made by those overly bright *Islamic* scholars with their camels and curly-toed slippers. All this newly available "wisdom" suddenly prompted a renewed interest in philosophy in the west, and in particular in the newly re-discovered works of *Aristotle*, and as a result was set to kick-start a whole new movement in western philosophy.

12

The Church Discovers Aristotle

"Love takes up where knowledge leaves off"
Thomas Aquinas (1225 - 1274)

At some point during the year of 1095 the then head of the Christian church, Pope Urban II, seemingly had a particularly bad day, and as a result promptly ordered the good knights of Europe to unite and set off for the holy lands to regain the holy city of Jerusalem which had rather inconveniently been under Muslim control since the 7th century. Within a year several huge armies of armour-clad knights hyped-up with religious fervour had set out on the long march to Jerusalem on a Crusade to rescue the holy lands from the Muslim usurper, and thus starting a 200 year long period of holy Crusades against the Muslim Empire (by the end of the 12th century a total of no less than seven, largely unsuccessful, major Crusades had been mounted).

Outside of the mostly teeth gnashing and holy wailing of the Crusades, one plus point was to come out of all the bloodshed and war-mongering (all in the name of what was effectively the self-same God for both parties, God is presumably God whatever name you choose to give him), namely that the great Western thinkers of the time who were till then still tucked away in their comfortable monastic isolation, now suddenly found themselves with access to the new, fresh ideas and knowledge which were now starting to filter back from the Islamic Empire, which itself was at the time experiencing its cultural peak. As such, and most importantly to our own little story, it now provided these mediaeval Christian philosophers with access to the long lost works of the great philosophers from antiquity, and in particular to the works of *Aristotle*.

Up until this time European philosophers had looked to the thinking of *Plato* to help them reconcile philosophical reasoning with the church and its doctrines (as we have seen *Plato's* ideas around "ideal forms" and a human eternal soul had put something of a ecclesiastical grin on the leaders of the Christian church, enabling them as it did to conveniently draw parallels with God and heaven), while *Aristotle's* own take on things which seemingly discounted the ideas of an immortal soul, or any notion of a "heavenly" other-world, had caused much of his work to be largely and rather conveniently ignored by the all-powerful church leaders. The result was the unhappy circumstance that early mediaeval philosophers were largely oblivious to the works of *Aristotle* and his philosophy apart from the availability of the limited translations made by a Roman philosopher named *Anicius Boethius* (480 - 525), which themselves only focused primarily on Aristotle's works in the field of logic.

However, Arabic philosophic literature was now starting to find its way back to Europe as scholars eager for new knowledge rode on the coat-tails of the Crusaders (or more likely at a suitably safe distance somewhat behind those holy warriors dressed up as tin cans) to gain access to the *Muslim* world and its scientific and philosophical works, and so within a very short space of time all manner of *Muslim* knowledge, books, and works from antiquity, were being translated from Arabic into Latin ready for eager western scholars to enjoy as bedtime reading.

With this reintroduction of the newly translated works of *Aristotle* and other early Greek thinkers, it was not long before a new school of thought started to emerge in the newly formed universities that were popping up all over Europe. *Scholasticism* was a method for critical thinking which came to dominate academic teaching from around 1100 onwards. Not so much a philosophy as a method of learning, *scholasticism* placed strong emphasis on logically analysis and dialectic reasoning (primarily by turning to the newly available bestselling paperbacks of *Aristotle's* ideas around logic) to resolve what were seen as contradictions, points of disagreement, or contention, between early philosophical works and church doctrines.

Although it began as an attempt to reconcile Christian doctrine with classical philosophy (reason), *Scholasticism* quickly became known for a somewhat overly rigorous method of analysis and for going to almost absurd lengths of applying rigid rules and formal logic (enter Mr. Aristotle) to decide questions and contradictions. In many cases even individual words were often analysed for possible ambiguity, and logic applied to try and prove that contradictions were merely down to reader interpretation.

Thus, in terms of those who followed this all new shiny *scholastic* method (which by the mid 1100's was now just about everyone who wore a cassock to work), philosophy was now becoming considered a subject that required robust analysis and enquiry, and something better left only to those well versed in the subject's technical vocabulary (logic) and those with a deep familiarity with all known philosophical schools and traditions. In short, *scholasticism* was in part creating a breed of philosophical snobs who would spend days on end in an obsessive and convoluted process of analysing an issue, analysing it again, and then just for good measure giving it all another good kick of the tires just to be sure, before declaring any conclusions.

However, *scholasticism* did now offer the great thinkers of the day a way around *Neo-Platonism* and its focus on unifying everything under a single "truth", and allowed them to focus on logic, words, and analysis, without stepping on the church's rather over-sensitive holy toes. This method of rationalizing Greek thought and Christian doctrine eventually came to define and dominate Catholic philosophy for the next several centuries.

One of the key issues of the time was trying to prove whether God actually exists or not (a rather fundamental issue you would have thought given God's somewhat central role in the whole religion thing). Although to those already committed to the church a belief in God's existence was simply a matter of faith, a bit of a given, Christian thinkers were keen to see if logic and rational argument could also be used to prove God's existence? *Saint Anselm* (1033-1109), an Italian monk who went on to be made Archbishop of Canterbury, took up the challenge and used *Aristotelian* logic to try and prove just that. What *Anselm* came up with has become known as *Anselm's Ontological Argument*, and is an argument for the existence of God based on two logical premises. Firstly that God is "greater than anything else that can be imagined", and secondly that "existence is superior to non-existence".

As such, *Anselm's Ontological Argument* states that if something is perfect, it must exist, since non-existence is a sign of imperfection. The most perfect thing we (or at least *Saint Anselm*) can think of is God, therefore, because God is perfect, he must exist. Thus, the very definition of God implies his existence. Easy, job done.

Now some would quite rightly argue (and many did) that the same logic could just as easily be applied to prove the existence of say the most perfect car, or most perfect pair of shoes, all depending on what you believe is the most perfect thing you personally can possibly imagine. But in fairness to *Saint Anselm*, he did not intend his proof as way to persuade non-believers to suddenly "see the light" and become immediate Christian converts, he merely looked to make the existence of God a little clearer to those who already believed in God as a matter of faith.

Today of course, it is generally accepted that there can be no logical proof either way for the existence of God (or the perfect pair of shoes), it really is just a matter of faith, (in both religion and cobblers). Interestingly, in a later attempt to offer something of a more rational reason to accept a belief in God, *Blaise Pascal* (1623-1662) a mathematician of some note, proposed that even given we can have no logical proof of God's existence, it is still a better bet (more rational) to believe in God than not to believe (just to be on the safe side).

Pascal's wager, as it became known, consists of weighing up the pros and cons in terms of possible consequences for believing or not believing in God. According to *Pascal*, if we choose not to believe in God then we have two possible outcomes, firstly if God does indeed turn out to exist then we run the huge risk of eternal damnation in hell (not good), if however it turns out He doesn't actually exist, then it would actually make little or no difference to us at all. Likewise, if we do choose to believe in God and He actually does exist then we stand to gain eternal paradise in heaven (very good), and similarly, if it turns out He actually doesn't exist then again it makes little difference to us (other than maybe some lost opportunity for a little flaunting of the ten commandments). Thus, weighing it up rationally (or more simply put, by playing the percentages) we have far more to lose if we chose not to believe in God than if we do. For the gambling man then, it would seem a far safer bet to actually believe in God.

The cause of mediaeval scholastic philosophy was also notably progressed by one *Peter Abelard*, a French philosopher, theologian, and also seemingly a notable lover, poet, and composer of some repute, who was born near Nantes in France in 1071, and who was described by many of his peers as the keenest thinker of the 12th century, and so all in all, Monsieur Abelard was something of a mediaeval rock-star.

However, despite his numerous contributions to mediaeval philosophy and thought, *Abelard* is today rather better known for his well-documented tragic love affair with *Heloise d'Argenteuil*, an affair that has been elevated to almost legendary "Romeo and Juliet" status amongst latter day playwrights, poets, and the hopeless romantics of the world.

Abelard began a secret and passionate love affair with *Heloise*, the ward of a fellow canon (who was also *Heloise's* uncle) at the cathedral school of Notre-Dame de Paris where *Abelard* taught, and most notably while all three were actually living under the unsuspecting ward's roof. The couple were eventually forced to separate by the understandably furious and red-faced uncle once their illicit affair was discovered.

However, as with all great love stories, the couple continued to secretly see each other, but this only resulted in *Heloise* eventually falling pregnant (although clearly a man of immense intelligence, *Abelard* apparently lacked the common sense to use suitable birth control), and on discovering that not only had the two lovers continued their relationship but that *Heloise's* honour had now been tarnished even further and in a way that was plain for all to see, her ward was naturally less than pleased. To protect *Heloise* from the wrath of her uncle, *Abelard* sent *Heloise* to the convent at Argenteuil, however, this act of compassion was completely

98

misunderstood by the now irate uncle who saw this merely as *Abelard* trying to get rid of *Heloise* after getting her pregnant.

Suitably furious, Heloise's ward dispatched thugs to "deal with" *Abelard* in a way seen as best befitting his "crime", and not ones to shrink from their duties the thugs once having found *Abelard*, duly castrated him. *Abelard* was eventually forced to become a monk for his own protection while *Heloise* remained at Argenteuil where she herself eventually became a nun. However, it seems star-struck lovers continued to exchange heart-felt love letters until their dying days. Such was love in mediaeval France.

It's a testament to *Heloise's* enduring love that the object of her desires through the latter part of her life was to all intents and purposes a castrated monk. As for *Abelard*, his contributions to philosophy fortunately appears to have remained unaffected by either their tumultuous love affair, its eventual painful consequences, and his resulting physically abbreviated stature in later life.

Despite his painful romantic woes, *Abelard's* prime importance to our story here lies in his role as one of the key driving forces behind the general adoption across Europe of the *scholastic* style of philosophizing. As such, *Abelard* was instrumental in establishing *Aristotle* as the key philosophical reference of the day, albeit not receiving formal approval from the church's major movers and shakers until almost half a century after his death.

In terms of his own philosophical musings, *Abelard's* key contribution was in his approach to what is known in philosophical circles as the *problem of universals*. *Universals*, what *Aristotle* called "qualities" (although obviously in Greek), can be seen as defining certain characteristics (hardness, roundness, skinny, fat, etc) that can be applied to any number of particular things, for example, a blue ball, the sky, your Grandma's blue rinse hair, and Smurfs, all share the *universal* of being blue. For philosophers, the problem of *universals* really just boils down to an argument over whether a *universal*, such as blueness, can actually exist as a real thing in its own right, completely independently of the particular things that exhibit it (like a ball or your Grandma's hair).

Before *Abelard* came along with the collective works of *Aristotle* firmly tucked under his arm, there were two conflicting views, firstly the *realists*, who took the view that, for example, all blue things are blue by virtue of the actual existence of a *universal* that is "blueness", a single independent abstract thing that is part of all things blue, and something that actually exists itself somewhere out there in "abstract-land" and (using *Plato* and his *theory of forms* as their reference point) that manifests itself wherever there are blue things.

On the other hand, in the opposing corner were a group known to philosophical bods as the *nominalists*, who saw universals as mere words, and as such to them they only have a verbal existence, nothing more. For *nominalists* there is no such universal of blueness (or hardness, or roundness, or any other such "something-ness") that exists anywhere, not in some mystical world of *forms*, or in your head, (or even in *Plato's* sizable head), and thus they have no corresponding external reality at all, in fact they deny the existence of any such *universals* altogether. To nominalists, *universals* are all just intellectual humbug, to them blue is just a word we use to describe "blueness", nothing more, nothing less.

Then came along Monsieur Abelard, who wanted to bring some new found *Aristotelian* thinking into the mix, and so tried to find a middle ground between the two opposing camps, and who thus speculated that it is actually our own minds that abstract such common likenesses (qualities) such as blueness. So unlike the *realists*, Abelard did not see such *universals* as having their own existence somewhere out there in some wondrous *world of forms*, but then unlike the *nominalists* he believed they are more than just mere words. To *Abelard* such *universals* are actually concepts of the mind, and they are constructed solely by the virtue of their conception. *Abelard* and his *conceptualist* view thus held a middle ground between *nominalism* and *realism*, basically stating that *universals* do exist, but exist only as concepts of the mind.

Now you may well quite rightly ask yourself, who really cares? Does it really matter if blueness, fatness, or hardness, actually have an existence or are merely just words? Well, to those early mediaeval philosophers it did, because the existence (or not) of such *universals* raises the more fundamental question around whether such things as an ideal truth that applies to all, or a heaven, or even God himself, can all actually exist. By creating a view that such *universals* do indeed exist, albeit as concepts of our minds, *Abelard* was able to reconcile such *universals* (along with *Aristotelian* thinking), to religion, and with God, who was himself being viewed as more or less defined as "mind" in the basic ideas of mediaeval *Neo-Platonism*.

However, the most famous of all Christian thinkers of this period was *Thomas Aquinas* (1225-1274), an Italian Dominican friar (a highly intellectual order of friars by all accounts founded by Saint Dominic in 1216) who was ultimately recognized as a saint by the Catholic church in 1323. *Aquinas* was a great believer in the thinking of *Aristotle* and is often called the great "synthesizer" of Christianity and *Aristotelian* philosophy.

Actually *Aquinas*, as a good Dominican friar, believed that the teachings of the church must always be accepted, without exception or compromise, but held that *Aristotle's* philosophy did not necessarily contradict such Christian teaching. He believed that if we reason correctly, such reason will not come to any conclusions other than that which agrees with that of churches doctrines. *Aquinas* saw Christian beliefs and reason (courtesy of *Aristotle*) as coming from the same source, namely God (although of course *Aristotle* didn't know it at the time), and as such could never contradict each other.

As an example of *Aquinas'* synthesizing views we can look to his thinking around the creation of the universe. According to church doctrine the universe has a very clear beginning, and the bearded man in the flowing white robe created it. *Aristotle* on the other hand believed that the universe was eternal, it has no beginning, it is, and has always been, constantly changing, and as such there could never have been a "first-cause" that kicked the whole thing off in the first place (whether in a flowing white robe or not). It would seem then that as far as their thinking as to the creation of the universe goes, the church and *Aristotle* were about as far apart as a vegetarian and a battery chicken farmer.

Now *Aquinas* clearly had a problem here. As a good and faithful Christian he had absolute belief that the universe was indeed created by God and thus had a beginning, but then at the same time he also wants to show that there is no flaw in *Aristotle's* reasoning. Something of a head-scratcher then for Friar Aquinas.

However, presumably after a suitable period of much heightened mental processing, *Aquinas* claimed that church doctrines may well have simply just confused two different points, namely that first God created the universe, and secondly that the universe had a beginning. To *Aquinas'* astute mind, *Aristotle's* position of the universe having always existed could well be true, even if it is also true that God created the universe.

At this point it's likely that the response from the collective minds of the church was a resounding "Puh-leez!" (I'm paraphrasing here), but *Aquinas* explains that although God did indeed create the universe, he may well has created an eternal one (He's God, he could apparently do clever stuff like that), a universe eternal in its appearance to us mere mortals at least (effectively, if the universe exists, then God must exist, as only God has the blueprint, materials, and tools to create the universe). Thus, to *Aquinas* it is entirely possible to believe in an eternal universe that was created by God, and thus confirming Christian teaching without contradicting the reasoning of *Aristotle* who in his defence *Aquinas* claims, clearly had no access to Christian revelation during his time.

Aquinas also used the above idea of God as the "first-cause" of the universe (a kind of "uncaused cause") to also help create what has become known as his *cosmological argument* for the existence of God. In brief, having already argued that God must have caused the universe to exist, he argues further that although the universe clearly does exist (your sitting here reading this book is proof of that), it is also conceivable that in some other strange set of circumstances it might well have not have come to exist, and thus its very existence is completely dependent upon that first-cause. This first-cause itself then cannot conceivably "not exist" as it is not contingent upon anything else. As we understand God to be this first-cause, it thus follows that God himself must therefore exist.

Throughout his life, *Aquinas* was to doggedly stick to his unwavering belief in both the church's doctrines and the reason of *Aristotle*, and that properly understood the two would never necessarily contradict each other, even when they were placed in seemingly stark contrast, for example as in the case of the Christian belief that a human soul survives our physical death compared to Aristotle's very clear belief that the soul is tied to the body and so survives only as long as it does. A contradiction that must have given our good friar many a sleepless night trying to reconcile.

Aquinas' synthesis of *Aristotle's* thought with church doctrines now made room for a higher regard for the natural world and our place in it (in contrast to earlier *Neo-Platonic* church thinking which emphasized the unreality of the natural world in comparison to the heavenly world of *forms*), and thus started to provide a well needed leg-up for the study of natural sciences which had largely taken a back-seat under earlier mediaeval thinking.

By the time mediaeval Europe was moving into the 14th century (and headlong towards the Black death and a hundred year war between France and England) many scholars were now starting to question the rigorous *Aristotelian* approach to logic adopted by *scholasticism,* believing that such a rigid and formal method was often leading to overly complex abstract logical concepts, classifications, and conclusions (in short scholars were becoming so focused on method they were often missing the simple and obvious truths that were right in front of their eyes). One such scholar was *William of Ockham* (1285-1349) and English theologian and philosopher. *William of Ockham* believed in using the evidence of observation and experience as the basis for any rational argument, and was a strong believer in the "simple is best" approach to problem solving.

Ockham is best known today for his principle, known as *Ockham's razor,* which states that when there are two or more alternative explanations for something, the simplest explanation or solution is usually the one which is the best. Consider the story of the philosophy master looking to set his class a philosophical problem, he walks to the front of the class and silently puts a chair on top of an empty desk. He then asks his somewhat bemused students to write a paper convincing him that the chair does not actually exist. The students spend the next hour furiously scratching their heads and putting pen to paper citing numerous complex philosophical theories, abstract thoughts, and obscure philosophers from history, all in an attempt to prove that the chair does not exist. At the end of the test all the students hand in their papers most of which cover numerous pages of high-brow spouting, all except one. This one student handed in his paper which consisted of only two simple words, "What Chair?". Philosophy, if nothing else, should be simple.

A pupil of *Ockham's, Jean Buridan*, took a slightly different tack on the paradox of rational choices between alternatives, *Buridan's ass*, as his paradox became known, tells the tale of a hungry ass placed exactly halfway between two equally attractive and nourishing bales of hay. Caught between the decision as to which bale of hay he should go to, the ass is unable to make a decision and eventually just starves to death. The moral of the tale being that when faced with two equally convincing arguments we can get so caught up in analyzing the alternatives we run the risk of choosing neither, when in reality (in the world of common sense) it makes little difference as long as we do chose one (at the end of the day, any hay is better than no hay).

Nikolaus Von Kues (1401-1464), also known as *Nicholas of Cusa*, a German philosopher and Cardinal of the holy Roman Church, also pushed back against the rigors of the *scholastic* style and its increasingly abstract approach to knowledge, *Von Kues* adopts a rather novel approach stating that all knowledge comes from God, who himself came before everything else, and as such God is actually unlike anything that our rather crude and simple human minds can possibly grasp, and so it is simply impossible for anyone to have any real knowledge or understanding of God at all, so we should just stop trying.

Von Kues went on to state that as God himself is thus the only reliable source of the real truth, and as we cannot truly know God, everything we as humans know, our observable reality, is thus flawed and full of contradictions, and really just shows how little we humans really do, or can, know. *Von Kues* called this acceptance of our ignorance *"learned ignorance"* (all we really need to know is that we can't, and don't, know). However, he did not suggest that we should stop thinking about God and religion altogether (he was a Cardinal of the church after all), but instead we should view our understanding of the world, of religious doctrines, our knowledge, as

104

just ways of thinking, as relative, and more as just approximations of the "unknowable" real truth.

In suggesting such an approach, all the religious dogma and beliefs that army's of *scholastic* pupils were feverishly trying to prove (or disprove) through thorough analysis and *Aristotelian* logic, could now take on a different meaning, they could all now be view not as absolute truths, but more as simply a way of thinking, as valid interpretations (presumably along with many other equally valid ways of seeing and thinking about such truths). *Von Kues'* view allowed scholars to now start to see religion and the universe in shades of grey, not just as black or white.

William of Ockham and *Jean Buridan* helped to get philosophy focused on what was observable rather than overly complex ideas and classifications, *Thomas Aquinas* and his great synthesis of *Aristotelian* reason and church doctrines got people thinking about the natural world again, while *Nikolas Von Kues'* notion of *learned ignorance* helped get philosopher's feet firmly back on the ground. All of which opened the door for alternative interpretations and ways of viewing the world, and in doing so started to prepare the way for the next chapter in philosophy and science, it started to prepare the way for what clever historian bods called the *Renaissance*. Going forward, it was to be a victory of rational scientific discovery over centuries of Christian dogma that would now epitomize the thinking of the time.

13

Science Fights Back

"Knowledge is Power"
Francis Bacon (1561 - 1626)

The Middle Ages in Europe are generally viewed as a bit of a cultural wasteland. Europe was gripped by rampart feudalism which meant that unless your name was King, Queen, Lord, Lady, or Sir something or other, it was always going to be a pretty miserable existence. For most, the Middle Ages offered little other than a constant stream of plague, war, or famine, and if you were particularly unlucky (which usually meant poor) all three at once.

Mediaeval science was also pretty limited as scientific theories continued to be mixed with superstition and legend, and so most mediaeval scientists (and I'm using the term loosely here) spent most of their time just dabbling in the mysteries of alchemy, vainly trying to turn lead into gold, or frogs into Princes. Medicine was also pretty much non-existent, the standard treatment for just about everything was basically to just either cut it out or off, or wait it out and see what God decided, not ideal in either case, and certainly not given to a high recovery rate. On the plus side, we were treated to such literary delights as Chaucer's Canterbury Tales and Dante's Divine Comedy, but even today a quick scan between their respective covers will only highlight that as masterful as they may be as literary works, they still remain almost completely unreadable to most of us even today (primarily because no one it seems bothered to check their spelling) .

As for philosophy, church led scholars held a firm grip on pretty much all scholarly activity, and spent most of their waking hours solely focused on searching for ways to reconcile church doctrines with reason, and thus in the process ruthlessly squashed any reasoned thinking that even slightly brought into question any such church doctrines or faith in God and his handy-work.

Of course there is a lingering romantic perception that there were still aspects of the Middle Ages that seemed rather glamorous (kings and queens living in fairytale castles, and knights riding around slaying dragons for the love of a princess), but overall the reality was that this was not a great time to be poor, illiterate, sick, or as it turns out a dragon.

However, as the Middle Ages made their way into the 14th century a wind of change was slowly starting to gather steam. The Holy Crusades (which overall had achieved very little of significance other than confirming that fighting in full armour in the heat of the Holy Lands was a very uncomfortable experience) had at least provided the unexpected side-effect of slowly making available *Muslim* texts and inventions to eager western scholars. Those at the top of feudalism's social tree were now slowly starting to topple from their lofty cushioned perches, and philosophers such as *William of Ockham* and *Nikolaus von Kues* were starting to question the church's icy grip on scholarly activity, and so the scene was set for the dawn of a new cultural movement to emerge in Europe.

The *renaissance*, whose literal translation from French means "rebirth", was a cultural movement that spanned the period roughly from the middle of the 14th to the 17th century, beginning first in Italy in the late Middle Ages, and later spreading to the rest of Europe. It refers to a "rebirth" of arts and culture around Europe after the perceived "dark times" and cultural wasteland of the Middle Ages. As a movement, the *renaissance* was to profoundly affect European intellectual life with its influence being felt across literature, art, music, politics, science, religion, and most importantly for our story, philosophy.

Like most cultural change, the *renaissance* didn't just happen overnight. Whole nations across Europe did not all just collectively wake-up one sunny morning and decide to hang-up their cod-pieces and tights in favour of heavily padded jackets and furs while suddenly also feeling the urge to question their fundamental beliefs in religion and the fact that the Earth was the centre of the universe. No change happened slowly, over time, starting in Italy and not reaching Britain till some time later (in fact there are parts of Essex today where it seems it has still yet to arrive).

The central driving force in the development of the renaissance movement was a renewed interest and connection with classical antiquity (Greek and Roman philosophy, literature, art, and science). The philosophy that underpinned this interest in classical antiquity is referred to as *humanism*, and is really based on a renewed celebration of humanity and its ability and power to create and discover new ideas, inventions, artistic and scientific works. This new breed of *humanists* believed in a naturalistic view of the universe, they drew especially upon facts of science, and had ultimate faith in humankind, believing that human beings themselves possess the power and vision to solve their own problems through reason and scientific method.

In many ways *humanism* was not so much a philosophy but a method of learning. In contrast to the mediaeval *scholastic* method which had doggedly focused on resolving contradictions between faith and reason, *humanists* would study ancient texts and appraise them through a combination of both reasoning and empirical evidence. There was thus an emphasis on such classics providing what became known as a "classical education", and developing in the scholar more "humanistic" qualities. Above all, *humanists* asserted the "genius of man", the unique and extraordinary ability of the human mind. It was a movement that would now view humans, not God, as its center.

Contrasting to the biased mediaeval emphasis on the apparent sinful nature of man, man was now starting to be considered infinitely great and valuable. Mediaeval thinking had God as the point of departure, while the *humanists* of the *renaissance* now took as their point of departure man himself. Thus began an almost unrestrained worship of genius as the "ideal man" became what today we call "renaissance man", a man of universal genius embracing all aspects of life, art and science. Man no longer seen as existing just for God's sake, and so he was now free to delight in the here and now, and express himself accordingly.

The movement was fuelled by such recent inventions as the printing press, which had been pioneered in Germany by *Johannes*

Gutenberg (1398-1468) in 1450, and which now allowed for the rapid transmission of all those newly rediscovered works from antiquity, along with the teachings and ideas of *renaissance* reformers and philosophers, which now in print reached the hearts and minds of a much wider audience, something that earlier great thinkers were unable to do (although it seems that pamphlets detailing daily horoscopes, recipes, Sudoku puzzles, and celebrity gossip were to prove more popular even at this early stage of the printed word's history). Importantly however, such freely available printed works also started to force the church to give up its role as the sole disseminator of the written word (it also left a small army of monks who to that point had spent every waking hour painstakingly transcribing great works by hand, needing to now find something else to do with their time).

However, the *renaissance* is perhaps best known for its artistic and scientific developments and the contributions of such polymaths as *Leonardo d' Vinci* and *Michelangelo*, who are recognized today as the pinnacle of the term "renaissance man". However, even these shining examples of mankind at its best were themselves not without fault. The great *Leonardo da Vinci*, the man who gave the world the Mona Lisa, flying machines, scuba gear, and the armored car, was in fact the love-child of a peasant woman and a lawyer, and an ambidextrous, paranoid dyslexic, who strangely could draw forward with one hand while writing backwards with the other. Even *Michelangelo* (whose full name, Michelangelo di Lodovico Buonarroti Simoni, was as remarkable as his talent), and who gifted us such masterpieces as the statues of David and the Pieta, as well as the fancy ceiling job at the Sistine Chapel, was also famous for his poor hygiene. He rarely washed, and often slept in his clothes and his boots, he was also known for his terrible temper and fearsome personality (imagine a kind of bad tempered hobo who just happened to be a dab hand with a paint brush and a chisel, and you'll have a pretty good picture of Mr. Simoni).

In the sciences there was now a new willingness to question previously held truths and to search for new answers resulted in a period of major scientific advancement. Some have seen this as a "scientific revolution", heralding the beginning of the modern age with significant changes in the way the universe was viewed and the methods used to explain natural phenomena. There was now a completely new approach to science, this "new scientific method" was really a process of investigating nature and its phenomenon through the senses, as opposed to what had been up to this point an exaggerated belief in reason, a belief that problems could all be solved purely by thinking (shut your eyes really tight, think really, really, hard, and presumably the answer will appear). This new method however took the opposite view, that scientific investigation should now be based purely upon observations and experience, supported by the introduction of systematic scientific experiments which were now being expressed in precise mathematical terms.

At the forefront of this new scientific method was *Francis Bacon* (1561-1626), an English philosopher who was interested in knowledge for its own sake, believing that the more we know, the more we are able to help ourselves (on the face of it not an unreasonable idea). He was thus not only keen to find ways to help us learn all we can, but also to ensure we avoided mistakes, and was thus critical of knowledge based purely on reason as preached by earlier scholastic scholars.

Bacon presented a series of psychological barriers that he saw we humans faced in the pursuit of such scientific knowledge, barriers that lead us to mistakes in understanding, and what he collectively called "idols of the mind". First of these is what *Bacon* called "idols of the tribe", which is what he sees as the tendency for humans as a species (a tribe) to over generalize things, there are then "idols of the cave", being the human tendency to impose our own preconceptions on nature rather than see what is really there, in defining "idols of the marketplace" *Bacon* saw as our tendency to let social conventions distort our experience, and "idols of the theater" being the distorting influence of the prevailing philosophical and scientific dogma of the day. According to Bacon, the scientist must battle against all such "idols" before he can gain any true knowledge of the world.

Francis Bacon's ideas around knowledge and scientific observation culminated in his work *Novum Organum,* published at the turn of the 17th century, in which he advocates scientific process of observation, analysis of data, formation of an hypothesis, and confirmation through experimentation, a scientific method that was to form the basis of modern scientific practice from that point forward, and still used today by men and women in white lab coats.

This new scientific method, coupled with the use of new mathematical expression for proof of observations and hypothesis, along with the recent invention of such scientific instruments as the telescope, soon led to the rather earth shattering proclamation by Polish astronomer *Nicolaus Copernicus* (1473-1543) in 1543 that the Earth actually moved around the sun (something of a shocker at the time, and known for evermore to science as the "heliocentric world view"). This clearly came as quite a shock to most given the centuries held belief (as preached by the church) that the Earth was actually the center of the universe, and thus everything revolved around it. This new "heliocentric" view gained further weight when German astronomer *Johannes Kepler* (1571-1630), spurred on by some rather clever mathematical jiggery-pokery, proved that the planets (including the Earth) indeed moved in elliptical (oval) orbits around the sun.

The scientific icing was then put on the cake by *Isaac Newton* (1642-1727) who not only described how planets moved around the sun, but went on to explain just how they were doing so using his "Law of universal gravitation" (which for completeness states that every object attracts every other object with a force that increases in proportion to the size of the objects and decreases in proportion to the distance between the objects, which is why you "fall" to the Earth rather than the Earth coming "up" to meet you), a theory he apparently happened upon due to a bump on his head caused by a falling apple.

Newton is widely recognized as one of the most influential scientists of all time and a key figure in the scientific revolution of the renaissance. His book *"Mathematical Principles of Natural Philosophy"*, first published in 1687, is widely regarded to be one of the most important books in the history of science, in which *Newton* showed how a universal force, gravity, applied to every object in every part of the universe, a view that dominated scientific thinking around the mechanics of the universe (actually right up until the time

111

a certain wild-haired German named *Albert Einstein* came along 300 years later, and once again was to change the scientific landscape).

However, even the great *Sir Isaac Newton* was also not without flaws. It seems that he more than dabbled in alchemy in a fruitless attempt (as far as we know) to try and turn lead into gold, it is widely reported that he once stuck needles in his eye to test his theories on optics (a sign of either complete commitment to his experiments, or one of complete madness), and was by all accounts a chronic loner who died a virgin. But despite all this, it would be hard to under-estimate the impact Newton had not only on science but also on philosophy.

Of course, the upshot of all this new scientific discovery was that the Earth, and so mankind, lost its "special" status in creation and the order of things, (a similar seismic shift was also to happen some 200 years later when *Charles Darwin* proved that man was not made by God in his own image, but rather from slightly more hairier tree-dwelling origins). For the church, life had been far simpler when the Earth was to be firmly found at the centre of the universe (known to science types as the "Geocentric world view", or now more precisely as just simply "wrong"), and which had been the core of church doctrine for centuries. However, now (courtesy of Messrs. *Newton, Kepler,* and *Copernicus*) the church was left with its proverbial pants down, and understandably it was not too happy. From this point forward, man, and more importantly the church, had to get used to the idea that we were in fact just living on some random planet, and as it turned out nowhere near the centre of what was turning out to be a vast universe.

However, Earth's (and thus man's) relocation from the exact center of the universe to somewhere in its outer reaches was not the only embarrassing blow the church was to receive from this new *humanist* way of thinking about the world. With its new view of man, philosophy and science were now gradually braking away from the church, and thus many now looked for a more personal relationship with God rather than one via the intermediary of the church, its leaders, priests, doctrines, and rules.

Desiderius Erasmus (1466-1536), also known as *Erasmus of Rotterdam* (although it appears he lived there for only the first four years of his life, never to return), felt that current church teachings were missing the point. *Erasmus* felt that the true message of the church should be that people can live quite happily together if they just have faith in God, live simply and with humility, and show love to God and one another. He also believed that all the intellectualizing and issues that scholars had spent the last thousand years arguing about were unimportant, for *Erasmus*, we each just need to understand God, the Bible, on our own terms.

Erasmus believed that true belief can only be based upon faith, never on reason. He was critical of the mixing of Christian doctrines and Greek philosophy by those earlier mediaeval philosophers such as *Augustine* and *Thomas Aquinas*, stating that it was all their intellectualizing, synthesizing, and just down-right tinkering with faith, which was at the root of what he saw as the current corruption of the church. Instead, *Erasmus* advocated a return to simple beliefs with individuals forming their own personal relationships with God, and not ones that were prescribed to them by the Catholic Church and its doctrines.

An Augustinian monk teaching at the University in Wittenberg, Germany, named *Martin Luther* (1483-1546) also believed that people did not need the "help" of the church or its priests in order to receive God's forgiveness, and neither was God's forgiveness dependent upon the buying of what he called "indulgencies" (reciting prayers, or giving alms and sizable donations to the church) from the church. *Luther* believed that every man was equal in the eyes of God, and that priests, and particularly the Pope, held no special place at God's knee, and so had no "special powers" to grant any such forgiveness or redemption from sin (not surprisingly, *Luther* never found himself on the Vatican's Christmas card list).

Luther felt very strongly that no one received God's forgiveness purely by just following church rituals, and thus believed that the church was effectively "selling" forgiveness and salvation by way of such "indulgencies". In Luther's eyes, this was nothing more than allowing people to bribe their way into heaven (it didn't really matter what you did in life, just pay the appropriate indulgence to the church, and you will still find a welcome mat for you at the pearly gates of heaven).

113

In 1517, *Luther* decided to take matters into his own hands, and so put quill to parchment to express his concerns over the authority of the Pope and what he saw as the abuses of the Catholic church, a document known as "*The Ninety-Five Theses*", presumably because Luther had ninety five concerns (apparently he did stay up all night but just couldn't think of another five to make it a nice round number). He went public by symbolically nailing the document to the doors of the Wittenberg cathedral, and thus triggered the start of what became known as the *Protestant Reformation*, a formal break from the Catholic Church (which to that point had been the only game in town for Christian believers in western Europe), and thus created the break-away Protestant church.

The duly excommunicated *Luther* went on to translate the Bible into German, believing that every man should be able to read the Bible at any time (well at least those who could read German anyway) not just the clergy, and so in a sense allowing everyone to become their own priest, and thus receive God's forgiveness and redemption from sin through their own faith alone.

The *reformation* spread quickly throughout Northern and Central Europe, although in truth in the case of Tudor England at least, the *reformation* was driven more by the raging libido of Henry VIII, his quest for a male heir, and the then Pope's refusal to annul Henry's marriage to Catherine of Aragon, rather than any wider concerns with the Catholic Church as expressed by *Martin Luther*.

The rapid spread of *reformation* ideas and beliefs was greatly helped by reformers who, by taking advantage of *Johannes Gutenberg's* handy-dandy printing press which had by now found its way across most of Europe, made heavy use of inexpensively printed pamphlets as well as a stream of newly translated Bibles which were now readily available in most European dialects, ensuring that there was a swift movement of both ideas and documents to the masses. From 1517 onwards, religious pamphlets flooded much of Europe, so much so that by 1530, it seems that over 10,000 publications were readily available, with a total of 10 million copies. In this respect, the *reformation* can also be seen as being the first media revolution.

All in all, the *renaissance* should be viewed as primarily a rebirth in art and science, but this in turn was to have an impact on the philosophical thinking of the time. Philosophers were now starting to move away from seeking to reconcile reason with God, or asking questions about the nature of the universe which were seen as now being empirically addressed by science.

The political upheavals of the *renaissance* period and the *reformation* were now focusing philosophical minds more and more in the realm of political thinking, while the philosophical thought of others was also now moving towards questions concerned around such things as "how can we know what we know?", and "what is our role in this world?". Philosophy was now starting to focus its attention on politics and the murky world surrounding the nature of the human mind.

14

Political Science Raises its Head

"The ends justify the means"
Niccolo Machiavelli (1469 - 1527)

From the 12th century and right through the *renaissance* period Italy it seems was, politically at least, quite a different place to the rest of Europe (even though today's uniquely Italian traits of the man-purse, Vespa scooters, unnecessary soccer theatrics, pizza, and spaghetti, had all still yet to be invented). While most European countries of northern and western Europe were still struggling under the grip of monarchies and a rather painful feudal system (well painful at least if you were short of either money, a castle, or a title), Italy had uniquely evolved into a rather strange collection of small independent City States.

Under the great European monarchies such as France and Spain, the absolute power of the king tended to stifle political freedom, commerce, and the merchant class, primarily due to the threat (perceived or otherwise) to its power and control of the people, and of course not to mention their own personal wealth. However, in Italy, where no formal unified state or overall sovereign had been established (they were all too busy planning the soon to be revolutionary man-purse), and with the subsequent unrestricted development and growth of commerce and the merchant class, many large cities such as Genoa, Verona, Venice, and Florence, became large trading centres and were able to obtain their own independence, creating city-states that established themselves as republics or ruled by the local powerful merchant families.

These city-states effectively controlled all trade along the Mediterranean sea, were each ruled independently and almost as little nations unto themselves, and where the merchant class wielded considerable power and influence. Relationships between the city-states were often governed by their commercial interests, and were based upon political and economic agreements aimed at mutual benefit. However, being in direct competition with each other, these city-states often engaged in shifting alliances and wars to secure their positions as commercial centres and control of trade routes, and often employed tactics that would make even the most feared of today's Mafia bosses turn pale. The period was marked by what was in effect a giant ongoing turf war over trading routes and merchant rights, where the individual king-pins of each ruling merchant family or republic were in a constant tussle for dominance and power.

To further complicate the political landscape, successive Popes waged wars against several of these Italian city-states on behalf of the Holy Roman Empire in an attempt to increase both the papal influence and their own coffers, while cities often fell from power as France, Spain, and even the normally peace-loving Swiss, often joined the political upheavals in pursuit of regional influence and control of their own.

And to make matters just that little more unpredictable, city-states too small to raise their own armies often employed mercenary leaders to defend their cities, and as a consequence political and military alliances continually changed as such mercenary leaders (a fickle breed who had no allegiances other than to their own pocket) often changed sides without warning based upon who was willing to pay or promise the highest reward for their services, all of which led to the rise and fall of many short-lived leaders and governments. Actually, the whole region politically was about as chaotic as your Mum's Tupperware cupboard.

It was into this political chaos that one *Niccolo Machiavelli* was born, (to be precise he was born in Florence, on May 3rd, 1469). The city-state of Florence had been under the control of the powerful Medici family for over 30 years, and quite by coincidence the year of *Machiavelli's* birth also saw Lorenzo de Medici succeed as ruler, and with him began a period of great artistic activity in Florence as

Medici money funded much of the flourishing *renaissance* that was gaining full steam around this time. Indeed, Lorenzo's patronage was a driving force behind the *renaissance* movement in Florence and he quickly became known to all as "Lorenzo the Magnificent", but then promptly died in 1492, and was succeeded by his son Piero.

However, Piero was clearly not quite as "magnificent" as his father, as within 2 years the French had crossed the Alps and invaded, and Piero was forced to surrender the city, and in the process gaining for himself the rather less flattering name of "Piero the Unfortunate". Florence itself was quickly rebranded as a republic the same year, and in 1498 *Machiavelli*, by this time a budding politician and diplomat, became Secretary to the Chancery in the new republican government.

Unfortunately, Florence was not a particularly powerful city-state, and to help keep the republic safe from the many political wolves at its door, *Machiavelli* spent the next ten years or so travelling between other city-states and the great nations of Europe on many diplomatic missions. It was during the course of his travels that Machiavelli was to come cross paths with one of the most infamous families in history. The Borgia's.

There a few families in history who have been collectively more tainted in sin, corruption, sexual depravity, and scandal than the Borgia family. The head of the family was Rodrigo, who had reputedly bribed his way to the papacy, and who thus became Pope Alexander VI in 1492. His daughter, Lucrezia, was cast as a whore, a murderer, and a witch, who reputedly slept not only with her father but her brother too, and who is rumoured to have poisoned her way through several husbands in order to fill the Borgia coffers. Her brother, Cesare Borgia, probably the worst of all, killed his elder brother in a fit of jealousy, and embarked on a campaign of ruthless conquest and slaughter aimed at carving out a kingdom across Italy's scattered city-states. Clearly, the Borgia's were not a family to just bottle-up their feelings and one who you'd not want to upset in a hurry.

But in the current climate of constant and ineffectual infighting amongst the city-states, *Machiavelli* saw in the Borgia's, particularly Cesare Borgia, just how effective individuals could be in both seizing and maintaining power when they were prepared to do "whatever it takes" to ensure they both gained and held onto that power. Cesare Borgia, although a significant threat to the Florentine state (and clearly not the most pleasant of men) nonetheless impressed *Machiavelli*, and was to prove a huge influence in his later political thinking.

Eventually, diplomacy and even some nice little gifts sent on birthdays and Christmas proved not enough to save Florence, and in 1512 a combination of the papacy and Spanish troops dissolved the republic and restored the Medici family as rulers of Florence, and *Machiavelli* quickly found himself out of a job. Things soon took a further turn for the worse for the now unemployed *Machiavelli* when he was subsequently falsely accused of conspiracy against the Medici family, imprisoned, and tortured.

Machiavelli was released from prison less than a month later (presumably having stood up to whatever methods of torture were employed against him, thus proving his innocence), but his political career was effectively over. And so he decided to use his now ample spare time to write a book outlining his political theories which he had evolved over his years as a diplomatic ambassador and which were heavily influenced by the many leaders and political movers and shakers he had met, and in particular Cesare Borgia.

The resulting book, *The Prince*, is effectively a practical handbook on how to ruthlessly gain and exercise power, in which *Machiavelli* argues that the goals of a ruler (the Prince) justify whatever means he uses to obtain them. He completely sets aside any notion of Christian morality or justice, indeed, *Machiavelli* holds that a ruler cannot be held to any standard of morality, but rather must do whatever it takes to secure his success.

In doing so the ruler should strive to be both feared and loved by his people (although being loved seems to be argued more as a "nice to have"), but should avoid acts of cruelty or mistreatment that would make the people hate him, for hatred would lead to rebellion which is clearly to be avoided at all costs. He should act with compassion, but issue harsh and swift punishment where warranted in order to maintain control and social order.

Machiavelli further argued that the stability of the state are paramount, and the ruler must be positively willing to act immorally if needed to ensure such. For *Machiavelli* "the ends justify the means" even if that meant coercing, deceiving, bribing, or just plain removing the heads of any threat to his rule from rivals or a rebellious population. As ruler, maintaining power is far more important than any notion of winning the hearts of the people.

Machiavelli's philosophy marked a huge shift in political and moral philosophy, effectively preaching that actions should be judged not by their intentions, motives, or means, but purely on their consequences, the results of an action are the only basis for judging the rightness of the conduct, a philosophy known as *consequentialism* (consider for example of the use of the atomic bomb against Japanese cities to accelerate the end of WWII), and the only consequences that should concern a ruler is the stability of his power and that of his state.

However, *Machiavelli* believed that such conduct is only justified for the ruler, for he has the higher responsibility for the nation as a whole, and thus must be free to do whatever is needed to secure its stability, while the conduct of a nations citizens must be held to the rule of law, morality, and virtue. It's OK for a ruler to do whatever it takes to get the job done, but having the population running around free to do whatever they want in pursuit of their own goals just would not do.

Machiavelli's radical political ideas have seen him often referred to as the "father of modern political theory", but since its first publication *The Prince* has both attracted and repelled politicians and leaders in equal measure. Its positive encouragement of immorality, deceit, manipulation, and a mixture of love and fear in support of gaining and retaining power, had a profound impact on political thinking throughout the west. So much so that the term *Machiavellian* has entered the language as a derogative term to describe anyone (but in particular politicians) who is seen as willing to ruthlessly deceive and manipulate others for their own personal gain and power (maybe we are all just a little *Machiavellian* at heart). And we need look no further back in history than the 20th century examples of Hitler, Stalin, and Mussolini, to see that

Machiavelli's philosophy still carried weight right through to modern times.

In popular culture, to be "*Machiavellian*" is to be a moustache-rolling, evil-laughing, villain, a byword for treachery, ruthlessness, and unfettered ambition, probably not quite what *Machiavelli* had in mind when he wrote his political treatise, but whatever his intentions his name has now become associated with any act where the "end justifies the means",

Just over a 100 years later another of Europe's great countries had also found itself in the midst of some uncomfortable political upheaval and war. By the time England had moved into the 1640's it appears its reigning monarch, Charles I, had successfully alienated many (if not all) of his now not so loyal subjects with his religious policies, his ruthless taxing of people to fund his many excursions to quell an ever-growing number of rebellions, and his apparent determination to rule with or without the approval of parliament.

Unable to resolve their differences, by 1642 civil war had broken out between the King's Royalists, the "Cavaliers", and the Parliamentarians, the "Roundheads". By the time all the dust had settled Charles I had found his head separated from his shoulders for treason (at only 5'4" tall Charles I is generally recognized as England's shortest ever king, a title further enhanced with the removal of his head), Oliver Cromwell had been installed as "Lord Protector" and effectively ruling as a dictator over of the Commonwealth of England, Scotland, and Ireland, but then promptly died, was succeeded by his son who proved to be just about one step up from useless at the job, and so by 1660 with the government in a shambles Charles' son was invited to resume his father's throne (albeit with a much reduced job description).

In the middle of all this mayhem one *Thomas Hobbes* (1588 - 1679), an English philosopher, found himself facing a bit of a problem. As a staunch royalist he feared the reaction of the "Roundheads" to his writing, and so he did what any self-respecting academic would do under the same circumstances, he packed his bags and fled to France where he stayed for the next 11 years.

However, *Hobbes* did not idle away the years just loafing around in Parisian coffee houses, he used the time to write his best known

121

work, a treatise on the nature of society and government, and the resulting book, "*Leviathan or The Matter, Form and Power of a Common Wealth Ecclesiastical and Civil*", but simply known (primarily in the interest of time) as *Leviathan*, is considered to be one of the most influential books on political philosophy ever written.

Hobbes' political theory is based around his account of human nature. For *Hobbes*, everything in the universe is entirely material in nature, including man who is thus merely made up of "matter in motion", and as such *Hobbes* has no truck or time for the existence of anything even vaguely immaterial such as a mind separate from the body, spirits, or a soul. Man (his body, brain, mind, and senses) is nothing more than a flesh and blood biological machine subject to the same physical laws of the universe as everything else.

This type of thinking was popular around this time given the rapidly growing knowledge in the physical sciences driven by such scientists as *Newton, Galileo,* and *Kepler,* (*Hobbes* was apparently something of a drinking-buddy of *Francis Bacon*), and there was a growing faith that the physical sciences would ultimately provide the answer to any and all questions about the nature of what was being perceived more and more as a wholly mechanical universe. For *Hobbes* there is nothing spiritual or magical about either the universe or man, there is no mystique to it, no one sat around a fiery cauldron throwing in eye of bat and tongue of newt, everything is completely made up of material matter and wholly mechanical in nature.

As such, the natural state of man is not one of trusting, peaceful coexistence wrapped in the loving arms of an harmonious and just society, it is far more a "dog eat dog" world, one of unlimited freedom where everyone acts in their own self-interest, free to rape, plunder, pillage, and murder to their hearts content, each person pitted against all others in a constant battle for survival where their actions are bound only by their own personal power and conscience, a war of "all against all". *Hobbes* called this natural state the "state of nature", and in his own words is one in which the life of the individual is "solitary, poor, nasty, brutish and short".

In the *Leviathan, Hobbes* goes on to conclude that to avoid this clearly rather unsatisfactory state of affairs for all, men will come to an agreement with each other to establish a "civil" society through what *Hobbes* calls a "*social contract*", a contract in which all gain security and prosperity in return for subjecting themselves to an absolute sovereign. Hobbes offers several options as to what or who this sovereign could be, a single ruler or a an assembly of men, but as a staunch royalist his vote was clearly for a single ruler. The sovereign may himself be a tyrant, cruel, and unjust, but to *Hobbes* even this is better than the outright anarchy of living the "state of nature".

Hobbes defines such a *social contract* as being a consent by all individuals to surrender some of their freedoms and rights (their natural rights under a state of nature) and submit to the authority, laws, and rule of the sovereign. In exchange each individual receives social and political order, and the protection of their remaining rights from the sovereign. Such a *social contract* clearly puts restrictions on the freedom of the individual, but it offers in return protection from the chaos, and lawless anarchy of the alternative, the state of nature. In short, individuals willingly agree to limits on their individual freedoms as fair exchange for the benefits of the state (if you provide me protection against rape, pillage, and murder, then in turn I will also promise not to rape, pillage, or murder. Seems fair).

It's important to understand that according to *Hobbes*, law, social, and political order are not seen as natural, they are human creations (what's natural is everyone running around with a club in their hand, raping and pillaging at will, the state of nature). As such a *social contract*, and the order it creates, are merely a means to an end, the mutual benefit of the individuals involved, and thus remains viable only to the extent that all fulfill their part in the agreement.

Social contract theory remained a cornerstone of political philosophy right through to the 19th century, it was used to address questions around the origins of society and the legitimacy of the state over the individual, and to answer the question of why a perfectly rational individual would seemingly quite willingly consent to give up their natural freedom to obtain the benefits of political and social order.

Both *Leviathan* and *the Prince* are seen as two of the most important works in the field political philosophy, *Machiavelli* may be painted as a moustache-twirling cad, and *Hobbes* as a "man is a machine" automaton, but they are both seen as founding fathers of modern western political philosophy, and as such remain greatly revered by pipe smoking pointy-heads and political radicals alike.

15

Defeating the Evil Demon

"I think, therefore I am.... I think"
George Carlin (1937 - 2008)

At roughly the same time as *Thomas Hobbes* was busying himself grappling with the political implications of his wild "state of nature" and its limitless freedom to rape, pillage, and murder, just across the water in deepest darkest France a somewhat different philosopher was emerging who was less concerned with social stability and keeping his head attached to his shoulders, and far more concerned with understanding the limits and roots of human knowledge.

Rene Descartes was born in 1596 in La Haye, in the Touraine region of France (the town itself since been renamed Descartes in his honour). He was the son of a nobleman, which in a remarkable stroke of luck for *Descartes* meant that he never had to work a day in his life, and just to add a little icing to the cake, perceived poor health as a child resulted in him also being granted permission to stay in bed every morning until 11am, a habit he not unsurprisingly kept throughout his life. Not an altogether unsatisfactory start to life then.

Despite his leisurely start to each day, *Descartes* nonetheless went on to study law, although he never went on to practice (probably due to the fact that court cases of the day would have necessitated an earlier than 11am start), instead he decided he wanted to travel the world and thus maybe somewhat surprisingly he decided to become a soldier. However, he quickly discovered he was clearly not cut out for a military life (those annoying early morning roll-calls, and the fact that the whole of Europe was being torn apart at the time by the rather bloody and cruel Thirty Years War (1618-48), all of which meant that being a soldier at this time was probably not such a great career move, and certainly not one conducive to a life of leisurely travel and sightseeing). He thus rather hastily left the military choosing instead to now pursue a somewhat gentler (and clearly less life-threatening) life of the mind.

Descartes had always been interested in mathematics and science, and it seems that sometime during November 1619 he had a series of dreams, in which it appears that they told him that through the use of mathematics there was a way in which all human knowledge could be made into a single unified whole, and not being one to doubt his dreams his course was firmly set, and *Descartes* spent the rest of his life in pursuit of fulfilling that dream.

There was a growing belief amongst scientists of the day that mathematics, rather than religion, held the key to understanding the universe and so like many of his day, for *Descartes* the universe was wholly mathematical and mechanical in nature, and thus in theory at least, entirely predictable. *Descartes* hoped to show that there was also an underlying unity to all the different branches of knowledge, believing that all human problems could eventually be articulated in terms of mathematics, and thus resolved through reason.

In 1637 *Descartes* created the first of his great works, *the Essays*, which was primarily a scientific work about optics, meteorology, and geometry, all of which has long been forgotten as it is in the introduction to the work where we see the key ideas of his philosophical ideas starting to take shape. In the introduction, rather long-windedly called the *"Discourse on the method of rightly conducting one's reason and seeking the truth in sciences of the mind"* (but nowadays in the interest of time and saving ink, it's known simply as the *"Discourse on the method"*), *Descartes* carefully lists the rules that he sees need to be followed if scientific investigation was to be more than just a haphazard mixture of intuition and guesswork. *Descartes* attempts to show how it is possible to discover "true" knowledge just by using a few central rules.

Descartes' basic method was that if we accept only that which he calls "clear and distinct" to your mind, ensure we split large problems into smaller ones, argue from the simple to the complex, and finally, check everything carefully when you have finished, then eventually science and mathematics will reveal all knowledge to us.

126

We can immediately start to see that *Descartes* was a committed *rationalist*, believing as any good *rationalist* does that the only reliable knowledge we can have comes to us from our use of pure reason, and usually reason deduced via the use of mathematics and science.

Thus, to the perennial philosophical question of modern time, "do these jeans make my bum look fat?", according to *Descartes* if you have a "clear and distinct" idea of exactly under what circumstances a pair of jeans can indeed make a bum resemble a sack of potatoes, a calculator, and a tape measure, then reason, mathematics, and a quick double-check of your measurements, will provide you your indisputable answer in a matter of minutes. Job done.

But *Descartes* was also a confirmed skeptic, and in his next great work, *Meditations on First Philosophy*, published in 1641, he uses doubt to ruthlessly question everything he believes he knows, even the certainties of his beloved mathematics. In the book, *Descartes* realized he must first start from a position of first doubting absolutely everything he knows, demolishing all knowledge completely, and to start again right from scratch if he truly wanted to establish a wholly certain and reliable basis for human knowledge.

In the book, *Descartes* asks himself where all human knowledge comes from, and concludes that there are only two possible sources of knowledge (if we choose to ignore the brainy kid with the glasses sat at the front of the class), our senses and our reason. *Descartes* starts by asking if even these fundamental sources of knowledge could themselves be doubted.

As a confirmed *rationalist* he gives short shrift to the idea of knowledge coming from our senses, seeing them not unexpectedly as wholly unreliable. Although *Descartes* never doubts that we do have sensory experiences, he believes we have no way of confirming their validity. To support his argument he uses what has become known as the "dream argument", in which *Descartes* argues that we have no way of proving that anything we experience through our senses is not all just part of one big dream. Your senses tell you are reading this book, but how do you know that you're not just dreaming you are reading it, and so whatever knowledge you may (or as is more likely may not), gain from its reading cannot thus be trusted.

You may think you're alive and well, the birds are singing, you have a perfect long-legged, size six model wife, you have blonde, blue-eyed mini-Einstein's for kids, a house measured in acres, and a car that is more rocket than automobile, but it may (unfortunately) all just be a blissful dream, and we have no real way to prove otherwise. In fact, how do we know we are not dreaming we are dreaming? It leaves us all in a rather awkward position of not knowing if what we sense as reality is actually real or just a confusing dream state, and so (according to *Descartes* at least) any and all supposed knowledge we perceive through our senses must continue to be doubted, and thus cannot be trusted.

So much for the senses then, but for *Descartes,* as a confirmed rationalist, knowledge produced from rational thought is harder to question, but it seems he had a cunning plan. *Descartes* imagined that there may well be an "evil demon" who is continuously tricking us all into thinking that our rational thoughts are correct, and so even the very idea that two plus two equals four may just be a trick this dastardly demon is somehow convincing us is true. Clearly no sober, sane, or half-way educated person with an IQ above single digits would accept that such a demon exists, but on the other hand, none of us can really definitively prove that he (or she) doesn't.

Descartes would thus seemingly have us all believe that there is no knowledge we can trust at all that can be understood as "clear and distinct" in our minds, either from our senses (it all just be one big dream) or even from our rational thought (the evil demon is tricking us into believing we are correct). And so at this point, for *Descartes,* it seems that everything we believe we know, absolutely everything, can all seemingly be doubted and thus there is nothing that we can truly believe, and so rather than gaining any true knowledge we are all just seemingly wandering around inside our heads with a white stick. For someone whose goal was to find a way in which all human knowledge could be made into a single unified whole, *Descartes* seemed to have backed himself into a bit of a corner.

However, going through this process of "doubting everything" eventually led *Descartes* to discover something rather extraordinary, what he realized was that there was always one thing that he could never doubt, and it was the simple fact that he was doubting, and thus thinking. And thinking can't just happen out of thin air, there needs to be a consciousness or a mind doing it, and so by the very act of doubting *Descartes* proves that he actually can't doubt that he exists. And hence we have *Descartes* now famous declaration, "*Cogito ergo Sum*", or in plain English, "I think, therefore I am" (actually more accurately put, there are some thoughts, so there must be a mind).

Thus, remarkably (and paradoxically), the very act of doubting you exist actually proves that you do indeed actually exist, and it is a truth that has no dependency on those pesky senses, and is also immune from the attentions of the evil demon, and so at last *Descartes* has a single perfect and indubitable piece of knowledge that he can "clearly and distinctly" believe. This simple and remarkable truth is the first principle of all *Descartes'* work and it remains one of the most important discoveries of Western philosophy.

With this first simple undeniable, fully certified, and "demon and dream proof" truth, *Descartes* had his starting point. But if he was going to use this truth to help him reinvent the foundations and structure of all human knowledge, he needed to discover just what it was about this truth that made it so certain. He needed to be able to uncover a universal rule which could then presumably offer him a similar guarantee of certainty about all other kinds of knowledge he cared to put his mind to, and to this end it seems that *Descartes* had yet another cunning plan up his seventeenth century sleeve.

Descartes' plan revolved around an argument that went something like; knowing that "I am" is now indisputable, and thus the fact that I clearly and distinctly perceive that "I am" is a true fact, therefore, whatever else I "clearly and distinctly" perceive will also then be true. In reality *Descartes* had merely returned to his first rule form the "*Discourse on the method*", but he now believed that this "clear and distinct" rule gave him just the spring-board he needed to enable him to jump from this starting point to a broader, more flexible certainty about all other kinds of knowledge.

But there was a problem with this "clear and distinct" rule that *Descartes* could not ignore, and it was with that annoying evil demon again. What's there to stop the cunning little demon from inserting ideas of such breathtaking clarity into our heads in order to fool us into believing them to be clear and distinct? *Descartes* was facing a problem, he needed to once again remove the threat of the evil demon, but this time he was forced to resolve the issue by falling back not on his trusted mathematics, but on God (when in doubt call on God). God, *Descartes* optimistically assures us, will never deceive us and will always guarantee that any clear and distinct ideas that enter our mind will be true.

But if *Descartes* was going to use God to guarantee the truth of any clear and distinct ideas we may have, he first had to prove that such a philosophy-friendly God actually existed, and to do this *Descartes* uses what has become known as the "Trademark" argument. When a manufacturer makes a product they usually stamp their own logo onto to it, just so everyone knows exactly where the product came from. *Descartes* thus clearly sees God as the ultimate marketing machine, as he believed that when God made man he stamped the innate idea of Himself into our minds, and as such we are all born with the certain knowledge of God's existence firmly imprinted in our brain, imprinted with God's "trademark".

However, this argument for the proof of God is more than a little flawed, primarily because it uses God Himself as one of the premises for own His existence. You can't guarantee a clear and distinct rule using a truth-telling, non-deceiving God, if you claim that you know He exists only because you have a clear and distinct idea of him in your brain put there by the very God you are trying to prove exists in the first place. It seems *Descartes* needs God to guarantee his rule, and the rule to guarantee that God exists. Clever philosophical bods refer to this somewhat gaping hole in *Descartes* logic as the "Cartesian Circle", many others just called it plain wrong.

And so *Descartes'* proof for his "clear and distinct" rule is that no less a being than God Himself has created eternal truths about us and the world in which we live, and that if we perceive them as clear and distinct ideas, then they are guaranteed by God Himself (and you can't get higher up the approval chain than that), and thus this time *Descartes* uses nothing short of God to defeat the evil demon.

But *Descartes* is still left with problem. If God so helpfully guarantees such clear and distinct ideas, why is it then that the good and right thinking folks of our species still make mistakes? (And it would seem, lots of them). *Descartes'* solution was based around a belief that when we make judgements about whether something is true or not, we are actually exercising two of our innate faculties, our intellect and our free-will. Now, according to *Descartes*, as long as we always choose only truly clear and distinct ideas, then we cannot and will not make mistakes (good to know), but the problem is that we often choose to believe confused and unclear ideas, or ignore the clear and distinct ones because it suits our free-will to do so. The idea that the world was flat had no clear and distinct basis for its belief (no one had ever stood at the edge of the world, stared over the precipice, and reported back to prove its existence), yet people still chose to believe its truth because it suited them to do so.

It seems that we often allow our free-will to be more influential than our intellect. We are told that our freedom to choose is part of what makes us human, but it is the overriding power of this free-will which is the reason why we often fall disastrously into error. For some reason best known to God (or evolution) we have been given total freedom of choice but limited understanding (a dangerous combination under any circumstances), and it appears we tend to exercise that freedom of choice way beyond the confines of clear and distinct ideas. The only remedy according to *Descartes*, is for us to restrain our will and abstain from unclear judgement, and restrict our knowledge claims only to those truly clear and distinct ideas.

So by this point Descartes believes he is on something of a roll. He has a rule for establishing truth (his "clear and distinct" rule), he has proved God's existence (well almost), proved the fact of his own existence (in mind at least), explained why we humans make mistakes (the dangerous cocktail of unlimited free-will mixed with limited understanding), and that God is the guarantor of certain ideas in our minds (and we have God's own "Trademark" stamp to prove it). But *Descartes* was not going to stop there.

With his now famous "I think, therefore I am", *Descartes* believed he had proved that he could doubt the existence of the physical world including his own physical being, but he could not doubt the idea that his mind existed because the very thought of doubting was itself a proof of his mind's existence (maybe a better

131

catch-line would have been "I doubt, therefore I am"). Thus, for *Descartes* it was now just a small step to conclude that his mind, his thinking, reasoning consciousness must itself also be separate from the physical world (it's at this point that for many *Descartes'* philosophy officially goes "left-field").

Descartes saw the human body as just a kind of sophisticated machine which can be defined in the same way as everything else in the physical world (it has length, width, weight, density, hard bits and floppy bits), and thus can presumably be measured and explained solely through science and mathematics. But *Descartes* saw the human mind as different, for him the mind is not physical, it exists only because it thinks.

Descartes thus came up with the novel idea that humans are actually made of two distinct substances, a conscious mind (a non-physical substance that thinks, doubts, hopefully remembers your wife's birthday, and can deduce that two plus two equals four), and matter (the physical stuff that walks, talks, poops, sees, touches, and apologises for forgetting your wife's birthday). According to *Descartes*, our mind is wholly distinct and separate from our body, meaning that you can increase the size of your boobs, reduce your amount of fat, add some hair, lose a leg, your teeth may even fall out, but none of that it seems will affect your mind or its ability to think.

Actually *Descartes* goes one step further stating that he cannot be certain that he exists at all when he is not actually thinking, and so his very existence depends on his thinking, and thus what defines us as human beings is that we think, not that we have a physical body, and accordingly the "I" in "I think, therefore I am" is entirely distinct from the body. It would seem then that to *Descartes* our existence depends entirely on our continued thinking, and so presumably if heaven forbid we were to ever stop thinking, then apparently we would effectively cease to exist and just disappear altogether.

This idea that man is made of two wholly distinct substances is known as *Cartesian Dualism* and is fundamental to *Descartes'* philosophy, and *Descartes* based this dualistic theory on the premise that he felt he had proven beyond doubt the fact that he exists (because he thinks), while the fact that he has a physical body can still be doubted (you can't trust your senses), and thus his existence must be independent of his body. Interestingly, *Descartes* believed that only humans were such a dual creature, in his world all other animals were completely made of matter and were without mind, and so for *Descartes* animals are thus in effect merely living, breathing, mechanical machines made of matter, and with no ability for reason or thought.

All this sounds great, but actually for someone who puts such ultimate faith in mathematics and logic, this idea of man being a dualistic being is not actually very logical at all. Just because we are unable to doubt that we are thinking, but can doubt that we have bodies, doesn't necessarily prove that we exist separately from our bodies. *Descartes* implies that if something can be doubted, then we should proceed on the assumption that it is false, rather than just simply "uncertain". *Descartes* seems to use the act of doubting as a kind of proof.

And then of course there is the whole issue of just how would such a dualistic mind and body interact (telepathy, via some as yet unknown dualistic language translator, email, twitter)? If we are to believe that human beings do consist of two utterly distinct substances, then logic would dictate that they just can't interact, but clearly they do, a mental event can cause a physical event to occur (I may think that all *Descartes* ideas are all complete hokum, so my brain tells me to throw his book in the bin), or vice-versa (if I accidently drop the same book on my foot, I can be sure that the physical pain will quickly register in my mind). So where, and how, would such interaction take place?

Descartes answered this by stating that there must be a part of the brain in which the interaction occurred (actually he believed it was the pineal gland in the brain was where the mind or soul lived and interacted with the body), but even if this were true, determining "where" such interaction takes place does not explain "how" it would take place. It was all very unsatisfactory.

Descartes died of pneumonia in 1650 at the tender age of 54 (his mind presumably stopped thinking at that point too), however his legacy lived on way past his death, and philosophers spent the next 150 years or so looking for ways to either support, or refute, his theories. It's easy to see now, nearly 400 years later, how there would be a queue of pointy-headed intellectuals queuing up at *Descartes'* door with a long list of holes they wanted to point a stick at in his theories (the over-reliance on God, the now disproven idea of "mind-body dualism", the rather unclear definition of what is "clear and distinct"), but this should not take away from his importance to the field of philosophy and science as a whole.

Descartes use of scientific method as a way of questioning and proving knowledge became one of the driving forces for new ways of thinking that we now call "scientific", but he is mostly remembered for his insistence on our ability to think for ourselves, and it is this shift that pushed philosophy away from merely being based on the thoughts of great thinkers of the past and ancient scriptures, and focused upon the individual mind of the philosopher himself. For this reason alone, *Descartes* is rightly remembered not only as the man who gave the world philosophy's most well known saying (I think therefore I am), but also by many of today's pointy-headed intellectuals and philosophers as the father of modern philosophy.

16

Could God's Name Be Ronald?

"We feel and know that we are eternal"
Baruch Spinoza (1632 - 1677)

Descartes' theories and ideas started a veritable stampede of new philosophers suddenly wanting to align themselves with his rationalist thinking and scientific approach to philosophy. It should really come as no surprise then to find that many philosopher's of the seventeenth century were thus also scientists, mathematicians, and logicians, but while *Descartes* had concerned himself with doubting everything he knew in a search to find true knowledge, many of these new rationalists were now more concerned with finding some understanding for the meaning of life and their role in this world.

Many of this new breed of rationalistic philosophers were also somewhat less than enthusiastic about *Descartes'* notion of mankind being a dual-beast, composed of two distinct substances, mind and body, with most still seeing the idea as making about as much sense as packing a bathing-suit for a trip to the North Pole in winter. One such philosopher was *Baruch Spinoza* (1632-1677).

Spinoza was born, lived, and died in Holland (in fact it appears he never travelled more than 100 miles from his birthplace throughout his short life), where his family, who were Jews from Portugal, had come to escape the Portuguese inquisition (a rather nasty invention of the Catholic church of the time to identify Catholic converts who still secretly practiced Judaism, unfortunately such "identification" was made by ruthlessly torturing suspects in some rather inventive ways until they confessed, guilty or not).

It seems that even from a young age *Spinoza* developed some highly controversial ideas regarding the Jewish faith and its reliance on ritual and the Hebrew Bible, and so it was no surprise that by the age of 23 he had been shunned by the local Jewish religious authorities, exiled from his own community, and eventually even outcast by some members of his own family. It should be no real shock then to find that *Spinoza* spent the rest of his life in seclusion, living a rather solitary, chaste, and frugal existence (by all accounts he also had no notable relationships, female or otherwise), making a living as a lens-grinder (optics were a field that seemed to particularly excited *Spinoza* the scientist), and in fact his early death at the age of 44 of a lung related illness was very likely brought on by the fine glass dust he inhaled while grinding optical lenses (clearly a high-risk occupation).

Spinoza's masterwork is his book entitled *Ethics Geometrically Demonstrated*, its title giving a rather strong clue to the fact that in the new rationalist tradition of *Descartes, Spinoza's* philosophical work uses scientific method and mathematical logic to demonstrate his philosophical reasoning and ideas. Thus *Ethics* (philosophers tend to refer to the work as such, probably in an attempt to stop it sounding like a 9th grade math book) is crammed full of mathematical axioms, deduced theorems, and abstract proofs, and as such make the work almost completely unreadable to all but the keenest math professor or science savvy philosopher. But despite its "clear as mud" style, at its heart is a philosophical view of the world that attempts to answer most of philosophy's burning questions all in one hit, "why does anything exist?", "how is the universe composed?", "what is man in the grand scheme of things?", "are we truly free?", "why do lens grinders die so young?".

Spinoza was also a leading voice against *Descartes'* view of mind–body dualism, primarily based on an argument that, if mind and body were truly two different "substances", then it is not clear at all how they could communicate with each other (it's a bit like your eccentric old Aunt who claims she can talk to her cat, we smile nicely and agree just to be polite, but you know she's likely long overdue a visit to the local psychiatric ward).

To counter such claims for *dualism*, in his *Ethics Spinoza* proposed that actually everything, mind, body, the universe and everything in it, all consist of just one single substance, but that this substance exhibits an infinite number of attributes, but only two of which can be conceived of by man, that of both physical (you, me, flowers, rocks, old pairs of socks, even your mad Aunt and her talking cat) and mental (thoughts, logic, ideas) attributes, which although being different attributes they still emanate from the same source, the same substance, it is everything from a duck-billed platypus to a thought about a duck-billed platypus.

This notion of a single universal substance is known to clever bods as *monism*, and provided *Spinoza* with a solution to the problem of interaction (or lack thereof) between the separate material and non-material substances proposed by *Descartes' dualism* (namely, they're actually just two attributes of the same substance). But there was much more to *Spinoza's* single substance view of the universe than just being a way to prove that although brilliant in many ways, *Descartes* was actually barking up the wrong "substance" tree.

Despite being shunned by his church, family, and community, for his ideas, *Spinoza* remained a deeply religious man. He believed that God exists, but not a God in the same traditional sense as taught by religion (old man, white robe, long grey beard, talks like Morgan Freeman), not a God that first created and now rules over the universe by virtue of his divine providence, a puppeteer who sits outside our world making changes, tweaking things here and there, and bringing flood, famine and plagues of locusts when He's having a bad day.

No, *Spinoza's* God is a God that is not outside of our world, but nor is He in it, *Spinoza's* God is the world, surrounding us, within us, part of us. It should then be no big leap of understanding to see that having already declared in his *Ethics* that everything that exists (both mental, physical, and everything in between) is composed of one single substance, *Spinoza* goes on to declare that this substance and God are actually (surprise, surprise) one and the same thing. In fact for *Spinoza*, God, the Universe, and Nature, are all names for the same single all-encompassing substance (in reality he could just as easily have called his single substance Ronald, or a Frankfurter, but God seemed a little more appropriate).

Thus *Spinoza*, viewed God and Nature as just two names for the same reality, namely a single, fundamental substance that is the basis of the universe and of which all lesser "entities" (namely you, me, cats, dogs, thoughts, feelings, songs, poems, earth, wind, fire, water, yesterday's socks, and tomorrow's dinner) are actually all just differing variations. We are all then part of God's manifestation, part of nature's whole, everything is conceived in terms of God or Nature, as variations of the one substance, and a such are wholly dependent upon it. Everything exists in God, as a variation of God, and as such is dependent upon God. This belief that God and Nature are one and the same thing is known as *pantheism*.

And *Spinoza* wasn't done yet, just to complicate things a little more *Spinoza* goes on to deduce that since everything is made of that single substance, a substance that has multiple attributes including both mind and physical body, everything that exists should then also be conceived in the same two ways, as containing varying degrees of the same two attributes.

This is easy to understand from the perspective of ourselves, we clearly see that we have both a mind and a body, the two attributes being expressed as the walking, talking, thinking, dreaming, pooping, being that is you. But things get a little strange with the implication that every other object in the physical world would also have its mental counterpart, in short, *Spinoza* is telling us that even rocks, trees, tables, chairs, a can of Coke, and a dirty old sock, are all also composed of all God's attributes, and thus are composed of not only a physical attribute but also a mental one too.

On the face of it this makes about as much sense as a chocolate tea-pot, but *Spinoza* assures us that we only need to see the universe in the same way that God does, from the infinite and eternal view of nature, as everything being part of the greater whole, for everything to become clear to us (maybe your eccentric old Aunt can speak to her cat after all, and her armchair, teapot, and walking stick).

It seems that according to *Spinoza* we all are bound by the laws of nature, the laws of the single substance that we are all a part of. As such, *Spinoza* is supporting a strong *determinist* view, the view that absolutely everything that happens occurs through the operation of necessity, for a reason, out of nature's law of cause and effect. For him, even human behavior is fully determined, with "freedom" actually only being our capacity to know we are "determined" and to understand *why* we act as we do.

138

We must all follow nature's law, we are not free to choose otherwise, just as a lion cannot suddenly wake up one day with a new found love for other animals and decide to suddenly become a tree-hugging vegetarian, we too cannot suddenly decide we can fly, live underwater, or leap tall buildings in a single bound, we are constrained by our own manifestation of that single substance, of God, bound by the laws of nature.

That we humans presume to have free will, it is merely a result of our awareness of what *Spinoza* called "appetites" (greed, desire, self-importance), which affect our minds and our ability to understand the reasons why we want and act as we do. For *Spinoza*, only God, or Nature, is truly free, truly of "its own cause", and thus free to act with complete freedom.

According to *Spinoza*, reality is perfection (it's all the manifestation of God after all, and it's hard to put a cherry on top of that), and so if circumstances are seen as unfortunate to us it is only because of our inadequate conception of that reality. *Spinoza* urges us to see ourselves as one with God, nature, everyone and everything else, and see our lives as determined by the necessity of that greater whole, only then will we be truly happy.

Spinoza's philosophy thus urges us to see our lives in a cosmic context, as part of a much bigger whole, a whole that is an infinite manifestation of a single substance, a manifestation of God as part of everything and everyone, everything being related, everything being part of nature's whole, part of God. He wanted to demonstrate that not only is life subject to the universal laws of nature (God, or Ronald if you prefer), but also then to the laws of logic, science, mathematics, and reason, and as such we must free ourselves from our feelings and passions (our ego) and see ourselves not as unique individuals but part of that whole, see ourselves in terms of nature's eternity. For *Spinoza* then, the highest virtue of man is the intellectual love God or Nature (or just Ronald to his friends).

Similarities between *Spinoza's* philosophy and early eastern philosophical thought are obvious. There seems to be many overlaps between *Spinoza's pantheist* view of the universe and the teachings of both *Lao Tzu*, and the Veda traditions of India, with his single universal substance easily being seen as similar (if not the same) as either *Brahman* or the *Dao*, each seeing everything and everyone as being just a small part of a single whole, and that true happiness is only to be found when we understand our role as part of that single whole. However, where *Spinoza* reached his glorious vision of the universal whole via (some somewhat unreadable) logic, proof, axioms, and reason, history seems to find no record of those early Eastern thinkers reaching their own conclusions based upon any such scientific approach, with hours spent with an abacus, or at the chalkboard.

Another of this new breed of rationalist philosopher was *Gottfried Wilhelm von Leibniz (1646-1716)*, a German philosopher and mathematician of some note (primarily famous for his claim to have been the inventor of calculus, rather than the slightly more famous Sir Isaac Newton, although in reality it seems that they had in fact both invented it independently at around the same time). However, where *Spinoza* led a secluded, lonely existence, *Leibniz* was something of a "mover and shaker" socialite, meeting and corresponding with all the leading lights of the time, but it seems all that socializing clearly took up a great deal of his time as he actually published very little in his lifetime.

Leibniz too was also not all that taken with *Descartes'* dualistic view of mankind, but where *Spinoza* had preferred to see the universe and mankind as composed of just one substance (possibly a frankfurter, or a God who may be named Ronald), *Leibnitz* went for a somewhat different approach. *Leibniz* saw the universe rather being made of an infinite number of simple substances (so actually, the complete opposite of *Spinoza*), and also unlike *Spinoza*, *Leibniz* actually managed to settle on just one name for all these substances, calling them *monads*, each of which was considered as self-contained and completely independent of all the others. In *Leibniz* view, God (he too still needed a God to support his theories) was effectively the "*super monad*", the creator of all others.

Now according to *Leibniz*, these *monads* are apparently rather clever little things, they each contain a representation of the whole universe, collectively they offer the infinite variety of the universe, and are all connected, logically, as part of a greater whole, and as such they all exist in a "pre-established" harmony, a harmony

140

established by the *super-monad* himself, God. Thus *Leibniz* saw that through their in-built understanding of the universe and their connectivity to that whole, it should be possible, in principle at least, for each *monad* (or more accurately any creature, thing, gas, liquid, or solid, composed of that *monad*) to presumably understand everything there is to know about the universe, they just needed to tap into their in-built understanding.

However, for a start, clearly we humans don't understand the universe or our connection to it at all (presumably *Leibniz* could only confidently speak on behalf of his own particular *monad*). But *Leibniz* explains this rather glaring hole in his theory by surmising that rather unfortunately it seems that each *monad* is only endowed with its own limited ability to understand that inner representation (thus not surprisingly a rock, or your old brown shoe, likely has absolutely no ability at all to understand the universe, why it is in it, or its own connectivity to it), and even the human mind with its superior ability for reason and logic (and so presumably superior type of *monad*), itself can still only comprehend only a small portion of the universe as a whole. For *Leibniz*, it seems only God has a mind "infinite" enough (as the *super monad*) such that it can fully comprehend everything in terms of its connectivity and harmony, and thus only God can see the true big picture.

Under this universal connectivity and harmony, like *Spinoza*, *Leibniz* believed that nothing happens without a reason, and since God created the universe (the *super-monad*, the creator), all reasons must be God's reasons, and thus we can safely assume that such reasons must all be good reasons, indeed they must be the very best reasons. In fact, this thinking led *Leibniz* to one of his more famous declarations, that this then must be "the best of all possible worlds", for if God chose to create this world out of what we must assume was an infinite number of possibilities, then this indeed must have been the best option of the bunch (sickness, earthquakes, famine, wars, spandex, and boy-bands included).

Remember, *Leibniz* was a rationalist, and so he came to this remarkable conclusion by logic and reason alone. His logic seems to have been that firstly there would be no world at all if God (the *super-monad*) had not chosen to create a world (all other *monads*) in the first place, and so having clearly chosen to create the world, and being both all-powerful and morally perfect (*Leibniz's* words not mine), God must have created the best of all possible worlds. For *Leibniz*, being all-powerful and morally perfect, God could not have created a world that was anything other than the best (if then this world of ours is the best of all possible worlds, you do have to wonder just how bad all the other options were).

As for the evil in our world, it seems then that for reasons best known to God we apparently need such evil as part of our seemingly "best of all possible worlds", and *Leibniz* assures us that it is only due to our own limited vision, our *monad's* inability to fully comprehend the bigger picture, that we see this evil as evil, and not just a necessary part of the bigger picture. In a strange twist then, it seems that *Leibniz* is telling us that without such evil, our world would actually be a worse place, and so it seems the likes of Jack the Ripper and Attila the Hun were actually all part of God's bigger picture, part of what constitutes the best world possible.

The logic of both *Spinoza* and *Leibniz* may well be questionable, both leaning more than a little on their particular version of God (either as a frankfurter or a *super-monad*), but both had taken up the baton handed down by *Descartes* to reach their philosophical conclusions via reason and logic alone, to use scientific method to prove their theories, and to reinforce the notion that we can only truly know what we know by pure reason alone. For this new breed of thinker, logic was not just something to apply to science and mathematics, it was the whole basis for the universe, reality, and how it all hangs together.

But across the English Channel a small group of philosophers were about to offer up their own theories around knowledge and how we know what we know (or don't know), indeed challenge the whole idea of rationalist thought altogether. *The Empiricists* of England, Scotland, and Ireland were about to loosen their stiff upper lips and make their voices heard.

17

Seeing is Believing

"No man's knowledge here can go beyond his experience"
John Locke (1632 - 1704)

While the Continental European types were enthusiastically pushing *rationalism* as the only way forward for philosophical thinking, their more stiff upper-lipped counterparts across the North Sea were formulating their own far more practical view. To these great British minds of the early 18th Century, who lived in an environment far more attuned to scientific discovery, technological advances, industrialization, bacon and eggs, and a distinct distrust of anyone with even the whiff of a foreign accent, *rationalism* was merely continental humbug, and just more proof that your average "Johnny-Foreigner" just can't be trusted with matters of the mind, and so firmly belonged out there alongside beliefs in fairies, unicorns, or that the moon was made of cheese. You were no more likely to find a *rationalist* in London than a herd of wild elephants roaming around Trafalgar Square.

Empiricists hold the view that all human knowledge must come from our experiences of the world that we acquire solely through the use of our senses, in other words, unless you have seen it, felt it, smelled it, touched it, or heard it, you shouldn't believe it. This of course is polar opposite to such *rationalists* as *Descartes*, who believed that we humans are in fact born with innate ideas, ideas that can give us knowledge about the world around us independently of anything we may experience through our senses, and thus the firm belief that knowledge can be gained purely through a process of reasoning.

The first of the British *empiricists* of any significance was *John Locke* (1632-1704), who was impressed with the new "scientific method" as proposed by *Francis Bacon* and his chalk-board loving friends, a method which adopted a far more empirical approach to scientific proof and investigation based upon observation and experience, and who looked to extend this thinking towards understanding just where we get our ideas and knowledge from.

Unlike *rationalists*, *Locke* firmly believed that as humans we are born with minds that are actually as empty as a church on a week-day, and thus we all start life with our minds effectively just a blank slate waiting for experience to fill in the empty pages with knowledge and understanding through the constant influx of information from our senses.

In support of this "blank slate" start to life *Locke* argues that there is not one jot of evidence to suggest that the minds of infants are anything other than completely blank at birth (no baby has ever been born who straight out of the womb was solving quadratic equations, knew what an apple or pear was, that fire burns, or that the correct place to poop and pee is in the washroom), and thus any theory that supports the existence of innate ideas must therefore be false.

Despite his strong views against any notion of us being born with any innate ideas, *Locke* did not however reject the notion that we humans have innate capabilities. In fact *Locke* details that it is our possession of innate capabilities such as perception and reasoning that are central to how we process all the sensory data our senses are merrily passing us every waking moment of the day.

In *Locke's* view of the world our minds are not just passively receiving information from the outside world via our senses, rather he sees that each piece of sense data is worked on by our mind's innate capabilities which thus give rise to our understanding of the world around us. For instance, in the act of eating an orange we do not sense the whole orange as a single sensation, rather we receive a whole series of independent sensations from our senses (we see something round and orange in colour, taste its sweetness, smell its aroma, feel the sting as the juice squirts into our eye), our minds then process all this sensory data putting it all together such that we come to the idea of what we then go on to call an "orange". However, ultimately, despite our innate ability to process all our in-coming sensory data into something that makes sense of the world, it is still only our senses that provide the necessary raw data.

Locke also distinguished between what he called "primary" and "secondary" qualities. By *primary* qualities he means our sensory perceptions of things in terms of their shape, size, weight, quantity, and so on, believing these are qualities which our senses can reproduce objectively and in the same way for everyone. But *secondary* qualities are how we sense things in terms of beauty, taste, comfort, feel, these do not reproduce the "real" qualities that are actually inherent in the thing themselves, they record only the effect the object has on our senses, and thus can vary from person to person. We will all hopefully agree that an orange is round and well, orange (no one sees an orange as square and purple this side of a drug-induced hallucination), but we may all argue as to whether the same orange is sweet or sour, juicy or dry, tasty to the palette or leaving a nasty taste on the tongue.

Irish philosopher *George Berkeley* (1685-1753) embraced *Locke's* ideas and then rather took them to their extreme. *Locke's* empirical view of the world still assumed that there was indeed a "real" world out there that our senses were perceiving, a world that must then have "substance" so that all the things we perceive do actually physically exist outside of our mind and senses. That orange that we hopefully have all agreed is round, juicy, and orange, did actually grew on a real tree, was picked by a real farmer, who shipped it off to market in a real truck ready for you to buy with your real (or the credit card company's) money.

But *Berkeley* argued that how can *Locke* be sure that these things do actually really exist, do actually have substance? Sure our senses send us messages telling us they exist, but these messages are not the same as actual substance, they are after all just messages. For *Berkeley*, the only place he can really be sure something actually exists then is in his mind, and thus in order for something to exist someone has to first perceive it in their mind, and thus logically (for *Berkeley* anyway) if no one perceives it then it just doesn't exist.

So where *Locke* saw a material world existing outside of the ideas of things in his mind, *Berkeley* saw that he could only be sure that the ideas of things themselves existed in his mind, his senses could

145

not tell him that the things themselves actually existed. Thus for *Berkeley* the only logical conclusion was that nothing exists outside of the mind, a position that is known as "*immaterialist idealism*", meaning that he believed that there was only one kind of substance in the universe (*idealism*) and that this single substance was not material (or actually a physical thing in any way) but purely mind, or thought.

In *Berkeley's* world then there is only perceiving minds receiving and processing sensory data, or the ideas that those minds create, there is nothing else, and as such "ideas" are all we can ever experience, a world constructed purely of thought (this book, the clothes you are wearing, your bank overdraft, all that washing up lying in the sink, all have no material existence, they are just "ideas").

But then this leaves us with a bit of a problem. If something can only exist for me because I have perceived it then it means for instance that the tree my orange grew on, the farmer who picked it, and the truck that took it to market, all do not exist as I personally did not "perceive" them, I only perceived the actual orange sitting on the grocer's shelf. Similarly, and probably a little more worryingly, it means that even when I have perceived something such as the chair I am sitting on, as soon as I get up and leave the room it too presumably now ceases to exist too as it is no longer being perceived. All very confusing.

But it seems that *Berkeley* had an answer all ready in his (perceived) back pocket to address this worrying little issue. *Berkeley's* response was that actually nothing is ever "unperceived" as even if I am not present to perceive something, it still exists as everything is always perceived by God (it should come as no surprise that *Berkeley* was also a Bishop of the Anglican church and so was always likely to somehow squeeze God into his philosophy somewhere). *Berkeley's* theory therefore depends on the existence of God, and a God who would seem to spend most of his time "perceiving" everything in the universe to make sure it all exists.

But actually, *Berkeley's* philosophical vision of God is more complex than just being a full-time perceiver of everything in the universe. *Berkeley's* view of the world is that everything exists purely as ideas, ideas that exist only in our minds as and when we perceive them through our senses. But we do not control what our senses perceive, we cannot choose what our senses experience, the world simply presents itself to us (as much as I may want, wish, and pray to see my orange as square and purple, the world will always present it to my senses as round and orange).

Berkeley thus concludes that the cause of all my ideas about the world are not mine at all, they are God's. God is the cause and generator of all our perceptions, all our ideas, God is the cause of everything, everything we see, feel, touch, hear, and smell. God is the cause of all our ideas and perceptions that we are constantly subjected to, the whole world in fact exists in God. For *Berkeley*, God is the one cause of everything, and we, our perceptions, our ideas, everything exists only in the mind of God.

In *Berkeley's* eyes then, God not only creates us as perceivers in our own right, he is also the cause and generator of all our perceptions. Thus, basically, *Berkeley's* idea is that God is up there somewhere not only busying himself perceiving everything in the universe, but also constantly tapping out an endless stream of sense data to us all (presumably on some massive cosmic web-site to which we are all tuned in 24/7).

Ultimately though *Locke* and *Berkeley* agreed in that all we can ever believe is what our senses tell us, they merely disagreed about whether the real world consists of material substance or just God's world-wide web.

The age of British *empiricist* thinking was to reach its peak with the arrival on the scene of Scottish philosopher *David Hume* (1711-1776) who by all accounts was something of a child prodigy entering the University of Edinburgh at the tender age of just 12, and whose ground-breaking philosophical work, *A Treatise of Human Nature*, published when he was 28 years old, was by *Hume's* own admission apparently a fully formed philosophical concept in his mind by the time he was only 15.

Hume divides the contents of our minds (however right, wrong, or limited in content they may be) into two kinds of phenomena, "*impressions*", being the direct sensations and perceptions we receive through our senses, and "*ideas*", being our thoughts, reflections, and imaginings around those *impressions*. *Hume* was particularly interested in how these two phenomena of our minds related to each other.

Hume believed that our *ideas* about the world around us are formed as our minds attempt to combine all the sensory perceptions we receive (*impressions*) that it believes somehow resemble one another or that we experience together into the *ideas* that we then go on to believe to be true knowledge of the world around us. For instance, throughout your life your mind has received numerous different *impressions* of certain 4-legged furry creatures that drool, bark, bite, have wet noses and wagging tails, aimlessly chase other smaller 4-legged creatures, and which generally do what you tell them if you give them treats, and eventually over time your mind puts all these *impressions* together to formulate your *idea* of what a dog is.

However, *Hume* believed that this process of combining associated *impressions* to formulate *ideas*, what *Hume* called *associationism*, actually leads us away from true *empirical* knowledge, stating that it is put together in our minds merely out of coincidences and connections that may themselves not be reliable. For *Hume* the problem is that we very often draw conclusions and formulate *ideas* about the world around us that we go on to believe to be true knowledge about the nature of the universe, but which are just not supported by our *impressions* (our sensory evidence).

To understand what he means we need to understand that *Hume* sees only two kinds of statement that truly express knowledge. Firstly what he calls "*demonstrative*" statements which are wholly self-evident in that denying the statement involves a logical contradiction. For example the statement that two plus two equals four is a *demonstrative* statement in that it is self-evident and requires no additional experience or empirical evidence to prove its truth (you did not have to experience owning two chickens, then in the process of buying two more you miraculously discovered that this resulted in you now owning four future Sunday dinners).

Hume also defines what he calls "*probable*" statements of truth. Unlike *demonstrative* statements, *probable* statements are not self-evident, they need a degree of empirical evidence for them to be known to be true or false, they need some kind of experiment to prove their validity. Take for instance the statement that I can't pay for the double decaf tall skinny vanilla latte with chocolate drizzle on top that I just drank. This statement needs me to first open my wallet and show the empty space where any cash or credit cards should be to prove its validity to the understandably irate barista.

According to *Hume* to understand if a statement is true or false we must first ask if the statement can be seen to be *demonstrative* (self-evident) or *probable* (provable by empirical experiment), if a statement is neither of these then we cannot know if it is indeed true or false, and it is thus a meaningless statement. This division of all statements of truth being only one of two possible kinds is known to today's bearded intellectuals as *Hume's fork*.

All this seems perfectly reasonable, but the problem comes when we apply *Hume's fork* to what today's brainy types call *inductive inference* or *inductive reasoning* as it is also known to other brainy types. *Inductive inference* is our ability to infer things (facts) from past evidence, which in simple terms just means that by observing something as always happening in a seemingly unchanging pattern, we believe (infer) that it will continue in the exact same way in the future. Such *inductive reasoning* is actually the basis of most scientific truths, rules, and laws, as by the use of experiments and observations science "infers" that such results provide sufficient proof for such truths to be understood as being undeniable laws of nature.

But *Hume* questions the validity of any such truths arrived at by *inductive inference*. Take for example the understanding that the sun will always rise again tomorrow. This seems a perfectly reasonable fact that we all happily believe to be true, after all we have experienced the sun rising without fail every day of our lives and have no reason to doubt that the exact same thing will not continue to happen every day in the future.

But if we apply *Hume's fork* the statement is clearly not *demonstrative* as its claim involves no logical contradiction given that the idea that the sun will not rise tomorrow (however unlikely and quite unthinkable in its consequences) is still a logical possibility. It is also not a *probable* statement as we cannot actually know (prove) for sure that the sun will indeed rise tomorrow. Thus according to *Hume* we actually have no rational basis for our belief in the fact that the sun will rise tomorrow, and thus the statement is effectively humbug .

According to *Hume* the same is true in our belief in *causality*, our belief that event A will always cause or be followed by event B. If we roll a white billiard ball into another similar sized but stationary black billiard ball we not unreasonably believe that the impact will "cause" the black ball to also move. Indeed, we believe we can verify (prove) the theory by observing such an event time and time again, never once observing that the white ball fails to "cause" the black ball to move, and so surely proving the theory to be true.

Indeed science bases much of its understanding of the nature of the universe on the understanding that nowhere in the universe can there be any phenomena that do not give rise to certain consequences and have not themselves been caused by other phenomena (a pin-prick causes pain, gravity causes objects to attract, water causes plants to grow, a sudden and obsessive interest in model trains will cause my wife to leave me), for science *causality* it is a fundamental universal truth.

But for *Hume* even *causality* does not hold up to real scrutiny. Again there is no logical contradiction in denying that event A will cause event B (however unlikely we believe it to be, the possibility that the black billiard ball will not move is still a valid one), nor can we prove empirically any causal event since we cannot observe every future instance of event A to see if indeed it is always followed by event B. Thus the idea of *causality* is also neither a *demonstrative* nor a *probable* truth, and thus according to *Hume* it must be rejected as a statement of truth as again there is no rational grounds for believing that event A will always cause event B (even though our experience tells us it does). Thanks to *Hume* it seems that the whole of science itself was now on very shaky ground.

However, *Hume* does fortunately go on to throw science a bone by stating that even though there can be no rational argument or justification for any laws of nature derived through *inductive reasoning*, it does not mean that they are not useful. After all, science still has a very reasonable claim to expect that something will happen based upon past observations and experience. What *Hume* tells us is that in the absence of any rational justification for *inductive inference*, our own human nature creates belief in what we believe our mind's associated *impressions* and *ideas* tells us, which itself becomes a not unreasonable guide. *Hume* goes on to state that in fact it is such belief that sits at the heart of most of our claims to knowledge rather than *reason* itself.

Such "facts" based not on reason but rather on beliefs reflect the way our natural instincts, force of habit, our conditioning, and social conventions have formed our view of the world. According to *Hume*, a great deal of how we think depends on human nature and not on *reason* or even *empiricism*. Such beliefs may not always be logically or empirically true, but we still need them to think and function in our everyday lives, and it seems that science needs them just as much too. The problem is that scientists mistakenly make assumptions about such beliefs as being scientific truths and laws, when it seems that (according to *Hume* anyway) they can be neither *logically* or *empirically* proven.

Unfortunately *Hume's* innovative ideas were somewhat ignored when they were first published, apparently he was better known at home for being the author of *A History of Great Britain* than for his philosophical ideas. However, across the English Channel, particularly in Germany, his ideas were to cause something of a stir (but obviously not in a *demonstrative* or *probable* way) and were to become the catalyst for several great *rationalist* thinkers to start to question their own philosophies.

18

Les Philosophes

"I do not agree with what you say, but I will defend to the death your right to say it"
Voltaire (1694 - 1778)

In 1789 Europe felt the full force of what was to become a watershed event in European history, however, as historically significant as it was, this event was not the election on February 4th of George Washington as the first President of the United States, the "Father of the Nation" who had sent the British packing with their tails between their legs some six years earlier. Surprisingly maybe for some, nor was it the much publicized mutiny aboard the Royal Navy ship HMS *Bounty* in the South Pacific on 28 April led by one Fletcher Christian which went on to inspire numerous Hollywood movies. No, this particular watershed event was the storming of the Bastille in Paris on July 14th by a large mob of French-types unhappy about the price of croissants and onions (amongst other things), an event which would mark the start of the French Revolution.

The French Revolution would ultimately see a nation teardown and then redesign their country's political landscape, uproot centuries-old institutions such as the absolute monarchy and feudalism, and thus (although actually failing to achieve all its own revolutionary goals) subsequently playing a critical role in shaping today's modern nations by showing the world the power to be found when the will of people translates into action. In addition, although to some probably not quite as significant, it would also prove the catalyst for defining a country that would go on to eat snails, frog's legs and horsemeat, produce over 400 different varieties of cheese, invent the hot air balloon, the submarine, and the parachute, and a people seemingly obsessed with sex, wine, and garlic, and where to this day it's still illegal to name a pig Napoleon.

As the 18th Century drew to a close the excessive and extravagant lifestyle of the then understandably unpopular French king, (King Louis XVI) had left France on the brink of bankruptcy. This, along with two decades of poor harvests, drought, high taxes, and soaring prices for baguettes, garlic, and croissants, all led to more than just a little unrest amongst France's peasant population. Not unsurprisingly then, the garlic starved people of France eventually expressed their unhappiness in a wave of revolutionary fervor, culminating on July 14th 1789 when rioters stormed the Bastille fortress in Paris (a date still celebrated today in France as an excuse to take an even longer lunch-break than usual), and thus officially starting the French Revolution.

By the time it was all over in the late 1790's, King Louis and his queen had been separated from their heads, radicals such as Maximilien Robespierre had unleashed a bloody "Reign of Terror" that saw thousands follow the fate of King Louis as they too were unceremoniously introduced to "Madame Guillotine", and the revolution itself had degenerated into a chaotic bloodbath. The revolution eventually culminating in 1799 with an overly ambitious General named Napoleon Bonaparte seizing power and appointing himself as France's First Consul, eventually promoting himself to the lofty rank of Emperor. In short, France had merely replaced an out of touch overly extravagant monarchy with a pint-sized soldier with ambitions on the whole of Europe.

Despite the obvious influences of a king hell-bent on a "rock'n'roll" lifestyle and the sky-rocketing prices of the average Frenchman's beret and onions, many believe that the French Revolution was primarily influenced by the thinking that grew out of the *Enlightenment,* and particularly by the group of thinkers who collectively (and rather unimaginatively given their collective brains) called their little band of intellectuals *les philosophes* (the philosophers), and who formed what became known as the *French Enlightenment* (although it should be said that not all the great thinkers associated with the movement were themselves strictly French).

153

The *philosophes* were a somewhat diverse group of thinkers who lived in France in the 18th century, and although credited by many for creating the language and ideas that were to drive the French revolution, none of them actually took part in the revolution itself, handicapped by the fact that by the time the doors of the Bastille were being kicked down by hungry French peasants most of the prominent members of the group were already buried under six feet of French soil. Few were primarily philosophers, most *philosophes* were more "public intellectuals" (essentially smart-Alec's who weren't afraid to voice their opinions in public on the issues of the day) who applied reason to the study of many areas of learning, including philosophy, history, science, politics, economics, and social issues.

The *philosophes* themselves believed in the existence of a natural order, consistent with the dictates of reason, and believed that any rational being had an immediate sense of what was just and unjust. For the *philosophes*, this manifested itself most clearly in the sense of outrage they felt for the illegitimate use of force and the oppression of the weak by the strong. Oppression to them was an insult to both nature and reason. They agreed with their British counterpart *Locke* in arguing that political authority was based on a contract between the government and the governed, claiming that nature gave no one person the right to rule and that freedom itself was a divine gift, and they applied this notion to all forms of government, but particularly against the existing French monarchy.

They also had a strong belief in progress, and the fundamental importance of the progress of science and technology, describing the history of the world as the history of the progress of the human mind. François-Marie Arouet (1694-1778), who is more widely known by his adopted nom de plume *Voltaire* and who was effectively the figurehead for the *philosophes*, focused in particular on the ways in which advances in scientific knowledge had changed human behaviour in all aspects of life. For *Voltaire*, progress in the arts and science went hand in hand with better government and a decrease in religious and political passions.

However, *Voltaire* also insisted that the *philosophes* themselves were neither a religious sect nor a political party, and tried to downplay their influence, which he insisted was limited only to intellectual pursuits and thus could not possibly threaten civil peace (you have to assume he had his fingers crossed behind his back when he said this). Of course no one, either then or now, believed that to be the case, and saw his comments being designed to be more around keeping himself out of a French prison, particularly when such mere "intellectual pursuits" would go on to lead to a full scale revolution a mere eleven years after his death.

Indeed *Voltaire* was no stranger to either controversy or the inside of a French prison. He developed a tense relation with the authorities of the time through his critical views, views that would have him experience the pleasures of the French penal system and receive several one-way tickets to England as a forced exile from his native home (Although likely relieved to be free of the arm of French law, such one-way trips to England were quickly tempered with the sudden realization that he would now have to suffer English food for the foreseeable future).

On one such three year exile to Britain, following an insult exchange with a French nobleman (a not uncommon occurrence for *Voltaire*), *Voltaire* became curious about the country's relative freedom of speech and religion, as well as its constitutional monarchy, as opposed to the absolute monarchy his fellow countrymen were being subjected to just 26 miles away across the English channel. He also became a big fan of *John Locke's* political philosophy, all of which resulted in a collection of essays which attacked both the French monarchy and the Catholic church.

However, *Voltaire* did not actually write what most people would think of as philosophical works (dry, lengthy, theoretical tomes more inclined to induce sleep than revolution), he preferred to express himself in more literary terms, using essays, plays, poems, and novels, to express his ideas and attack those he saw as the enemies of those ideas. His work is often seen as witty, mocking, satirical commentaries and scathing critiques, which were always seen as controversial, but at the same time accessible to not just to his fellow intellectuals, but also to the very people who were suffering at the hands of the very injustices he was trying to highlight.

Voltaire himself was *deist* (meaning he believed in God, but believed that God once having created the world now has little or nothing to do with its nature or day to day running, probably assuming that He likely had better things to do with his time than worrying about what was happening on one unassuming planet in a remote corner of the universe), and as such believed we cannot know much about God one way or another, and so we certainly shouldn't be making any assumptions about how he should be worshipped. For this reason *Voltaire* strongly opposed organized religion, believing that God allows people to exercise their own reason rather than rely solely on faith or doctrine. Distrust (and in many cased outright hostility) to organized religion, particularly the Catholic church, was a shared trait amongst the *philosophes*, who viewed religious fervor as the single biggest threat to civil peace everywhere.

In an period where French culture and ideas were the centre of western thought, *Voltaire* was probably the most famous (or infamous) intellectual in Europe, and even today is probably only eclipsed by Napoleon, Joan of Arc, and the 1998 French FIFA World Cup winning team, in France's "most famous list". No *enlightenment* thinker had a career as long, a voice as creative, a body of work as large, or a readership as devout and widespread (he also probably holds the record for most days spent either in either exile or inside a French prison cell for the crime of merely voicing an opinion). He was despised by the Church, and by the monarchs and nobility who tasted his ridicule and suffered his scathing satire, while at the same time he became a hero and inspiration to a countless number of your average Jean-Paul's, and as such his ideas, representative of the entire *French enlightenment*, meant that he was likely the first philosopher to truly go "mainstream".

However, as broad and wide-reaching as *Voltaire's* writings were, the two greatest political philosophers of the time associated with the *philosophes* were *Montesquieu* and *Rousseau*. *Charles-Louis, Baron de Montesquieu* (1689-1755) believed that people can develop laws that are reasonable if they are given the freedom to do so, but that any such reasonable laws for one society may be different from those of another society. Good law, according to *Montesquieu* depends on what a particular society is like. This idea that something is good or bad depending on the way a particular society works is known as *relativism* (for instance giving a thumbs-up sign to indicate that everything is ok will generally be met with a smile of acknowledgement in most places around the world, but will likely get you killed in the Middle East where strangely it's seen by people as a sign that you would like to shove your thumb up somewhere rather unpleasant about their person) and as a concept had been understood since the early thinkers of ancient Greece, *Montesquieu* was however one of the first thinkers to apply this to the law.

Montesquieu's point was that laws should be based on the way people live and think rather than on the desire of rulers to hold power over their subjects. He was particularly opposed to despotism (the arbitrary use of power by a King, a style of rule that has never really worked out well for the particular ruler's subjects) as was the case in 18th century France under the rule of Louis XIV. *Montesquieu* believed that laws and government should be set up to allow people as much freedom as possible, and he saw the best way to do this was for a government to be moderate and allow human nature and social custom to do most of the work in regulating people's behaviour, rather than the arbitrary power of a king (this of course was all rather dependant on a belief that human nature was inherently good, and that left to their own devices people would naturally devise a fair and just society rather than just fall into anarchy and chaos).

Montesquieu particularly admired the way England was governed, ruled as it was by three separate bodies, the House of Commons, the House of Lords, and the monarch. These three bodies worked together while at the same time limiting the power of each, and *Montesquieu* believed that this form of government, which became known as the "separation of powers" encouraged personal freedom and religious tolerance. *Montesquieu* strongly felt that France should adopt such an approach and although he would not see such in his lifetime, this principle remains today part of both the U.S. constitution and the constitution of the French Republic.

Jean-Jacques Rousseau (1712-1778) was born in Geneva, Switzerland (so not really French at all then), moving to France at aged 16 trying to make his name as a musician and composer. However, in 1740 he met *Denis Diderot* and *Jean d'Alembert*, two prominent *philosophes*, who apparently sparked his philosophical interest (likely he was also proving to be no great shakes as musician), and from that moment on his main interest became political philosophy.

Rousseau's controversial political views saw much of his work being banned in France, and even leading to warrants being issued for his arrest, and so like *Voltaire,* he ended up "vacationing" for a period of time in England where he became strongly influenced by the work of the English philosophers, and in particular the works of *Thomas Hobbe*s and his ideas around "*social contract*". However, admiring and agreeing are clearly two different things as *Rousseau* it seems took an almost completely opposite view to *Hobbes* on what the great English thinker had seen as mankind and his brutish "natural state" (how we would all live if there were no laws, ethics, or society),and the subsequent need for a *social contract* to provide some much needed peace, love, and social harmony.

Hobbes saw life in mankind's "natural state" as a one of where everyone would just act in their own self-interest, free to rape, plunder, pillage, and murder to their hearts content, where everyone was pitted against each other in a constant brutal fight for survival. To avoid such lawless anarchy and mayhem *Hobbes* believed that mankind came to an agreement with each other to establish a "civil" society through what *Hobbes* called a "*social contract*", a contract in which everyone would gain security and prosperity in return for giving up some of their "natural" rights and subjecting themselves to the rule of law (no more rape, plunder, pillage, or murder and in return everyone will live without having to sleep with one eye open).

However, *Rousseau* argues that what *Hobbes* saw as the savage and brutal "natural state" of man he sees much more as a state where man is born free, happy, innocent and independent, a state where everyone is born fundamentally good, virtuous, and compassionate. Effectively *Hobbes* saw mankind in its "natural state" as a world full of club wielding rapists and murderers, while *Rousseau* saw a world full of Mother Theresa's and Mahatma Ghandi's.

Rousseau goes on to state however, that as soon as the first man put up a fence around a piece of land, stuck a sign in the ground that announced that it was "private property - trespassers will be shot", he introduced the notion of property and ownership, and as groups of people then started to live side by side in their own "private" property they formed societies which they maintained through a system of laws. However, these societies and laws were designed only to protect property and are thus laws inflicted on the poor by the rich. In doing so, *Rousseau* states that such societies not only impose selfish and unjust laws, create inequalities and injustice, but we also at the same time lose touch with our "natural goodness", we lose touch with our true inner feelings.

For *Rousseau* the move from a "natural" to a "civilized" state merely brought about a move from freedom, innocence, and compassion, to one of injustice and enslavement, in short *Rousseau* believed that society corrupts and that although man is born free, the laws imposed by society condemn him to a life "in chains" (unless of course you are a rich property owner). What was needed was for us to stop using trying to use reason to solve our social problems, and all just get back to our true emotions. According to *Rousseau* then, human nature is itself inherently good, and it is in fact society that makes people corrupt.

Now clearly *Rousseau* wasn't advocating that as an alternative we should all just stay in our "natural state" with no imposed law and order, that would likely just leave us all living a version of the American wild-west with Wyatt Earp and Billy the Kid types running amuck across Europe (although clearly in a very loving and compassionate way), no what *Rousseau* proposed was an alternative civil society, one that was not run by wealthy aristocrats, land owners, the monarchy, or the Church, but one run collectively by all citizens.

Rousseau imagined a society where citizens are given full legislative powers and operate as a single unit, prescribing laws based on what he called the "general will", laws that would be agreed by all and would apply to everyone, and where everyone was considered an equal. Such a legislative process he believed would lead to the elimination of inequality and injustice, promote a feeling of belonging, a collective good, and individual freedoms, and one that would lead to liberty, equality, and fraternity for all, an ideal that was to become the motto of the future French Republic some forty or so years later.

By the time of *Rousseau's* death in 1778 revolution in France was imminent, and his pessimistic view of modern society as one full of inequalities and injustice and his ideas of a social contract in which the "general will" of the citizen body controlled the legislative process, offered would-be revolutionaries what they saw as a viable alternative to the corrupt system they were currently under. *Rousseau's* declaration that "man is born free, yet everywhere he is in chains" soon became a rallying cry for the French revolution, but his ideas around inequality and justice were also to find even more willing ears in the late 19th century where philosopher's such as *Karl Marx* took up and further developed his analysis of capitalist societies and the revolutionary means of replacing it.

19

You Kant Touch This

"Two things awe me most, the starry sky above me and the moral
law within me"
Immanuel Kant (1724 - 1804)

A man comes home to find his wife in bed with his best friend.
Before the man can speak his best friend jumps out of the bed and
says "before you say anything, what are you going to believe, me or
your eyes?". Although as a slice of humour this little joke will likely
not have stand-up comedians queuing up to include it in their routine,
it does however rather neatly sum up the two opposing schools of
philosophical thought that had bearded intellectual-types of the late
18th century scratching their brain-filled heads as to who was right
and who was wrong (if either).

By the early 1780's the philosophical battle lines had been clearly
drawn between the opposing views of the stiff-upper-lipped British
with their *empiricist* "it's all about the senses" philosophy, and their
rationalist "I think, therefore I am" philosophical counterparts over
in continental Europe. It appears that as far as philosophers went,
you either liked steak and kidney pie or garlic and onions, and as far
as anyone could tell neither of them seemed to be entirely right, yet
at the same time neither seemed to be entirely wrong, but certainly it
appeared that neither were going to back down.

Into this philosophical stand-off stepped *Immanuel Kant* (the
correct pronunciation of which being rather uncomfortable listening
for English speakers with a more sensitive ear), a German
philosophy professor, who had himself grown up in the *rationalist*
tradition, and who, primarily in reaction to *David Hume's*
"knowledge just comes from habit" philosophy, set himself the
somewhat formidable task of trying to prove that knowledge can

indeed be derived purely by *reason*. In doing so *Kant* was to inadvertently reconciling the two opposing philosophical camps of *rationalism* and *empiricism*, and thus laying down the gauntlet for a paradigm shift in philosophy. By the time *Kant* was finished philosophy would never be the same again.

Immanuel Kant was born in the East Prussian city of Konigsberg on 22nd April 1724, and went on to teach at the local university where he was required to teach on a broad range of subjects, including philosophy, and thus he becomes the first of our historical philosophy heroes who actually taught philosophy as a university professor (and so presumably knew his *Berkeley* from his *Bacon*). *Kant's* own early work however seems to have focused primarily on natural philosophy, although it appears to have not got off to the greatest of starts with most of his published early work being seen as idiosyncratic at best, highly speculative, and often just down-right strange.

Kant apparently had the idea that volcanic explosions could change the direction of the Earth's axis, and that the Earth's rotation was slowing down due to the friction caused by the tides against the seabed (and so presumably at some point in the future would just come to a grinding halt). He also developed a model of the universe composed of a series of concentric waves or rings, of which the "crests" were the regions of fully formed worlds, whereas the "troughs" were the regions of chaos, and argued that God must exist precisely because nature still manages to proceed even under such chaos.

To the outside world it also appears that *Kant* was also never going to win any "world's most interesting man" awards. His physical appearance appears to have been that of a small, rather ugly man, weak, and with a complexion once described as "drier than dust", he formed no close relationships throughout his life (with either women, pets, or "men-friends"), and never married thinking it would interfere with his work. His life was also extremely ordered, waking each day at precisely 4:55am, spending the morning writing or lecturing, and at 12:15 on the dot he would lunch, followed by a daily constitutional walk which was so exactly timed that it is said the inhabitants of Konigsberg actually set their clocks by it.

162

But despite the fact that most of *Kant's* most important philosophical works are considered as quite possibly the driest and most complex ever written, and almost unreadable to all but the most determined egg-head (in reality they are an insomniac's dream to read, and although the general public clearly appreciated the huge leaps *Kant* was making in philosophical thought they generally didn't have the faintest idea what any of it was about), he was destined to become quite possibly the greatest philosopher of all time.

Maybe due to a realization that his work to date was considered somewhat "off the wall", *Kant* spent the entire 1770's in philosophical silence, publishing nothing at all (readable or otherwise) during this period. However, it was during this period that *Kant* read *David Hume's* "all cause but no effect" philosophy, and this was to have a decisive impact on *Kant* and his ideas. *Kant* came to believe that such radical *empiricist* ideas at the very least demanded a response from the *rationalist's* camp, and so focused his full attention towards formulating his ideas around just how "pure reason" could indeed provide what he called "pure knowledge" (science, math, geometry, logic, and the undisputable fact that no one looks good in socks and sandals).

So after almost ten years of focused chin-stroking *Kant* would eventually publish his masterwork, *The Critique of Pure Reason*, (1781), a very long and insanely difficult volume that was met with great interest (and to be fair more than a just a few very confused readers just left scratching their heads), but which to this day remains one of the most important and influential works in philosophy. It is the "Sgt. Peppers" of philosophy, and it would turn *Kant* from an 18th century, overly-ordered, quickly-forgotten Prussian professor into the Bob Dylan of his day.

According to *Kant*, what philosophy should be focused on was not questioning the nature of the universe around us (no one had so far successfully found any answers to most of these questions anyway, least of all *Kant* himself), but rather on channelling philosophy's brightest minds towards a better understanding our mental faculties, defining the limits of knowledge, and establishing just how our mental faculties affect what we can know.

Thus, *Kant* was proposing to effectively turn philosophy on its head by arguing that we will only find answers to the nature of universe around us by examining the way we actually process and gain knowledge (what philosophy-types today call *epistemology*) rather than in any direct questioning (either by reason or via the senses) of the fundamental nature of being and the world that encompasses it (what the same philosophy-types call *metaphysics*).

Kant's great philosophical revolution was thus the shift from *metaphysics* to *epistemology*, the shift from trying to discover what reality is, to what we can actually come to know about reality and just how we can come to know it, effectively to stop thinking of the human mind as just passively recording the outside world, and seeing it as actively constructing its own reality.

As a confirmed *rationalist, Kant* had supreme faith in the power of *reason* alone to ultimately provide the answers to all of man's questions about the universe, our place in it, ethics, why men have nipples, and just what is the point of mosquitoes. However, *Hume* had given *Kant* a jolt of *empiricist* reality with his idea that not only does all knowledge come from the senses and not *reason* (Empiricist - 101), but that in addition we also can't assume any universal, necessary, and undeniable truths from what those senses tell us either (experience can teach that something is true in this instant, but not that it must be true in all instances), which of course was a bit of a blow for science as a whole.

Hume's radical tartan-clad ideas thus likely caused *Kant* a few well-reasoned sleepless nights, and it seems ultimately forced *Kant* into realizing that some kind of response to *Hume's* theories was needed. If *Hume* was right then science as we know it was actually all a bit of a waste of time, in fact our whole understanding of the universe based on the principle of "cause and effect" would be shot down like an application for an Atheist stall at a Baptist rally.

Thus, *Kant* set about the task of trying to prove that regardless of what a certain kilt-wearing philosopher had to say, knowledge that is undeniable and universal (science, math, geometry, logic) can indeed come to be known wholly through *reason,* through the processes of our mental faculties, and it is in that almost unreadable work *The Critique of Pure Reason* where he sets out exactly how.

For quite some time philosophers had broken knowledge down into two distinct categories, the first being knowledge gained completely independently of any experience at all, known as *A Priori* knowledge ("prior" to experience), and thus being knowledge that we just well, somehow know. Presumably we are all either born with such *A Priori* knowledge imbedded as part of our human starter-pack (if I cry I will get what I want) or we have derived such knowledge through *reason* alone.

Then there is knowledge that we gain through experience, known as *A Posteriori* knowledge ("after" experience), and thus being knowledge we gain through our senses, experience, and experimentation (if an apple falls on my head I will spontaneously invent the laws of gravity).

But then this is where we see *Kant* start to get a little creative as he then additionally defines two "types" of proposition. These he called *Analytical truth*, which he defined as a proposition that is true because in every circumstance it always conforms to some rule of logic or definition, and *Synthetic truth*, which he defined as a proposition that is true because of its connection to some new experience.

An example of an *Analytical truth* would be that "all bachelors are unmarried", as the concept of being unmarried is also contained in the concept of being a bachelor, it is, and always has been, true. In an *Analytical truth* we can always say that the concept "B" (in this case being unmarried) is always a logical part of what it is the concept of "A" (being a bachelor). Such truths do not actually add to our knowledge, they merely verify a truth. *Kant* believed that all *Analytical truths* are evidently true because to state the reverse would make the truth self-contradictory (I can't be married and yet at the same time say I am a bachelor, although many nightclubs are full of men who try).

On the other hand an example of a *Synthetic truth* would be "all bachelors are ugly" which although may seem to be evidently true in the case of your current boyfriend, you'd need to experience a little more "dating in the name of science" before you can assume it is true in all cases. In a *Synthetic truth* then we can say that "B" (in this case being ugly) is not a logical part of what we define as being "A" (a

165

bachelor), rather "B" extends our knowledge of "A", and thus we can say that *Synthetic truths* actually add to our knowledge (even if it's just adding the fact that it's clearly wrong). Thus, for *Kant, Synthetic truths* bring something new to the subject.

Thus we can see that with this little piece of creative thinking *Kant* was now left with four possibilities for how we gain and understand knowledge. We have the possibility of *A Priori* knowledge based on either *Analytical* or *Synthetic truths*, and we have *A Posteriori* knowledge also based on either *Analytical* or *Synthetic truths*. Of these four possibilities two were easily recognizable to the philosophers of the day, *A Priori/Analytical truths* are merely the realm of the *rationalists* while *A Posteriori/Synthetic truths* are the sensory world of the *empiricists.*

Kant also acknowledged that the idea of *A Posteriori/Analytical truths* was actually of little use to anyone since knowledge that is already deemed to be known as necessary and universally true does not need any subsequent experience to rediscover it (if I want to make a pot of coffee I don't need to rediscover the boiling point of water every time). But it is in the fourth option, *A Priori/Synthetic truths*, where *Kant* would hopefully find his response to *Hume's* anti-science ideas, and find a source for true universal knowledge that can itself be extended, not just verified, and yet done so only through the processes of "*pure reason*".

Kant argues that it is in the realms of mathematics and the principles of science where we find the "Holy Grail" of such *A Priori/Synthetic truths,* first arguing that all mathematical solutions must be *A Priori* by definition (not based on any empirical evidence), because they are universally true, and cannot be contradicted. As an example let's take the simple sum, $7+5=12$, we all (hopefully) know this statement is true, it is and always will be true, it is necessary and universal (there isn't a far distant galaxy out there somewhere in the universe where we would suddenly find that $7+5$ actually equals 13), it is therefore *A Priori*. At first glance we would also expect it to be clearly be an example of an *Analytical truth* (12 certainly seems to be a logical part of the sum of $7+5$).

However, (and here again we see *Kant* using his creative juices) *Kant* argues that we cannot actually know that 12 is the answer just by analysing the concepts of what the number 5 and the number 7 are, we can't actually deduce that the number 12 itself bares any logical relationship to either them.

What *Kant* argues is that the concepts of 7 and 5 do not themselves contain within them the concept of 12, thus, this information can only be grasped by going "beyond" the concepts of 5 and 7, and bringing in something else, something new, some *Synthetic truth*. Someone, somewhere, back in the annuls of time, a boffin with a large enough forehead was the first to rather cleverly use their fingers and toes to count 7, and then 5, and found the sum to be 12, they extended our knowledge of the concepts of the numbers 7 and 5 (that if you add them together you get 12), and thus for *Kant*, 5+7=12 (and thus by extension all mathematics) is not only *A Priori, but* it must also by definition be a *Synthetic truth*.

This was all starting to sound like *Kant* had hit philosophical gold, but how could such a proposition be possible, how could knowledge that, by *Kant's* own definition, must be outside of empirical experience (*A Priori*) but still be extended by a new concept (a *synthetic truth*)? How can a statement that gives us new knowledge about the external world, become known by *reason* alone?

Kant had found what he thought was his means for "new" knowledge that was also *A priori*, but now he had to explain just how on earth he thought such a seemingly contradicting idea would actually work, and this is where anyone reading *The Critique of Pure Reason* needed to really strap-in, as this is where it really did start to get insanely difficult. *Kant's* solution was his notion of what he rather mystically called, *Transcendental idealism*.

Idealism itself is the philosophical view that reality as we can come to know it is actually all just a construct of the mind, and key to *Kant's Transcendental idealism* was in his drawing of a sharp distinction between what he saw as the world as we experience it through our senses, and the world as it actually exists "in itself".

Kant saw that what our senses tell us about an object is never a complete picture, what we see, hear, touch, feel, and taste give us certain information about a thing, but that can never be the same as the real "thing in itself" (the idea being that something is more than just the sum of the sensory data you form of it). I can see, smell, and hear you, I can feel you (in an appropriate way of course) and even taste you (should we both be so inclined), but even with all that sensory information, I still will not know what it is to be you.

Kant's called the world as we experience it through our senses the *phenomenal* world, while the world of "things in themselves", the reality that exists independent of our mind, where everything is actually the "thing in itself", he calls the *noumenal* world (we should note some philosophers believe this dual-world view makes no logical sense at all, and so will happily tell you that the *noumenal* world is where you will also likely find unicorns, fairies, and the end of the rainbow).

Thus for *Kant*, he sees the *noumenal* world as *transcendental*, (it exists beyond our senses and understanding), while the *phenomenal* world is actually the world that remains real to us as the world we perceive every minute of every day through our senses. Thus, *Kant* concluded that we can know nothing about things as they are in themselves, the *noumenal* world, we can only know the *phenomenal* world, the world of our senses.

According to *Kant*, our mind does not just passively receive "data" from our senses which then just haphazardly creates our view of the world, rather he states that the mind is an active organ which moulds and coordinates sensations into ideas, an organ which transforms the chaotic stream of sense data (experience) into an ordered unity of thought and ideas, actively shaping and making sense of that "data". It does this through the built-in structure and processes of our minds, and thus for *Kant* the truths of mathematics and science derive their necessary character (*A Priori/Synthetic truth*) from that built-in structure and processes by which our mind operates (clearly it did not seem to occur to *Kant* that our minds, for some of us at least, may actually be inherently faulty, but that's a discussion for another day).

Kant states that actual experience (our physical and mental sensations) give us nothing but raw data, just a constant stream of bits and pieces of unrelated sensory data, but through what he calls the process of *sensibility* the mind constructs relationships between that raw data, collectively organizing it into a *perception* of the object or thought we are sensing. To achieve this the mind uses what *Kant* calls *pure intuition*, it is the means by which our *sensibility* enables us to perceive the relationships between all the random raw data to create that *perception*.

According to *Kant, pure intuition* uses two primary "*forms of intuition*" to organize the raw data presented to it, space and time. But for *Kant* space and time are not things we perceive in the normal sense from the outside world (your wristwatch and the room you are in), they are rather modes of *perception*, the way *sensibility* creates sense out of our *sensations*, they are constructs of our mind. The process of *intuition* uses the notion of sensory data perceived in both space and time to create the relationships between the raw data, and thus creating the *perception*.

As such, space and time must be *A Priori* to our minds because all experience pre-supposes them, we cannot experience anything without reference to space and time, as without them our mind would merely have a just a jumble of random raw sense data with no way to pull it all together into a *perception* of something. So for *Kant*, space and time are an *A Priori* part of the mental process we are all born with, and thus by definition they must precede every experience.

But we are not quite there yet. *Pure intuition* itself cannot create the possibility of an *A Priori/Synthetic truth*, to do that *Kant* tells us that the mind needs to take the *perceptions* created by the process of *sensibility*, and raises this *perceptual* knowledge into what he calls *concepts,* which constitute the relationships, sequences, rules, and laws, that we call knowledge, and the mind does this by the process of *understanding*.

Just as the mind arranged *sensations* around objects in space and time, so the mind now arranges those *perceptions* around what *Kant* called *categories*. *Categories* are the concepts around which every *perception* must be viewed in order for it to become an object of knowledge. *Kant* tells us that there are twelve *categories* that the process of *understanding* uses, including unity, negation, limitation, cause-and-effect, reciprocity, and necessity (which basically just means the relationships and effects of a *perception* with other *perceptions*)

Like space and time, these *categories* are applicable to whatever we experience, they are the means by which we process our experience. These *categories* are then also pre-existing structures in the mind into which *perceptions* are received, and by which they are classified and moulded into the ordered *concepts* of thought and thus knowledge, and as such they too must be *A Priori* to our mind. The *categories* are the bridge to the ideas that we have of the world, and thus all our understanding, all theory, is created by them.

With the processes of *sensibility* and *understanding*, *Kant* felt he had proven that the mind does not simply receive information, it actually shapes that information, and thus knowledge is something created by the mind by filtering our sensory experiences through our various mental faculties. *Sensation* is just unorganised raw data, *perception* is organised *sensation*, *conception* is organised *perception*, and these *concepts* become knowledge.

But most importantly, *Kant* believed he had demonstrated, through the formal *A Priori* processes of *pure intuition* (space and time) and the *categories of understanding*, that *A Priori/Synthetic truths* are indeed possible, and we can indeed infer universal truths (mathematics, science) through *pure reason*. We can grasp the nature of cause and effect, and that 7+5=12, not because *pure reason* has some insight into the world out there, but because *pure reason* has insight into the nature of our own mental faculties. And just for good measure, as a consequence of *Transcendental Idealism*, *Kant* had also managed it seems to score the bonus point of synthesizing the two opposing school of thoughts of *rationalism* and *empiricism* by demonstrating that we understand new *synthetic* knowledge via the use of *A Priori* (rational) mental processes.

However, this notion of *Transcendental Idealism* comes at a cost, as since all our knowledge of the external world is filtered through our mental faculties, via our senses, we can therefore only know the world that our mind presents to us, that is, all our knowledge is only knowledge of the *phenomena* world (the world in our mind), and thus we must accept that the *noumenal* world and anything in it is fundamentally unknowable. Science thus can happily discover things about the *phenomenal* world, but the reality of the *noumenal* world will always be beyond human understanding. For *Kant*, the issue with science is that it supposes that it is dealing with things-in-themselves, the real world, yet the whole material of science can only consist of the *sensations, perceptions* and *conceptions* that our minds create for us and thus are outside of the real world.

Having (in his mind at least) successfully refuted *Hume's* arguments, proven the case for *pure reason*, and thus single-handedly saved scientific theory, mathematics, and the universe from the potential chaos of "cause but no effect", you would expect that *Kant* would now just sit back, put his feet up, and bask in the adulation of the philosophical community (at least from those who could understand his work). But no, in 1785 *Kant* published his second great work, his *Critique of Practical Reason,* in which he outlines his philosophy around *ethics,* as supported by his concept of *pure reason.*

Kant's primary principle, the basis for his entire view on *ethics* is what he called the "*the supreme categorical imperative*", which in *Kant's* own words is the "unconditional command of our conscience to act according to the maxim whereby you can at the same time will that it should become a universal law". However, in words more clearly understandable to us mere mortals, what this really means is that an action is judged to be moral only if it is desirable that it be an accepted rule of behaviour for everyone, effectively, what's considered a moral action by you must also be considered equally moral for everyone else (if I think it's morally ok to steal from you, I must accept that it's morally ok for you to steal from me). For *Kant,* as with science and mathematics, the difference between right and wrong is wholly a matter of *reason,* and *reason* is the same at all times for all people, as such it is universal, there can be no exceptions. The *categorical imperative* it seems allows no excuse notes, no days off.

Kant's ethics are based upon an approach known to philosophy-types as *deontology. Deontological* (duty-based) *ethics* are concerned with what people do, and not with the consequences of their actions. Under this form of ethics you can't justify an action by showing that it produced good consequences, which is why it's sometimes called a *'non-consequentialist'* ethic. Duty-based ethics teaches that people have a duty to act accordingly, regardless of the good or bad consequences that may be produced. So, for example, *Kant* thought that it would be wrong to tell a lie in order to save a friend from a murderer (which is probably why Kant had so few friends).

Although his ethical vision as outlined in his *Critique of Practical Reason* follows his trend of publishing works so complex in their style and understanding that only those with the biggest pipes and sturdiest sandals can make sense of it, *Kant* nonetheless believed that he was putting forward something that would help people deal with the moral dilemmas of everyday life, and provide all of us with a useful guide to acting morally, based not on rules or doctrines from God, King, or the loudest voice in the room, but based on *pure reason* alone.

With *Kant,* philosophy began to flourish in the German-speaking world, and kick-started a century of German dominance in European philosophical thought, a period known as German *idealism. Kant's* own *Transcendental Idealism* inspired many followers (but likely far more were left just trying to understand just what it all meant), and his influence has been immense, even to the point where the people who we trust to know these things tell us that seemingly no philosopher since *Kant* has remained entirely untouched by his ideas.

Kant had turned philosophical thinking upside down by asking us to focus not on "what" we can know but on "how" we come to know, he put our mental faculties and the world it creates for us front and centre, and philosophy would never be the same again.

20

Romance and Spirit

"What if you slept?
And what if, in you sleep, you dreamed?
And what if, in your dream, you went to Heaven
and there plucked a rare and beautiful flower?
And what if, when you awoke, you had the flower in your hand?
Ah, what then? "
Samuel Taylor Coleridge (1772 - 1834)

While French and British philosophers seemingly ruled the philosophical-roost during the *Enlightenment*, from the 1780's onwards some overly-bright thinkers with decidedly more Germanic accents began to flourish, driven primarily by the radical new ideas proposed by philosophy's new shining star, *Emmanuel Kant*, and who is now seen as the first in a philosophical movement that became known as *German idealism*.

This period of *German idealism* was strongly aligned to the growth of a much broader literary and artistic movement that was sweeping across Europe which was turning the young poets, authors, painters, and musicians of the time into moping tortured souls who were filling their pages, canvasses, and score-sheets, with heart-felt visions of nature and all-consuming love.

Romanticism was Europe's last great cultural movement (mostly because Europe would spend much of the subsequent years fighting meaningless wars either amongst themselves or on a larger global scale) which started towards the end of the 18th century and lasted till around the middle of the 19th century. Its devotees were a new breed of artistic-types who were wholly concerned with human emotion, the individual, and who held a strong fascination with nature (nature in the spiritual sense rather than the "let's dissect a frog" sense). They were passionate about the individual and their connection to nature, and expressed their passion through their art and in the way they lived. They were rebels with an artistic cause, they took drugs, declared unquestioning and unrequited love, had numerous illicit affairs (seemingly with members of either sex), and had a morbid fascination with the "darker" side of human emotions. They were the rock'n'roll stars of the 19th century.

Romanticism itself was seen as developing as a reaction to the *enlightenment*, which was largely created by rich and powerful families concerned with progress, science, structure, and industrialization, but was also influenced by *Rousseau's* view of mankind's innate tree-hugging "state of nature" and *Spinoza's* view of everything being connected to and part of, well, just about everything else (God is nature, and nature is God, blah, blah, blah). The *Romantics* saw nature as a "world spirit", where everything was part of a single whole, and they were united in the idea that as part of that whole everything (from spiders, trees, rocks, you, me, poetry, language, art, music, entire nations, to even this book) is all just part one single living "organism". They were 19th century hippies looking for a tree to hug, and writing heart-felt poetry about the beauty of it all, but importantly they were also an artistic rebellion against the order and structure of the world.

But the *Romantic* movement was not (as you might first think) all about fluffy feelings, candle-lit dinners, sitting in your attic dashing off inspired verses of unrequited love, or the discovery of Valentine's Day cards, it was actually a movement far more concerned with the individual.

Most *Romantics* were themselves *idealists*, believing that everything comes from the mind of the individual. They felt that relying on their senses and experiencing everything in their own way was the only way to be truly free, and as such they looked to emphasise the positive powers of the human spirit and imagination. They liked their art natural, heart-felt, passionate, and spontaneous, and didn't like that life always had to make sense (not that it ever did anyway), be understood or controlled. They wrote, painted, composed, and lived exactly how they felt, they wore their hearts on their sleeves and stuck two fingers up to the establishment and just about everyone else. Of course on the other hand, many saw the *Romantics* merely as drug-addicted depressives with suicidal tendencies, who just moped around all day sulking about a love they couldn't have (It's fair to say they were probably more than just a little "misunderstood").

The *Romantics* were characterized by such tortured souls as William Blake, William Wordsworth, Percy Shelley, Samuel Coleridge, John Keats, Beethoven, Goethe, and Lord George Byron, and were usually seen as rebels, living their art, living recklessly, and in many cases dying young at their own hand (suicide was not an uncommon "romantic" solution for their often unrequited yet unattainable love). Indeed, a yearning for something distant and unattainable was to become almost a pre-requisite characteristic if you had ambitions towards becoming a *Romantic* (being moody and always wearing black probably also helped a little too).

But most importantly for our story, the *Romantics* did a great deal to help develop the idea of a "world spirit", and of people as individuals, individuals with their own identities, own needs and feelings. The whole notion of rebellion (in the sense of an individual rather than an unwieldy mob with pitch-forks unhappy with the King's taxes) came from the *Romantics* (if you are looking for someone to blame for that lazy teenager moping around upstairs in your house, blame the 19th century *Romantics*).

However, none of the developments of such a "romantic" view of the human condition would have happened without the all-pervading presence throughout Germany of a new kind of philosophy. *Idealism* at its core emphasised the individual, which was in stark contrast to the great thinkers of the *enlightenment* with their emphasis on *rationalism* and *empiricism* and their fixed, mechanical view of the universe which left very little wiggle room for the freedom and creativity of the human spirit. Philosophically then *idealism*, and thus by extension *romanticism,* represented a shift from the *objective* (the world as it is understood based purely on facts, and not influenced by any personal feelings, interpretations, prejudice, or what the man down the pub tells you) to the *subjective* (the world as you understand it from your own individual viewpoint).

Consider the moon, objectively it's Earth's only planetary satellite, it has no atmosphere and only about 17% of the gravity we feel on Earth, it orbits the Earth every 23 days, and is about a quarter of its size, which are all good, solid *subjective* facts that are scientifically true whether you look at the moon from your bedroom window or the North Pole, whether you are a fat-cat jet-set billionaire or a subsistence farmer in Outer Mongolia with only a skinny underfed goat to your name.

However, now imagine three very different individuals staring up at the moon, one a property developer, one an artist, and one a four year old child. Rather than a slow moving, gravitationally challenging, planetary satellite devoid of any atmosphere, the property developer would likely see the moon as a potential investment opportunity for homes with "stunning views in a very quiet neighbourhood". The artist would probably only see all the numerous shades and subtleties of colour and form, while the four year old would very likely just see a huge ball in the sky which they presume is made of cheese. Each individual is seeing the moon from their own unique perspective, a viewpoint that for each of them is perfectly correct based upon their own *subjective* understanding of the world. This is how the *Romantics,* and *idealists*, viewed the world (although probably not as all made of cheese).

The move from the *objective* to the *subjective* was a direct result of *Kant's* idea that human beings do not see the world directly, we do not see "things-in-themselves" (what *Kant* called the *noumenal* world), we only understand the world through our own human, individual point of view, and that what we actually experience as the "external world" (*Kant's phenomenal* world) is one created by our minds. *Kant* (presuming you could make sense of his philosophical works of course) had opened the door for the individual to shape their own world (whether they be a tortured artist or a four year old child with a cheese fixation).

The leading *Romantic* philosopher of the time was *Friedrich Wilhelm Joseph von Schelling* (1775-1854), and whose main philosophical goal seems to have been to show us all that both the human mind and nature are all just an expression of one great Absolute, what he called the *"world spirit"*. For *Schelling* nature is

176

visible spirit and spirit is invisible nature, and thus the natural world and the spiritual world are actually just expressions of the exact same thing. Effectively, for *Schelling*, the trees, mountains, your mind, body and soul, along with the chair you are currently sitting on and the washing-up that's waiting for you in the sink, are all just expressions of *world spirit*, all part of one giant universal whole.

For *Schelling* then *world spirit* can be sought not only in nature but also in one's own mind, and so it follows that the human mind itself must also hold within it this *world spirit*, and through it the whole universe, we merely need to look within ourselves to connect to all its joys and wonders. In fact it was *Schelling's* goal to show that by looking within yourself through art, poetry, music, and philosophy, we can all connect to this *world spirit,* and thus connect to the universe as a whole, effectively uniting mind and matter as one entity, united under the universal "*world spirit*". *Schelling* called this view *absolute idealism.*

However not content with merely uniting mind and matter under one Absolute, one *world spirit* (something that would have already had the budding *Romantics* of the time rattling off heart-felt lines of prose in search of their inner connection to the universe), *Schelling* also proclaimed that this *world spirit* exists as one continuous organic, growing process. He believed that nature is a living thing, continually seeking to grow towards a highpoint of development, a highpoint which he saw as the point where human consciousness rises to the level of nature, which itself thus becomes conscious, a point where mankind becomes nature arrived at a state of self-awareness. Not hard to see why *Schelling* became something of a leading flag-bearer for the soul-searching, nature loving, *romantics* in search of their own inner meaning and truths.

Johann Gottlieb Fichte (1762-1814) was another leading *Romantic* philosopher who was himself a student of *Immanuel Kant,* and who was particularly concerned with how it was possible for us to exist as ethical beings with free-will (which he presumably felt we all were) if we are given to believe that we actually live in a world that is causally determined, that is a world where every event follows on necessarily from the previous event according to the unvarying laws of nature and the universe. How can we as human beings have

177

any kind of choice in what we do, if everything is already determined by something else that exists outside of ourselves?

Fichte found his answer in a version of *idealism* very much in-line with his great mentor *Kant*. His answer was that we must come to understand that we live in a world that is the product of our own individual mind, everything we think of as reality is all just the creation of our mind, and that in this *idealist* world our "self" is an active being or "essence" that can thus exist outside of any universal laws of cause and effect (if this is merely a world that I created for myself, then I can rather conveniently ignore the rules that apply to the "real" world), and in this way our mind is thus free to think and choose independently of any such universal laws.

For *Fichte* then our mind creates a world for us that exists outside of the universal laws of nature, effectively saying that in the *"real"* *noumenal* world we have no free-will, but in the in the world our mind's create for us, the *phenomenal* world which according to *Kant* is the only world we can know, as a welcome bi-product we get to have free-will.

One of the more colourful of the German *Romantic* philosophers of the time was *Arthur Schopenhauer* (1788-1860), whose wealthy father had committed suicide and whose mother was something of a criticising nag. *Schopenhauer* himself earned something of a reputation as a philandering woman-hater having been convicted of assaulting a woman, having several rather public affairs, and avoiding marriage like the plague (he is purported to have once said "Marrying means to halve one's rights and double one's duties"). Not unexpectedly then he spent the last 27 years of his life living alone except for a succession of pet poodles that he named either Atman (meaning "soul" in *Hinduism* and *Buddhism*) or Butz (being German for hobgoblin).

Schopenhauer also agreed with *Kant's* view that the world is divided into what we perceive through our senses (the *phenomenal* world) and "things in themselves" (the *noumenal* world). But *Schopenhauer* took a somewhat different view on the nature of these two worlds, he saw them not as two different and distinct realities but as just two aspects of the same world, aspects that he tells us we perceive as *"will"* and *"representation"*. For instance we perceive our

178

bodies both in terms of a physical *representation* (arms, legs, and other various bits), and our consciousness which we can only experience within ourselves and is thus experienced as *will*.

When we look at things outside of ourselves (your car, house, this book), we only see their objective *representation*, but for *Schopenhauer*, just like us, they all each still have an inner reality, (an inner *will*), and as such everything exists (cars, houses, books, you, me) with both the inner (will) and outer (representation) reality of the same world.

Schopenhauer saw *will* itself as an energy that has no driving direction, goal, or purpose, but is nonetheless responsible for everything that manifests itself to us as *representations* in the physical world we experience. Observable reality (*representations*) then is just a physical expression of the universal *will*, and as such this universal *will* and our own individual "wills" are thus one and the same.

He also agreed with *Kant* that both space and time are merely concepts used by our minds to help make order of the experiences and perceptions it receives, and thus do not exist outside of the *phenomenal* world. Thus, by some rather clever logical deduction and much chin-stroking, *Schopenhauer* deduced that this universal *will* also then cannot be perceived as existing in space or time, and so must itself be timeless and indivisible. With a little more chin-stroking *Schopenhauer* deduced that the *phenomenal* world we experience must then also be controlled by this vast, timeless, yet ultimately motiveless *will*.

It is at this point however that *Schopenhauer's* philosophy takes a bit of a dark turn as he goes on to deduce that we must then all be at the mercy of this mindless, aimless, directionless, universal *will*. For *Schopenhauer* the world is neither good or bad, just meaningless, and so humans who try to find any form of happiness, meaning, or direction in their lives find at best gratification (money, power, fast cars, and even faster women), and at worst pain and suffering (penniless, powerless, a second-hand bike, and a nagging mother-in-law).

Schopenhauer had spent a great deal of time (when he was presumably taking a break from beating on women) studying Eastern philosophies and religions, and it was in the works of Eastern thinkers that *Schopenhauer* turned to provide what he saw as the only escape from such a miserable existence of chasing desire but finding only pain and misery. As in *Buddhist* and *Hindi* teachings, *Schopenhauer* says we must lose our desires and cravings (or in the words of *Siddhartha Gautama*, the *Buddha*, our "ego") by recognizing that our separateness from the universe is just an illusion, as our individual wills and the *will* of the universe are actually all one and the same thing, and thus ultimately meaningless.

According to *Schopenhauer*, we can all achieve this loss of will for desire by spending our lives in "aesthetic contemplation", which is just a fancy way of saying that we need to come to appreciate the universe as a single whole through the appreciation of art, poetry, music, and nature. Indeed, *Schopenhauer* (finally finding a note of optimism it seems) states that if we can all learn to see that our own will and the *will* of the universe are but one and the same, then such an understanding and empathy with everyone and everything else will give rise to moral goodness and compassion. This again is a sizable nod to the ideals of Eastern philosophies and religion, but where they search for a transcendent state free from desire and suffering (what *Buddhists* call "*nirvana*") *Schopenhauer* preaches the goal of becoming one with the universal *will* by the contemplation of art and nature.

In the end *German Idealism* and the *romantic* movement as a whole was really all about getting the individual to think and feel for themselves, and about the cues that an artist, poet, or philosopher was able to give the viewer, reader, or thinker to try and spark them into a little self-reflection. Ultimately though, as a full scale movement the *romantic* period had effectively fizzled out by the late 19th as the "modern" world slowly consumed the individual (industrialization, imperialism, mass urbanization, and the onset of some rather devastating wars). Modern society, and thus the individual, seemingly no longer had time to think, they only had time to do.

However, the legacy of the *romantic* movement lives on in society and culture today. In many ways, today's rock icons, artists, and film stars are the modern *romantic* equivalents of Keats, Byron, and Shelly, living outside of social norms and asserting their individuality, and echoing the *romantic* themes of rebellion and dissent. Modern *romantic* heroes such as James Dean, Jim Morrison, Jimi Hendrix, all died young living the way they wanted to live expressing themselves though their art, and so quickly became the idols and role models for a modern youth trying to find its own identity.

Unfortunately we can't all be James Dean or Lord Byron, but we all at some point want to be recognized as different, as a unique individual, live a more real and authentic way of life that is true to who we think we may really be, and maybe that's the real legacy of those early tortured *romantics* and the *German Idealist* thinkers who helped inspire them.

21

It's All About History

"A man is nothing but the series of his actions"
Georg Wilhelm Friedrich Hegel (1770 - 1831)

Despite the "romantic" influences of *Schelling, Fichte, Schopenhauer,* and their poetic "group-hug" vision of nature, the individual, world spirit, sauerkraut, frothy beer, and lederhosen, by far the most influential of the post-Kant German *Idealists* was *Georg Wilhelm Friedrich Hegel.*

Hegel was born in Stuttgart in 1770, was Head of Philosophy at the prestigious Berlin University at the time the city was becoming the intellectual centre of Europe, and who died in 1831 a victim of the great cholera pandemic that was sweeping across Europe at that time (bacteria clearly having little respect for either intellect or position), but not before his philosophy, *"Hegelianism"* (a mouthful in either German or English) had gained an enormous following at just about every university in Germany and across many parts of Europe.

As one of the major philosophers of the *German Idealist* period, *Hegel* organized and expanded upon the ideas held by many other *idealist* philosophers of the time, and his philosophical vision was as immense as it was complex (like *Kant* before him, *Hegel's* work is entirely academic in style, and thus dryer than a good chardonnay, and almost completely unreadable to anyone without a brain of planetary proportions). However, *Hegel* effectively succeeded in uniting and developing almost every idea that had surfaced during the *romantic* period, although at the same time being sharply critical of many of the *romantic* leading figures whose "it's all about the individual" ideas were in many cases just a little too self-centered for his own particular version of distinctly "non-romantic" *idealist* thinking.

Schelling, along with several other *romantic* thinkers, had said that the deepest meaning of life lay in what he called "*world spirit*", *Hegel* also used the same term but in an entirely new sense. When *Hegel* talks of "*world spirit*" he means the collective sum of all human ideas throughout time (regardless of whether they were good, bad, ground-breaking or what amounted to just plain stupidity), and thus in this sense his philosophy is centered around a vision of a *world spirit* seen as the progress of knowledge throughout history.

Fundamental to *Hegel's* beliefs is that there can be no fixed truths, rather he sees the very basis of human understanding changing from generation to generation, and the only fixed point philosophy can hold on to at any point in time is history. What *Hegel* was effectively saying is that every truth is only true at that point in time, it is grounded in the prevailing circumstances, society, the material conditions of the time, which way the wind is blowing and whether you have an "inny" or an "outy" belly-button, all of which determine how you think, and what it is you believe to be right or wrong, true or false. Thus according to *Hegel* you can never claim that any particular thought or belief you have can be held to be correct forever, it can only be correct (or presumably incorrect) from where you stand, correct at that moment in time, at that moment in history.

For instance, 5,000 years ago not even the most enlightened of thinkers in ancient Egypt would have thought that slavery was anything but the natural order of things, that's just how things were, indeed that's how things got done. As far as your average ancient Egyptian was concerned (at least those on the non-slave side of the ledger sheet anyway) there was absolutely no need to question the validity or moral legitimacy of slavery.

However, if I was to go down to my local town-square today with a large megaphone and a box to stand on, and start preaching the "benefits" of slavery there's a good chance that I would (rightly) not be making it home for dinner. However, what is clearly abhorrent and rightly considered as morally and socially wrong today, was to your average "Johnny Egypt" quite acceptable and an unquestioned truth.

The difference is that today we have a completely different (and fortunately better) basis for our judgements, but at that moment in time, some 5,000 years ago, slavery was indeed considered morally and socially acceptable. History then has changed the moral landscape to the extent where building a pyramid is now a somewhat more expensive and time-consuming task.

Hegel went on, stating that as new ideas and new context continue to be added, *reason* must then also be always changing, expanding, progressing. For *Hegel* then, *reason* itself is dynamic, it is a process, and there is no criteria beyond the historical process that can determine if an idea is right or wrong, true or false, morally acceptable or otherwise, and it can only do so when considered with reference to its own historical context. *Hegel's* philosophy is then more of a method for understanding the progress of this human knowledge through history, rather than a philosophy in its own right.

As far as *Hegel* was concerned our knowledge and understanding is always expanding, developing throughout history, from *Plato* to *Kant*, from Fred Flintstone to Albert Einstein. Knowledge constantly grows and expands with new ideas, and thus *Plato* it seems was no less right or wrong with his ideas than *Kant,* but only when taken in terms of his own historical context. However, as historical contexts changed (robes and sandals out, wigs and tights in), ideas were processed and subjected to subsequent generation's scrutiny and criticism, thus our understanding grew and new truths appeared.

History for *Hegel* then is just one long chain of reflections, and he further proposed that actually there are even certain rules that apply to this chain of reflections. It's rare that any one individual has a mind-blowing, game-changer of an idea completely independently of anyone or anything else (with the odd exception of the likes of Newton, Einstein, or the individual who first had the idea for the bikini), and thus as a rule an idea or proposition is usually proposed on the basis of other, previously proposed ideas or propositions. However, as soon as one thought is proposed (what *Hegel* calls the *thesis)*, *Hegel* argues that it will usually be contradicted by another (what *Hegel* calls the *antithesis*). A tension thus arises between these two opposites ways of thinking, a tension which continues until it is usually resolved by the proposal of a third thought (which *Hegel* calls the *synthesis*) which (hopefully) accommodates the best of both views. *Hegel* calls this a *dialectic process*, and shows the process by which opposites (usually) find resolution.

For example the *thesis* that grew out of *Rene Descartes'* "man is a dual beast" which gave rise to the distinctly continental view of *rationalism,* found its *antithesis* on the other side of the English channel under the British *empiricists.* This tension latest for almost 100 years until the cross-channel feud was finally resolved by *Kant's transcendental idealism,* the *synthesis* of the two into a new, clearer (at least once you'd found someone who could actually understand what *Kant* was saying and had them explain it to you), truth.

All ideas then, according to *Hegel,* are interconnected in this way, and the process of revealing those connections is what *Hegel* called his *dialectical method.* As such, *Hegel* explains that the *dialectic process* never ends (philosophy didn't end with *Kant,* and fashion didn't end with robes and sandals), this new *synthesis* itself becoming the starting point for a new chain of reflection (it becomes itself a *thesis*) which is then contradicted by a new *antithesis,* resulting in a new *synthesis,* and so on throughout history.

The key point for *Hegel* being that it is history that ultimately decides what's right and what's wrong, indeed, one of the big issues *Hegel* had with all philosopher's to that point (he was not a great one for making friends with his peers) was that they believed their truths, their reasoning, were truths not just of and for that time, but truths that would be true for all time. For *Hegel,* they had all missed the point, they were all correct in their thinking, but their truths would last only until history came along with the next batch of newly *synthesized* ideas consigning their ideas to the "that now makes no logical sense at all" heap.

People's views then of what is rational and right changes over time, we are all just products of our time, we inherit things and ideas from the past, change them, enhance them, and pass them on to future generations. This is true of science, language, political systems, institutions, religion, customs, and also of consciousness, perceptions, and understanding. And so for *Hegel* we as humans never begin from scratch, from a blank slate, but always within a certain "historical" context.

Hegel (clearly wanting to be seen as totally unbiased in his criticisms of philosophers past and present) thus also poked several large holes in *Kant's* philosophical vision in that where *Kant* saw our *reason* as working via innate, fixed and unchanging structures of consciousness (what *Kant* had called "*categories*"), *Hegel* saw such *categories* as dialectic, evolving, and thus subject to change. Where *Kant* believed in an unchanging framework of experience, *Hegel* believed that the framework of experience itself is subject to change, just like the world we experience around us.

All of this seems to make quite logical sense, we have a idea, and often with time we learn and discover more through other people's ideas, and so collectively our understanding moves on and presumably nearer to the truth. History shows that humanity has been moving towards an ever-increasing knowledge and self-development, and thus toward greater rationality and freedom. Despite the seemingly constant interruptions of wars, the odd despot, and natural disasters, historical development is as a general rule of thumb mostly progressive.

But now here's where *Hegel* straps on the long white beard and flowing robe and starts to go somewhat "other-worldly" on us, for *Hegel* took this idea of knowledge and understanding slowly moving to towards truth and stated that he believed that this was actually *world spirit* itself developing towards an ever-expanding knowledge of itself.

For *Hegel* history is actually the story of *world spirit* gradually coming to consciousness of itself. His central idea was that all phenomena from consciousness to political institutions, to you, me, and even your Mother-in-law, are all aspects of *world spirit* that over the course of time is reintegrating every new *thesis* back into itself, and through this process of growth is slowly moving towards its ultimate goal of self-realization.

In this respect *Hegel* is therefore a *monist*, believing that everything is just different aspects of a single thing, (which in this case is his version of *world spirit*), but also an *idealist* in that he believes that reality is something that ultimately is not material, for him reality is in fact *world spirit*.

As such, *Hegel* is really putting forward the idea that reality unfolds through time, and that reality is itself just a kind of giant mind (a mind that he as snappily called, *world spirit*) just trying to figure itself out. The point of reality then is to realise itself, to see what it is, and eventually to become that thing it sees.

Hegel's views came to blows with those inward-thinking individualistic *romantics* in that under *Hegel's* philosophical vision the individual is just a small part of a much bigger whole. *Reason*, or *world spirit*, only comes to light in the interplay between people (the *dialectic process* needs someone else to propose an *antithesis* to your *thesis*, otherwise it stops being a process and just becomes a dead-end). In *Hegel's* eyes no one can realize *world spirit* on their own, we need to find our place in history to realize *world spirit*, our place in what *Hegel* called the state. The state is more than the individual, one cannot then just adopt the *romantic* view and resign from society, stick two fingers up to the world and go off and "find" yourself all on your own.

According to *Hegel* it is only *world spirit* that "finds" itself, become conscious of itself, and since it is driven by a *dialectical process*, it must in some sense contain a particular sense of direction and an end point. *Hegel* calls this end point *absolute spirit*, a future state of consciousness where the *world spirit* belongs no longer to individuals, or the state, but which instead belongs to reality as a whole. At this point in its development knowledge is complete, and this knowledge is nothing more than its own completed essence. For *Hegel* even our consciousness is part of an evolving process, a process in which *world spirit* comes to an ever more accurate understanding of itself, culminating at the point where it finally achieves complete understanding, complete self realization, a point where *world spirit* becomes a fully self-realized *absolute spirit* (unfortunately, *Hegel* never did go on to explain just what would then happen next).

Hegel's use of *dialectic* put a whole new spin on the study of knowledge by suggesting that what we know and how we know it depends on where we stand in history. The *reason* that figures things out for us is not then the individual's own reason, as it was for *Descartes*, but the shared human consciousness at work in history.

We are all then not a separate constituent of reality, but just an aspect of how *world spirit* develops, and so all just a part of the process of historical development.

Many (particularly in the land of blond hair, blue eyes, lederhosen, and sauerkraut) hailed *Hegel* as a philosophical genius and embraced his ideas whole-heartedly. Some, like *Karl Marx*, even went on to form their own philosophical models based upon his thinking but looking at it from a more practical sense in terms of material human struggle rather than just an abstract philosophical conflict moving towards *world spirit* realization.

However, just as many were unhappy with *Hegel's* views on the individual and his idea that no one individual can realize this *world spirit* (or nature, or whatever the greater whole happens to be) all on their own, as far as *Hegel* was concerned realizing *world spirit* was a team game and not for the moping, tortured individual. And so began a philosophical backlash that once again tried to place the individual front and centre. Although *Hegel* may have figuratively speaking all but killed of the individual, philosophy was standing by with the defibrillator and paddles to make sure the debate was far from over.

22

Power to the People

"Workers of the world unite, you have nothing to lose but your chains"
Karl Marx (1818 - 1883)

When most people think about *communism* they think about the oppressions of the late Soviet Union, the poverty and failed policies of Mao Zedong's People's Republic of China, South American revolutionaries such as Che Guevara, Fidel Castro's Cuba, or the secrecy (and to be honest what seems to be just plain lunacy) coming out of North Korea. However, it seems that despite its many incarnations and attempts by numerous countries around the globe to install a regime based on its noble doctrines, the creation of a *Communist state* has unfortunately almost always ended up with a people no better (and actually often worse) off than when they started.

The first to make an attempt at setting up a *Communist state* was Vladimir Lenin (1870-1924) driven by his Bolshevik revolution of 1917. Lenin's plan was to setup a *Communist Worker's state* but with the little added twist of one being led by a dedicated revolutionary elite (a kind of round-table of communist party guiding leaders), with the resulting Union of Soviet Socialist Republics being formally established in 1922.

But it soon became clear that this ruling elite were more concerned about using subversion and a rather less than friendly secret police to "remove" all who opposed them rather than lovingly ensuring that communist ideals became reality, and along with their wholesale nationalization of industry and state control of agriculture, it all rather quickly led to peasant unrest, a rapid increase in Siberia's "labour camp" population, and probably most worryingly widespread shortages of vodka and turnips.

Lenin then unfortunately up and died in 1924, leaving a power struggle amongst his successors, and by 1929 a certain Joseph Stalin (1878-1953) had emerged victorious. Stalin quickly launched a series of five-year plans intended to transform the Soviet Union from a peasant society into an industrial superpower with his development plan centered on full government control of both the economy and agriculture. However, millions of farmers refused to cooperate with Stalin's orders and as a result many were unceremoniously exiled as punishment or just simply shot (somewhat against the communist ideal of a fair and just society for all), all of which only resulted in further widespread famine and a much reduced population of the new Soviet Union by millions.

Ultimately, Stalin ruled by terror and fear, he "eliminated" anyone who might have opposed him, expanded the powers of his secret police, and had millions of people killed or sent to forced labor camps (the infamous Siberian Gulags). By some estimates, he was responsible for the deaths of over 20 million of his own people during his brutal rule. As an example of a *communist* state then, the former Soviet Union became more of a warning for what happens when a ruthless megalomaniac is given power over one of the largest nations in the world, rather than as a shining example for the assumed benefits of *communist ideals*.

Undeterred by what was happening in the Soviet Union the communist ideal continued to inspire other revolutionaries around the globe, with the next to make a serious attempt at creating a *communist state* being Mao Zedong (1893-1976), who after a brief civil war (revolution is rarely a peaceful affair) proclaimed a People's Republic of China in 1949. The ousted Nationalists quickly fled to Taiwan to set up their own "off-shore" Nationalist government, leaving Mao in control of mainland China, where his first move was to setup a People's Liberation Army whose remit was to firmly secure the borders of China against any outside interference (China effectively remained a "closed" country right up until Mao's death in 1976), and to root out "class enemies" (which basically meant anyone who disagreed with the new self-appointed Chairman's ideals). It very quickly became clear that Mao's revolutionary vision was not going to include openness and freedom of speech from either within or from outside his borders.

Mao then quickly set out to reshape China under *communist ideals* with industry quickly coming under state ownership and China's farmers being organised into "collectives", and (seemingly following the example of his Soviet neighbours) all opposition was quickly and ruthlessly suppressed.

In 1958, in an attempt to introduce a more 'Chinese' form of *communism*, Mao launched the 'Great Leap Forward', which aimed at mass mobilisation of labour to improve agricultural and industrial production. The result was an unmitigated disaster, with a massive decline in agricultural output, which, together with poor harvests, led to the "Great Chinese Famine" and the subsequent deaths of over 30 million people. Sensing that losing over 30 million of your people to starvation was probably not such a great thing, and certainly not good for his image as a great leader, Mao quickly abandoned the policy.

In a further attempt to re-assert his authority Mao then launched the "Cultural Revolution" aiming to purge the country of "impure" elements (basically anyone or anything that reflected badly on him or his ideas) and so revive the revolutionary spirit. Those more aligned to Mao's methods may have called him merely over-zealous, but the net result of his cultural revolution was that nearly two million people were "purged" and much of the country's cultural heritage was destroyed. Ultimately, with many cities on the verge of anarchy, Mao was forced to sent in the army to restore order.

Today Mao is remembered not just by his "little red book" of quotations, but like Stalin also as a ruthless leader responsible for the deaths of millions of his people. But unlike Stalin, Mao is also seen as a somewhat incompetent leader (ruthless and incompetent, a dangerous combination at the best of times but particularly for someone in charge of a country with over one billion inhabitants). Mao once ordered the massacre of every sparrow in China believing that they ate the grain needed to feed the people, however, it was quickly brought to the attention of the clearly ornithologically inept "Chairman" that sparrows actually ate insects, and now with no sparrows to eat them, insect and locust populations ballooned, swarming the country and compounding the problems already caused by the Great Leap Forward and its associated famine.

Thus, the "glorious" *communist* experiments in two of the world's largest and most powerful nations had merely resulted in disastrous political policies, poverty, famine, widespread fear, and the deaths of millions. Probably not the outcome those who had so enthusiastically signed up for revolution were hoping for.

Although the ideas of a *Communist* state had been around for a while, it is the variation on its ideology more correctly known as *Marxism* that had become the blueprint for likes of Lenin, Mao, Castro, and their red-underpants wearing political comrades around the world. *Marxism* was the brain-child of *Karl Marx* (1818-1883), a German born philosopher, historian, sociologist, economist, and Santa Claus look-a-like, who lived much of his life in London at the height of the Industrial revolution, and who spent most of his days producing critiques on the perceived evils of *capitalism* and trying to convince people that *communism* (or rather his "*Marxist*" version of it) was the only way forward towards a truly fair, just, and equal society.

However, it would be a little harsh to put all the blame for the 20th century's seemingly disastrous experiments in *communism* entirely at the feet of *Marx* himself. Admittedly Marx clearly didn't have everything perfectly worked out, and he probably should have dedicated a few additional chapters in his writings to outlining the type of people we should trust to oversee such *communist* states (clearly the likes of Stalin and Mao had confused the ideals of *communism* with those of a ruthless dictator).

Indeed, *Marx's* own vision of *Communism* was one of a utopian society where everyone was free and equal, there were no class distinctions, wealth was evenly distributed, there was no private ownership property, education was free and available to all, it never rained, and your favourite soccer team won every game. The vision was of a perfect society, unfortunately the 20th century practical reality was of Gulag prisons and dead sparrows.

Karl Marx was born in Trier, Germany, in 1818, he studied law and worked as a journalist in France where he met his life-long friend and collaborator *Friedrich Engels*, before eventually settling in London where together with *Engels* he wrote an enormous number of books and papers mostly designed to outline the ills of *capitalism* which itself was now beginning to boom under the steam of the Industrial revolution. Technological advances in coal and steam driven machinery, abundant natural resources, along with bountiful rivers and natural harbours for the easy transportation of goods and raw materials, had seen a whole new manufacturing industry sprout up almost overnight across Britain, transforming the existing agricultural based society of self sufficient farmers and wealthy land owners into Europe's industrial centre and the world's first *capitalist* society.

Capitalism at its most basic (at least in late 19th century Britain) is really all just about making profit, profit for the few (those who own the factories) who will look to pay their workers as little as possible so they can manufacture their goods as cheaply as possible, allowing them to then sell their goods on to consumers (who were generally the very people who work in the factories in the first place) for the maximum profit. The picture is complicated a little when you start to throw in other factors such as supply and demand, market competition, greed, and fake handbags from China, but effectively this is still pretty much how three quarters of the world's economies run today.

Industrial Britain could now suddenly manufacture goods faster, cheaper, and on a mass scale in factories and mills driven by new technological advances run on coal and steam. Towns were soon flooded with people in search of work creating massive urbanization across the country and with it a whole new "working class" of people.

But this industrialization came at a cost. Urban slums quickly appeared, pollution from the coal burning factories created so much smog that city-dwellers rarely saw any actual sky, and the exploitation of the new working class in pursuit of profit led to untold poverty, child labour, unsafe working conditions, and working hours longer than a mother-in-law's memory. Ultimately the rich just got richer and the poor got decidedly poorer, creating an unequal

193

distribution of wealth, and it was this inequality that grew out of the new *capitalist* system that kept *Marx* awake at night.

In much of his writing *Marx* looked to outline what he saw as the primary ills of a *capitalist* society, primary among which was that *capitalism* forced everyone to put economic reasoning above everything else, to the extent that we believe that a person who doesn't work is worthless, that more than a few weeks of leisure time is somehow sinful, that more belongings will somehow make us more happy, and ultimately teaching us all to become competitive and overly anxious. According to *Marx, capitalism* effectively forces us to become obsessed with material wealth and to unfortunately forget that true happiness is not to be found in a new pair of shoes.

Marx also saw that work became increasingly insecure as *capitalism* makes human beings utterly expendable. As soon as costs rise workers are ruthlessly let go to save costs while factory owners will always look to shrink the wages of the workers to increase profit, which *Marx* saw simply as the theft and exploitation of the talent and hard-work of the workers. As humans we need to feel secure, that we always have a place in the world, that we are needed, but according to Marx *capitalism* merely reduces the worker to the level of a commodity to be used, abused, or let go depending on market forces.

Workers also now rarely felt a connection with the products they made. The rise of factory manufacturing generally meant that workers were usually forced to perform only limited specialized tasks and so rarely felt any sense of contribution or worth in the objects they made, they are merely a "tool" to help produce goods to sell and so feel disconnected from the fruits of their labours. *Marx* called this disconnection "alienation", and he believed that it led to workers feeling unfulfilled, worthless, and ultimately entirely disinterested in what they do.

Maybe most importantly of all, *Marx* saw that *Capitalism* also created a spiral of poverty for the working class who needed a steadily increasing income to meet the ever growing costs of their new consumer lifestyle, but with factory owners constantly driving down their wages in search of greater profit margins it became harder and harder for the working class to make ends meet.

Effectively, the better they did their job for the factory owner, the harder their own lives became.

Marx was strongly influenced by the philosophy of *Georg Hegel*, but where *Hegel* saw an historical process with ideas and reason as the source of change that led to increased freedom and knowledge, *Marx* saw the process driven by an entirely different force. *Marx* believed that it was in fact economic forces in society that actually created change and ultimately drove history forward and ultimately leading to political and economic freedom. *Marx* was what intellectuals with long beards and pipes call an *historical materialist*, believing that it was material factors in society that determined how we think.

Marx believed that throughout history there has been a constant conflict between two opposing forces in society, those who owned the *means of production* of the time, and the workers. This can be seen initially in the slave society of the Egyptians and Romans, then the feudal system of the middle-ages with the conflict between the feudal lords and serfs, later between the aristocrats and citizens, through to *Marx's* time and *the capitalist society* where *Marx* saw the conflict between the factory owners (who *Marx* called the *bourgeoisie*) and the workers (who *Marx* called the *proletariat*). Thus *Marx's* theory is known as a "conflict theory" because it states that society is in a constant state of conflict between the rich and the poor, the "haves" and "have-nots", seemingly constant cycle of class-struggles.

Marx believed that the *proletariat* were oppressed and that the *capitalist* system was designed to ensure that the poor stayed poor and the rich just kept getting richer. Moreover, Marx also saw that it is the ruling class that decides the rule of law for what is right and wrong, and since the owners of the means of production will understandably not voluntarily give up their power, change can only come through revolution.

Thus, as in the past, *Marx* believed that at some point the conflict between the *bourgeoisie* and the *proletariat* would eventually come to a head when the *proletariat* would realize that they had the power to actually change things (in *Hegelian* terms the *synthesis* of the conflicting political classes), and that this change would only be

195

achieved by revolution, a revolution where the workers would rise up and overthrow the ruling class.

The key to *Marx's* theory however is that out of that revolution, *capitalism* will be replaced by a society where the *means of production* would be owned by everyone, where all people are finally treated as equal, there is no private property or ownership, and thus finally removing the class conflict that has existed throughout history, and as a result (according to Marx at least) everyone will live happily ever after. The 20th century reality though felt like the boy who was promised a trip to Disneyland, but ended up with a visit to the dentist.

No other philosopher in history has had such a direct effect on world history, and although his vision of a classless, fair and equal society where everyone works for each other and shares in the collective benefit may have proven to be just a little too utopian to become a true reality, he stands as the one great philosopher who truly did change the world.

Inscribed on Marx's gravestone is one of his more famous quotes, "To-date philosophers have only *interpreted* the world, in various ways. The point, however, is to *change* it.", there are millions of people in the world today who daily lives are still governed as a direct result of just such action.

23

Victor the Hermit

"Life is not a problem to be solved, but a reality to be experienced"
Søren Kierkegaard (1813 - 1855)

While most of Europe's 19th century philosophers were all kneeling at the feet of *Hegel*, in some quieter corners of the continent some other enquiring minds were clearly not quite so impressed with this rather scary looking German and his impersonal and overly abstract take on mankind being just part of one great historical development of what he rather grandly called "world spirit". *Søren Kierkegaard* (1813-1855) was one such philosopher whose own philosophy developed as a reaction to German *idealist* thinking as a whole, but in particular to that of *Georg Hegel*. It's fair to say that Mr. Kierkegaard was never going to be seen at a *Hegel* appreciation dinner.

Kierkegaard felt that *Hegel's* philosophy had completely taken away any responsibility an individual may have for his own life, regardless of whatever historical context he happened to find himself in, and so wanted to examine what it meant to actually be a human being, an individual, and not just some bit-part player in some great *Hegelian* philosophical system. In short, he felt that *Hegel* had become so focused on mankind as simply being just a minor cog in a greater "world view" machine, that he had forgotten what was actually meaningful for each of us as an individual. Effectively, *Hegel* had forgotten that he was a human being.

Søren Kierkegaard was born in Copenhagen the son of a tradesman who although wealthy was devoutly religious and prone to depression (maybe made worse by the fact that his surname actually translates to be "graveyard" in English), all character traits that the young *Søren* was to inherit. So much so that later in life *Søren* would actually break-off the engagement with his fiancée of three years believing that his "melancholy" made him wholly unsuitable for any form of married life. These "family traits" would also go on to permeate his philosophical thinking.

However, *Kierkegaard* was nothing if not prolific. By the time of his death at the tender age of just 42 he had written more than 25 books outlining his philosophical views, although after his death most, if not all, slipped into obscurity as his ideas were largely rejected (or actually just plain ignored) by his contemporaries. *Kierkegaard's* philosophical vision had the sweeping ambition of Napoleon, but unfortunately in his lifetime he amassed about as many followers as an anti-gun lobbyist in Texas. The importance of *Kierkegaard's* work is actually in their rediscovery in the 20th century where they eventually revolutionized European thinking and became the catalyst for the philosophical movement that became known as *existentialism.*

Strangely, all of *Kierkegaard's* philosophical works were written secretly and published under such pseudonyms as "Victor the Hermit", "John the Silent", "Hilarius Bookbinder", and "Dirk Diggler" (actually I made that last one up, but you get the idea). However, very few scholars were in any doubt as to the true author of the works, despite *Kierkegaard* continuing to claim he had neither written the works nor indeed had any opinion on them. The books themselves were also hardly relaxed Sunday afternoon light reading, with titles such as *Fear and Trembling, The Concept of Dread,* and *The Sickness unto Death,* these were books not to be taken on lightly. *Kierkegaard's* "melancholic ways" certainly seemed to have led him to something of an obsession with the darker side of human experience, at least in respect of his book titles.

*Kierkegaard (*or Victor the Hermit if you choose to believe *Kierkegaard's* denial of any knowledge of the work) was interested in truth, truths in respect of what it meant to us as individuals, and particularly the roles both *objective* and *subjective truths* play is shaping who we are as individuals.

Objective truths are things that are true for everyone, regardless of whether you live in a city or the at the North Pole, an Egyptian slave from 3,000 B.C., or a modern day "fat-cat" entrepreneur.

Truths such as "two plus two equals four" are true because science and mathematics have proved them to be so. However, these truths are what clever philosophical types call "*existentially indifferent*", which is really just a fancy way of saying that nothing in your life would radically change if you suddenly discovered that one of these truths was actually false. If two plus two was suddenly proven to equal to five, although there would clearly be a lot of red-faced mathematicians in the world, as individuals we wouldn't suddenly start to behave differently or become a different person because of it.

However, on the other hand, *subjective truths* are truths that can't actually be proven by science or mathematics, or by some clever bod with a watermelon-sized brain, they are truths that are true only for you as an individual. Thus *subjective truths* are personal, there is no method, mechanism, or process by which we can project our own subjective knowledge onto another person (or though many of course try). The same clever philosophical types call these kind of truths "*existential truths*", as they are essentially related to how we live our lives, our own individual existence. For instance, if you think that causing unnecessary misery or harm to someone is wrong then such a belief will be expressed in your actions (you likely won't cheat, steal, lie, or generally act like a five year old spoilt brat or Jack the Ripper). But if you suddenly change that belief and now think that raping and pillaging the good folks in the next town over the hill is perfectly acceptable social behaviour, then likely you will all of a sudden start to go all Viking on everyone, and thus not only will your behaviour change, but you will also become a different person (and likely partial to wearing helmets with horns).

Kierkegaard believed that the only really important truths are personal, truths that are true for you as an individual, truths that define who you are and how you live your life. Thus, for *Kierkegaard* then the only important truths are *subjective truths*.

In line with his devoutly religious beliefs, the key *subjective truth* for *Kierkegaard* was whether God actually exists. *Kierkegaard* believed that this is not a question that can be answered theoretically, by looking it up in a book, or applying reason to derive a definitive answer (although many philosophers before *Kierkegaard* had tried), it is a question that can only be answered by each of us as an individual and in terms of our own relationship to the question. It is a question that can only be approached through our own individual faith.

Ultimately *Kierkegaard* saw the existence of God as a belief that every individual must reconcile for themselves, and do so entirely on their own. It doesn't matter whether Christianity and religious doctrines are true or not, or whether anyone else believes they can definitively prove that God exists, it only matters if it is true for you.

Through our *subjective truths Kierkegaard* believed that we actually become the authors of our own world, what we believe to be morally right and wrong, how we behave, who we are, and as such we must take full responsibility for that authorship. *Subjective truths* then are not pieces of knowledge to be picked up in a classroom or from the old man who sits in the corner of the pub, there is no objective criteria to establish their validity, they can only be developed by the individual themselves, and reflected in their decisions and actions. This discovery must be made by each individual entirely alone.

However on the downside it then follows that we can never truly justify our own morals or actions outside of our own existence, and so we can never truly be certain that we have chosen the "right values". For *Kierkegaard* this means that there is no such thing as existence without risk, and thus existence for all of us as individuals will always be experienced with a degree of anguish and dread.

Similarly, *Kierkegaard* also believed that our lives are determined by our actions, which themselves are determined by the choices we make, and so how we make those choices is critical to just what kind of live we will lead. But where *Hegel* thought that the moral decisions we make are largely determined by the historical conditions of our times, *Kierkegaard* believed that our moral choices were independent of any historical context, they are personal, intuitive, and completely subjective to us as individuals.

However, for *Kierkegaard* this freedom to make our own choices was far from being a reason for happiness, he felt this complete freedom of choice actually causes us nothing but anxiety and dread. Once we realize that we have complete freedom to make even the most terrifying decisions (effectively, whatever actions we choose are entirely down to us as an individual, and thus their consequences are also entirely down to us to live with) we experience what *Kierkegaard* called "the dizziness of freedom".

Take for instance your noisy neighbour. You have several choices as to how to deal with him. You could go round and confront him over his anti-social behaviour face to face, you could just play your music even louder than he does, you could up and move to another city, or you could just buy a rather large gun and simply make him an offer he can't refuse. Each will likely solve the problem, each has consequences, but the knowledge that only you can choose along with the fear of the consequences of your choice will likely fill you with anxiety and dread as to how to proceed. This is what *Kierkegaard* meant by "the dizziness of freedom".

However, although this anxiety induces fear, it can also shake us from blindly making quick, unthinking decisions made with little or no thought, as it ultimately makes us more aware of the available choices we actually have the freedom to make. This, according to *Kierkegaard* increases our self-awareness and sense of personal responsibility.

This brings us to what *Kierkegaard* called the "three spheres of existence", where he effectively looked to outline what he saw as the three possible modes of existence we may experience throughout our life, each with its own ideals, motivations, and forms of behaviour. We can voluntarily choose anyone of them as the model for how we live our lives, and we can move between them, up or down, but one of them, what Mr. K called the "aesthetic sphere", is more basic than the others in that even those who never make any conscious choice concerning their fundamental stance in the world find themselves in *aestheticism* along with all those who have consciously chosen it, it's effectively our default mode of existence.

The *aesthetic sphere* is all about being concerned only with the pursuit of pleasure, enjoyment, and the avoidance of pain. Individuals who live this way seemingly live carefree lives, avoiding all responsibility and living for the moment, but in reality they are simply slaves to their own desires and moods. But according to *Kierkegaard* the problem with a life devoted to pleasure and enjoyment (apart from the lack of sleep) is that the pleasure we derive is often fleeting, and then like a drug it often leaves us depressed and needing more. More importantly, the result of being guided solely by the "pleasure principle" is that we are never quite in control of ourselves, we are always governed by external desires and their often arbitrary nature.

In short, for *Kierkegaard*, those who live by such *aesthetic* concerns never achieve a truly "human" form of existence, they are driven by the exact same "instincts" and motives that drive say cats, dogs, amoebas, or slugs (pleasure and pain are fundamentally biological in nature after all) and so are only concerned with pleasure (whatever the form) rather than being a conscious, aware, thinking, and responsible human being.

However, *Kierkegaard* says that for those who become aware of the importance of their existence, they will eventually start to feel dissatisfied with such a life devoted to such fleeting pleasures (hard to believe but boredom does eventually set in), and they will then begin to experience a feeling of unfulfilment while gaining a sense of their own impermanence and insignificance which will ultimately fill them with dread. It is at this point when the individual will often make the leap to the next level, to the "ethical sphere".

It is in the *ethical sphere* that the individual starts to understand and become his true self, and recognizes that such an existence entails moving away from their old *aesthetic* self. For the first time the individual judges himself from some perspective other than through just pure pleasure. However, according to *Kierkegaard* it's not important that the individual chooses some particular ethical code, it is a more basic decision, it is whether to hold oneself responsible to any ethical code at all.

Once made, the decision cannot of course remain just an abstract thought, it must then be made real with a particular commitment to a particular ethical code, regardless of what code it may be (Buddhist, socialist, Christian, vegetarian, or even Hells Angel). The important point is that regardless of whatever ethical code you may adopt, it fulfills a personal commitment to self-perfection, and a commitment to other human beings. The issue of course is that at this point every future choice now becomes an occasion for self-judgement.

However, *Kierkegaard* goes on to describe a third sphere, a higher plain that quite frankly is probably not for everyone. This is where *Kierkegaard* reconciles his devout religious beliefs with his notion that everyone is ultimately free and responsible to choose their own way of living. In doing so, *Kierkegaard* introduces what he calls the "religious sphere". To help describe his *religious sphere* *Kierkegaard* uses the example of Abraham from the Book of Genesis (if you're going to define a religious sphere you might as well turn to the Bible for an example of its use) to help define just what type of person may choose to move to this loftier level of existence.

In the story God pays a surprise visit to Abraham (it seems that if we are to believe the Bible God was not averse to popping down to Earth and making surprise house calls on the mere mortals of the day. Sadly he seems to have stopped this practice in more recent times) and commanded him to take his people and begin a journey to a land that God would provide him directions to. In return God promised Abraham that Sarah, Abraham's barren wife, would become pregnant and father him a son who would in turn become the father of a great nation. All this sounded like the sort of deal he couldn't pass up, so Abraham quickly spat on his palm and shook on it.

Having delivered on his side of the bargain by delivering his people to the land of Canaan, as promised Sarah duly fell pregnant and gave birth to a son they named Isaac. As far as Abraham was concerned this completed a nice little piece of business, and overjoyed he got down to the tricky business of raising a son.

Then, just as everything was going so well, God paid another unexpected late night visit to Abraham and told him that he must take his son Isaac, place him on an alter and sacrifice him to demonstrate his love for God. Without hesitation (and likely much to the dismay of Isaac) Abraham took Isaac to the altar, said "sorry" and "goodbye", and started to sharpen his knife. But just as he was about to kill Isaac God again appeared and told Abraham that he had passed his test, that he need not sacrifice Isaac after all, he had successfully demonstrated his love for God.

Now this little story seems to have quite shocked poor *Kierkegaard*. To him, Abraham's actions are quite incomprehensible.

For starters how could he be so sure he had understood what God had asked him to do? Before you just jump straight in and sacrifice your first born wouldn't you at least first stop to ask why, or at least try and find a way to wangle out of it? Clearly Abraham was insane or had secretly harboured a long-term dislike for his son anyway. But the story is considered a remarkable show of faith, faith that God would not ask anyone to do anything unless he had a very good reason, even if we don't understand that reason, and even if it causes us great personal loss.

Kierkegaard, although a devoutly religious man, was not your typical presents at Christmas, chocolate eggs at Easter, and prayers on Sunday type of believer, he believed in a very personal faith, not one guided by the rules and doctrines of a religious establishment, but a faith that was very individual. For *Kierkegaard,* we can never know or prove that there is a God, rather we must passionately just choose to believe it.

Thus, *Kierkegaard* believed that the story of Abraham demonstrates a kind of "double-movement" that one must go through to fully commit to such a personal *religious sphere.* Firstly there is a movement of complete resignation, where in our story Abraham is willing to give up his son Isaac, to lose everything, to go against every moral standard he has (killing your own son is usually pretty high on people's "no no" list), and place his faith solely in God. But this is quickly followed by a movement of faith, as at the same time as losing everything, he suddenly gains everything but in a whole new way. He gained a complete and utter faith in God, a faith that although he may not fully understand His meaning or purpose, God will provide a way out of the despair and pain in the world. Abraham had to be prepared to first sacrifice everything (literally) but in doing so he gained even more.

Abraham may well be completely "unintelligible" in his actions to the rest of us, and if around today would likely be locked up in a suitable institution (anyone who hears voices in their head telling them to murder someone is not someone you want out there roaming the streets), but *Kierkegaard* argues he's not unintelligible to God. He had given up the *ethical* for what he took to be a higher *religious* purpose.

Kierkegaard stated that you can only reach this third stage through a "leap of faith" because there are no rational reasons for making this move. It can't be influenced by religious institutions, or justified by logic or philosophical reasoning, you cannot be taught or instructed to do so (presumably with the exception of voices in your head), it is a purely personal commitment made by the individual. But once the leap has been made it offers a way out of the despair of our world and gives a sense of permanent significance in your life.

The transition to the *religious sphere* is in many ways identical to the transition from the *aesthetical* to *the ethical sphere*, in each case one gains a new self at the expense of one's old self. But as *Kierkegaard* explains, the difference here is that this second leap to the *religious sphere* is far more terrifying, as in the first leap you merely fall away from your old "it's all about the pleasure" self, but in this second "leap" you fall away from mankind as a whole, and by anyone's measure that's quite a leap.

24

Who the Hell Killed God?

"In the beginning there was nonsense, and the nonsense was with God, and the nonsense was God"
Friedrich Nietzsche (1844 - 1900)

Friedrich Nietzsche is a late 19th century German philosopher who's had something of a bad-rap. No other philosopher throughout history has been so misunderstood, intentionally misinterpreted, and used as a philosophical justification for the horrors of war, genocide, racism, and the "death" of a deity. Not something even the most cold-hearted amongst us would want our name associated with, let alone a mild-mannered, if somewhat eccentric philosopher.

Nietzsche's cause was not helped by the fact that he was officially declared "insane" for the last eleven years of his short life, during which time his rather manipulative sister took control of the publishing, archiving, and editing of his work, and thus "reinvented" much of his philosophical thought to support her own anti-Semitic ideals (it also didn't help that she was later to form a friendship with a certain Adolf Hitler). Although to be fair, even when sane *Nietzsche* himself didn't always do himself the best of favours, at one point proclaiming that "God is dead", which itself was always going to cause a bit of a stir amongst the God-fearing folk of Europe (although by 1900 it seems that God was able to return the compliment).

But it's the apparent association between *Nietzsche's* philosophy, Adolf Hitler and all his Nazi chums that have been the main cause for his latter-day rather unsympathetic reception, and his portrayal as the "Godfather of fascism", where his work was often seen as being used to encourage and support violence, racism, fascism and white supremacy within the Third Reich (not an easy label to just shrug off).

However, *Nietzsche* was actually anything but a Jew-hating white-supremacist and would likely have choked on his morning cornflakes had he lived long enough to know of the Nazi's twisting of his ideas to support their own. Nonetheless, Nazi propaganda very clearly painted a picture suggesting *Nietzsche* was in favour of *eugenics* (effectively the breeding of a master race, which in this case was to have blonde hair, blue eyes, and a strong German accent), and thus supported their own philosophy of an Aryan-super-race, racially pure, and superior to all other races and ethnic types.

Clearly, most of *Nietzsche's* ideas were intentionally misinterpreted by the Nazi's who were only interested in the parts of his writing that could be spun to suit their own ideals, and *Nietzsche* would have been more than little disturbed to find that his ideas had been high-jacked in such a way that ultimately was at least in part responsible for the deaths of over six million Jews.

Because of *Nietzsche's* provocative style and his often outrageous claims such as "what doesn't kill me makes me stronger" or that "God is dead", his philosophy often generates passionate reactions, his work remains controversial, and as we have seen open to misinterpretation (intentionally or otherwise). Although actually the first challenge most of us face when first confronted with *Nietzsche* (apart from seeing past his very large mustache) is just how on earth do you pronounce his name, which apparently we are reliably informed is (in your best German accent) , "knee-cha".

Friedrich Wilhelm Nietzsche was born in 1844 in a quiet village in Eastern Germany where his father was the local priest. It seems he was a bit of a rock star at school, and by the time he was 24 he had already been made a professor at the university of Basle. However, it seems that ill health and just plain boredom with such an academic life meant he subsequently moved to the Swiss Alps to concentrate on documenting his philosophical ideas, although he often travelled frequently to find climates more conducive to what appears to be his rather fragile health.

At the age of forty four however *Nietzsche* suffered a mental breakdown apparently brought on by the sight of a horse being flogged by his driver. He was never to fully recover (apparently his subsequent mental state often led him to believe he was either Jesus, Napoleon, Buddha, or any one of several other well known historical figures, although thankfully not all at the same time) and he died 11 years later with his mental health having deteriorated to the point where he had already been declared mentally insane (enter Nazi sympathizing sister).

Nietzsche was a prophet of what he called "self-overcoming", the idea that a truly great man (what he called an *Übermensch,* or a "Superman" for those of non-Germanic descent) would rise above his difficulties and circumstances to embrace whatever life had to throw at him. *Nietzsche* wanted to teach us how to become "who we really are", and thus for *Nietzsche* philosophy had a very definite practical purpose, that being to facilitate the emergence of the great individual who dedicates their life to growth and self-overcoming in the face of life's suffering, pain, and tragedy.

Nietzsche main observation was that as human beings we should all "own up to envy", and believed that envy was nothing for us to be ashamed of or try to avoid, in fact it is envy that shows us the path towards becoming the *Übermensch* we all seemingly have inside us. Envy is a big part of our lives, but according to *Nietzsche* religion, and in particular Christianity, had taught us to feel ashamed of envious feelings, that they are an indication of evil and that we should hide them from ourselves and others. But *Nietzsche* said there was nothing wrong with envy as long as we use it as a guide for what we really want, and that we should see every person who makes us envious as a benchmark of what we could one day become, what we could be capable of being.

Unfortunately *Nietzsche* hadn't stumbled upon some magic formula by which we will all get what we envy (just by publically owning up to the fact that I envy George Clooney or the Dalia Lama doesn't mean I am one day guaranteed to be worshipped by millions, rich, handsome and famous, or George Clooney), but he was saying that we should face up to our true desires, try as hard as we can to achieve them, and then, and only then, accept failure with solemn dignity should we not quite reach the lofty heights we had aimed for. This for *Nietzsche* is what it means to be an *Übermensch.*

It should also come as no surprise then that *Nietzsche* was not backward in coming forward in his disdain for religion, and in particular Christianity, believing as he did that religion only served to protect people from their envy. For *Nietzsche*, in his usual "don't worry about sparing anyone's feelings" approach, believed that Christianity had only really evolved in the minds of what he saw as weak-minded Roman slaves who were too afraid to go after what they really wanted (freedom, their own villa by the sea, and free access to the local Roman baths) and so they created a religion for themselves that made a virtue out of what he saw as their cowardice.

Nietzsche called such hiding of envy behind religion "slave morality", and those who clung to its beliefs "the herd", who he saw as too inept to get what they wanted and so created a hypocritical religion that denounced what they really wanted (that villa by the sea), while praising all the things they didn't want (obedience, suffering in this life for the promise of a better afterlife, forgiving everyone, fish on Fridays, church on Sundays) but unfortunately happened to have. For *Nietzsche* then, Christianity was just a giant "denial" machine offering the reward of a non-existent paradise for those who conformed and obeyed.

Nietzsche saw a time when the beliefs around the purpose of life would no longer be driven by a belief in a God, a religion, or the "herd", and all of which would finally be exposed for what they truly were, mere myths and stories. It was in this belief that *Nietzsche* felt compelled to make his boldest statement of all, his proclamation that "God is dead". Of course such a statement was always going to piss off the church hierarchy from the Pope down to the altar boy, and it so it should be no surprise to hear that after his death his burial records written by church authorities noted that he was a "known anti-Christ".

Strangely *Nietzsche* also hated alcohol (he himself only drank water, only treating himself on special occasions to a rather less than exciting glass of milk), stating that just like Christianity alcohol is just served to numb pain, helping to convince us that things are fine just the way they are, and thus sapping us of the will to change things for the better. He referred to Christianity and alcohol as Europe's two great narcotics.

Nietzsche believed that although we each have the potential to become an *Übermensch* there clearly is more than a distinct possibility that your average weak-willed human will avoid confronting what he saw as their life's mission (to confront envy and strive to become all we are capable of being) and instead just follow their "herd instinct" and seek out the comforts of mediocrity as part of the herd, simply leading a life led by blind obedience to the accepted morality and distinctions of what is good and what is evil of their culture or religion. In all honesty it's just simply easier to follow the herd than put in the effort to confront your pain and envy and shoot for the goal of becoming an *Übermensh*, particularly when the "herd morality" instills in us a conviction that our weakness is not actually a fault at all, but instead a strength, and that those qualities which the herd lack, are a weakness and so are evil.

Again not pulling his punches *Nietzsche* goes on to point out that with herd morality as he put it "the sheep gains in respect", since sheep-like qualities are championed by herd morality as being 'good', herd morality pressures individuals into becoming good, that is, weak and obedient. The potential *Übermensh* however, if he is to ever achieve greatness must escape the clutches of herd morality, and renounce it in favour of his own self created and life affirming morality. Effectively what *Nietzsche* was saying is that we should all dump religion, dessert the herd, and strike out on our own to find our own way in the world.

But the path to becoming a shining example of *Nietzsche's Übermensh* is not an easy one. Firstly *Nietzsche* points out that in order to escape from the herd and live according to our own life affirming morality, it is essential to separate ourselves physically from the herd and live a life of solitude. *Nietzsche* believed that to achieve greatness in life, we must contemplate questions which the herd is too weak and scared to think about, and so to do this, we need solitude (presumably then all those that have indeed achieved such "superman" status are all to be found hiding out on various mountain tops around the world).

Secondly, confronting your inner fears, envy, pain and suffering is not an easy task. If the deepest question which confronts man is 'why do I suffer?', *Nietzsche* understood the need to first and foremost interpret suffering in a manner which would be life promoting rather than just a rather painful experience (otherwise why would we bother). So *Nietzsche* rather cleverly turned the whole experience of our pain and suffering on its head.

Nietzsche explains that any wannabe *Übermensh* would first need to realize that without their pain and suffering they would actually have no motivation (what he called the "will to power") to grow and overcome themselves, and thus would remain forever stagnant as part of the herd. *Nietzsche* preached the rather novel idea that a life without suffering and pain would actually prove to be a rather miserable life, for he believed suffering to be the precondition of greatness, as with great suffering comes great advancement. In fact, *Nietzsche* believed that as we progress along the path to our own self-realization we will start to understand that evil, pain, suffering, and tragedy are not ugly but actually have an inherent beauty to them, for within these aspects of our existence lies the potential for growth and self overcoming.

Nietzsche however did admit that the path to such greatness is an extreme challenge to the human spirit (you would suspect primarily due to the apparent need to "embrace" a shed load pain and suffering) , but in short It seems we should all look to embrace such envy, pain, and suffering as these are actually the true path to greatness, the path to becoming an *Übermensh*. We should all then just stop complaining, embrace our pain, as greatness awaits.

25

All Too Human

"Existence before essence"
Jean-Paul Sartre (1905 - 1980)

As far as most Brits are concerned, modern philosophers (and actually intellectuals as a whole) are all pipe-smoking continental-types who dress in black, have homosexual tendencies, hang out all day in coffee houses, and who as a breed collectively begin at Calais and generally gravitate towards Paris, where the fact that they seem to be idolized is seen as just yet more proof that the French, despite their obvious cheese and wine making skills, are all fundamentally unsound.

In fact, in Britain particularly, the word "intellectual" is often used far more as a "not so intellectual" jibe towards overly brainy boffin-types who are seen as clearly "too clever for their own good" and who just tolerate the rest of us who unfortunately have IQ's somewhat nearer to a well trained dog. As a rule then, on the continent intellectuals are seen as sexy, snappy dressers who are to be admired, while in Britain they are seen as merely socially awkward nerds and thus just an easy target for the butt of jokes and ridicule.

Thus, in general the typical image of the modern philosophical thinker is a continental one, and one which has been largely shaped around the embodiment of the late French "intellectual" *Jean-Paul Sartre* (1905-1980), and his radical "*existentialist*" philosophy (*Sartre* was French, lived in Paris, smoked a pipe, and very few people knew what on Earth he was talking about, so clearly then an "intellectual"). *Existentialism* however should not be mistaken for a philosophical system or set of doctrines to follow, it is probably better classified rather as a philosophical movement, a set of ideals shared by some like-minded "intellectual" types with beards and pipes (well most of them anyway).

However, although *Sartre* was the first to actually use the term *"existentialism"* (liberal use of a French accent optional), he was not the first to be associated with what became known as *existentialist* ideals. As a movement the ideas which were later to be collectively grouped under the general term *existentialism* first arose in 19th century Europe under the ideas of *Kierkegaard* and *Nietzsche* who are often now referred to as the founding fathers of the *existential* movement. However, it was not really until the early to mid-20th century, and particularly after World War II that *existentialist* thought was to really gain any sort of prominence, primarily through the works of *Sartre* and his contemporaries such as *Martin Heidegger* (1889-1976) and the author *Albert Camus* (1913-1960).

So what is it then that tied all these philosopher and author "Exi-types" together under the banner of *existentialism*? Well, in short, they all directed most of their considerable philosophical brain-power towards trying to understand exactly what it meant to be a human being, and the problems that being a member of that particularly complex species brings. They emphasized our individual existence, freedom and choice, and held the view that we humans should look to define our own meaning in life, and try to make rational decisions for ourselves despite existing in what they saw as an acutely irrational world. In short, they looked to see just how an individual can make sense of their own existence in a world that clearly made no sense at all.

Existentialist thinkers recognize the confusion of the human condition, and generally start out with an attitude of disorientation and confusion around their place in the world, a world which they cannot either understand or accept, indeed they coined the phrase that individuals can often feel *alienated*, that we are both strangers and alone in a world that makes no real sense (to them or anyone else). *Albert Camus* particularly was interested in what he called the *absurdity* of human existence, the fact that if we truly think about it none of it really makes any sense, questioning just what is the point of it all, and so according to *Camus* we all really just lead a rather meaningless existence.

213

However, *Camus* believed that rather than become depressed by the notion that there is no meaning or purpose in life at all (so why bother even getting out of bed in the morning), rather we should *"protest"* against it, if there is no meaning to life then as individuals we should give it our own meaning. *Camus* asks that we *"revolt"* against the nothingness we see and fill it with our own meaning, believing that we are all truly free to fill our lives with whatever meaning want.

Indeed, *Camus* believed that it is only when we fully accept the fact that life is meaningless and absurd can we actually then get on with living our lives fully. *Camus'* goal was that we should look to live our lives as he said *"without appeal"*, by which he meant that we are free to choose and do what we as individuals want to do, without any appeal to others for either acceptance or approval. However, *Camus* stressed that although we should live our lives without the need for permission or validation this did not mean we are free to just run around raping, pillaging, stealing old lady's purses, or ignoring red traffic signals in some free-for-all, "it's all about me", lawless society. We are all still responsible and accountable for our choices and actions.

Camus, like many of the modern *existentialists* chose to express his ideas through plays and novels, rather than through any formal philosophical papers, and in 1957 was ultimately awarded the Nobel prize for Literature. But in a strangely existential-twist of fate *Camus* was to die only three years later in a car crash aged only 46, having discarded a train ticket to rather accept a lift back to Paris from a friend. *Camus* lived the life he preached, he changed political affiliations several times throughout his life, was married twice and had many lovers, he was care-free and enigmatic, he embraced the absurd, lived in constant revolt against the meaninglessness of it all, and ultimately likely lived as freely as any man can live. He also looked remarkably like Humphrey Bogart.

As a rule, *existentialists* also strongly rejected any "all-encompassing" system, be it philosophical, religious, or scientific, which attempts to answer the meaning or purpose of life in a system which purports to have definitive answers to such questions that collectively apply to all human beings regardless of their colour, race, shape, sex, age, or favourite pop band. History is of course littered with such "all-encompassing" systems and would include the likes of the multitude of world's religions, stoicism, idealism, pagan worshippers, boy-band fan clubs, obscure religious cults, Goths, punks, Hells Angels, and people with a leather fetish.

These "all-encompassing" systems however are of course very appealing as they remove the massive burden an individual would have to face on their own were they to try to create any meaning and purpose for themselves. As a rule we humans are an inherently lazy bunch, and such generic belief systems (and there's a lot of them out there on offer) effectively offer us a quick an easy "off-the-shelf" solution for those still looking for some meaning and purpose in their life but who seemingly don't have the time, inclination, or will-power enough to turn the TV off and figure it out for themselves.

Clearly trying to understand the human condition and face all of life's problems as an individual without the assistance of say the direction of the Bible, the Koran, or a DVD collection of Star Trek, is always going to be very difficult. But this is exactly what *existentialists* advocate, finding your own personal meaning for your life, defining who you are as a unique individual, and doing so all by yourself.

But why bother, why spend the time and effort struggling with personal demons and searching for your own meaning for your life, why not just opt for finding your meaning and purpose in life through Christianity and the Bible, or Series One of Star Trek and base you whole understanding of the meaning of life around the philosophical musings of Mr. Spock? Well for the *existentialist* they believe that adhering to any one-size-fits-all system is actually detrimental to an individual's development into a truly unique and free human being, for them any such generic systems do not adequately take into account just what it is like to be a unique and individual "human".

Part of the problem is that many such systems see the meaning and purpose of life as coming from some magical and other-worldly realm, such as heaven, Plato's "world of forms", or the planet Vulcan, and in doing so they lose perspective of what it's like as an individual living on this Earth here and now, along with all the

215

hopes, fears, anxieties that are part and parcel of the human condition. For example, most of the world's religions will look to provide answers to many of life's questions from the perspective of an all-knowing and all-powerful God through the medium of Holy scriptures or prophets, but *existentialists* believe that what is needed is not a "divine" or "other-worldly" perspective of the human condition but a uniquely "human" perspective.

Key *for existentialists* is that any "divine" perspective does not really take into account one of the really quite fundamental parts of the human condition, that being the fact that we are mortal, and that at some point we will shuffle off our mortal coil and die. In fact most religions will actually deny that we will inevitably "truly" die at some point in the future at all by preaching a belief in some form of immortality (a passport to heaven, or a constant merry-go-round of birth, death, and rebirth).

In particular the *existentialist* philosopher *Martin Heidegger* believed it's important that as an individual we face up to the reality of our impending rendezvous with the Grim Reaper. He believed that once we come to accept that the only existence we can be sure of is in this life, the shock of this realization can actually give us the strength to stop living a daily drudge in conformity with everyone else in some generic belief system and a vain hope in some promised utopian after-life, and instead take control of our own lives and start to live by standards and values of our own choosing.

Heidegger believed that as humans we are all rather unceremoniously thrown into this world only to find that we have entered into an ongoing world that existed long before us, and as such our range of choices as to who or what we can become are limited by the place and time we are born. For instance as someone born in the late 20th century, even outside of the obvious fashion issues, it would be somewhat difficult for me to look to carve out a career as a soldier in a Roman Legion or a medieval Court Jester.

As humans we attempt to make some sense of the world we are thrown into by engaging in various "projects" such as getting an education, a job, getting married, or even dressing up as a Roman soldier at the weekend. But living this way is what *Heidegger* called leading an *inauthentic* existence, an existence driven by conformity,

216

and that it's not until we become aware of our own mortality, become aware of death as the ultimate limit of our possibilities, do we reach a deeper understanding of what it means to truly exist, and so make choices for ourselves with that limit in mind (once you accept the fact that you will die in the not too distant future you will generally make damn sure you live your life in a way that makes the best use of every single second of every day).

Heidegger stated that all beings (cats, dogs, Roman soldiers, Court jesters, you, me) are beings whose "furthest horizon of being is death", but that only humans can recognize this (cats and dogs have no clue that at some point in the future they will end up supporting the food chain), and only once we realize this can we start to live a life that is meaningful and *authentic* for us.

The idea of an individual being able to freely choose his own standards and values and create meaning and purpose in his own life is closely related to another fundamental *existentialist* idea, the idea that for humans our existence precedes our essence, an idea first put forward by *Jean-Paul Sartre*. But what on earth does such a statement mean?

Well, the concept of essence itself was first put forward by *Aristotle* who believed that every substance (you, me, fish, trees, flowers, even your neighbours 3-legged mangy old cat) has what he called an essence, and this essence can be seen as the necessary properties or characteristics that are required for the thing to be what it is. *Aristotle* believed that all substances in nature tend towards the goal of the actualization of their essence. For instance an acorn has a tendency to grow towards its essence of being an oak tree, a chicken egg into its essence of becoming a chicken, and a rock to become well, a rock.

For *Aristotle* he saw that the essence of human nature was to act in full accordance with *reason* (of course excluding the likes of Genghis Khan, Josef Stalin, and Adolf Hitler, who clearly had their own unique essence), but unlike other substances (cats, dogs, rocks) humans are actually free to choose whether we act in accordance with our essence (*reason*) or not. However, *Aristotle* did not believe that humans could create their own unique essence for themselves throughout the course of their lives, as such you either acted in accordance with *reason* or presumably went some way down the same path as Messrs Khan, Stalin, and Hitler, you could not however change your mind about who you were or decide you were going to grow your nose and be an elephant.

The same goes for those who believe that mankind was created by God, where in this case the essence of humans is believed to be predetermined by the all-powerful one before we are even born. Thus both in the case of *Aristotle* or any Divine being in long white robes, the essence of what it is to be human is preset for us even before we are born, and thus our essence precedes our existence.

But *Sartre* saw things as being completely opposite. *Sartre* agreed that when we make something (a chair, a table, or even a fuss about the washing up not being done) we do so for a purpose, and thus the purpose (the essence) of a made thing must come before its existence. But, as a confirmed atheist, and thus without the presence of God (the human manufacturer) to make us, *Sartre* believed that we humans were not "built" with any specific purpose or function in mind. Thus for *Sartre* we come into this world lacking any predetermined essence, and our ability to make free choices (unlike elephants, cats, dogs, rocks and plants) gives us the chance to sculpt a unique essence for ourselves during our lifetime (but clearly within the limitations of our physical being, we still can't become an elephant no matter how much we want to). As such, for *Sartre*, our existence precedes our essence.

However, *Sartre* saw this freedom to shape our own lives as our greatest responsibility of all, for we are not just responsible for the impact that our choices have upon ourselves, but also the impact they may have on mankind as a whole. In addition, he saw that as there are no rules to justify any of our choices or actions (no pre-defined essence), we have no excuses to hide behind for the choices we make. For this reason *Sartre* famously declared that we are all "condemned to be free".

Existentialism essentially says that life itself is absurd, it can be alienating and confusing, there is no meaning to any of it, but rather than seeing this as a reason for us all to just slit our wrists in despair, as unique individuals we should rather embrace the freedom it gives us to choose our own way, to find our own meaning in our lives. You can be born Jewish, black, French, crippled, gay, or feel like you're a woman inside a man's body, but you are still entirely free to decide what you make of yourself (and you don't even have to move to Paris, speak with a French accent, smoke a pipe, or even look like Humphrey Bogart to do so).

26

If someone tries to fail and succeeds, which did he do?

"Time is a great teacher, but unfortunately it kills all its pupils."
Hector Berlioz (1803-1869) - French Composer

Philosophy's lengthy history has filled the pages of many a book with more than its expected quota of interesting (for which you can loosely translate to mean varying degrees of challenging, off-the-wall, spiritually up-lifting, or what amounts to just plain madness on stilts) stories, thoughts, theories, and ideas, and just as many interesting (for which you can also loosely translate to mean varying degrees of complex, misunderstood, extrovert, moody, small, large, ugly, or just plain mad) thinkers, enough at least to fill the pages of this particular little book.

We've seen philosophers who have been ignored, laughed at, ostracized from their church and communities, and even seen those willing to die for their beliefs. We've seen philosophers get in touch with God, some deny the existence of a God all together, or even declare that actually there was a God but that unfortunately he was now dead (seemingly with foul-play having not been ruled out).

We've seen other philosophers find themselves, lose themselves, deny the existence of everything, doubt everything, just resign themselves to their fate, live the party life, believe only what their senses tell them or only what their reason tells them, and even deny that the world we live in even exists at all. We've even seen the notion that we exist only because we think, that our actions should be judged only by their consequences, or that whatever our actions may be the means justifies the ends. Some philosophers even appear to have given up trying to convince us of their theories all together and adopted what seems to be nothing short of a "if you can't convince them then confuse them" approach.

At the end of the day it all appears to clearly demonstrate that the history of philosophy has not been one steady march towards the answers and undeniable truth of life, the universe, and everything. Rather, it's been a journey littered with forks in the road, u-turns, dead-ends, and frankly periods of just wandering around aimlessly with a white stick. However, what our brief sprint through philosophy's history has shown us is that mankind has always, and will always, ask questions about the world around us, our place in that world, and search for some meaning to it all.

Now we've also clearly seen that throughout history those seeking the answers to such questions don't always come up with any clear answers, or if they do those answers will often make no sense to anyone else regardless of whether their IQ is closer to Forrest Gump or Stephen Hawking. But what we can see in that history are the methods and thought processes that many of history's great thinkers have used to come to their conclusions, regardless of how sane, valid, founded in logic, or just created out of pure blind belief they may be. Some of the conclusions may have be a little questionable, but the methods are sound.

I admittedly had started this book with some vaguely honourable intentions around inspiring the reader to consider dipping their own philosophical toe into the world of some of life's bigger (if not necessarily pressing) issues and questions, all driven by a quick rattle through what some presumably at least vaguely intelligent previous soul-searching individuals had come up with before, and all in the hope that it may just spark the reader into a little "naval-gazing" of their own.

Admittedly, I wasn't shooting for the miraculous spontaneous generation of some new Aristotle-like clone or Kant-wannabe, or even necessarily trying to inspire the reader to some crossed-legged gentle chin stroking as they considered some of philosophy's "big" questions for themselves. However, my rather lofty (and on reflection maybe also a touch overly lofty) goals were still around maybe inspiring a little philosophical thought around the reader's own individual life, and around their own individually pressing questions and issues. Philosophy after all should be about asking the questions that are relevant to you (should I cheat on my taxes, blame one of the kids for that big dent in the side of the car, feast on the joys of red meat or become a paid-up tree-hugging vegetarian, or even ignore the fact that I just drove past three homeless people as I pulled away in my overly-expensive shiny new car?), and not just necessarily about the big philosophical "A-list", deep and meaningful, change the way we all think and live type questions.

Now I'm sure the explanations of the thoughts, ideas, and theories of history's great thinkers as detailed in this book may well have many academic philosophers around the world biting down furiously on their pipes and ripping out great clumps of their ample beards all in shear disbelief around its simplistic, possibly misinformed, and maybe even in some cases down-right incorrect content. But academic accuracy (fortunately) was never my intention. However, hopefully there is still some key lessons we can all take away from such a "simplistic" review (no matter how high-level or factually dubious) of yesterday's great thinkers.

Firstly, and probably most importantly, must be that philosophy is as much about listening as it is about thinking, and as such we should acknowledge that as a rule you likely aren't learning too much when it's your mouth that's the primary focus of your brain's attention (a closed mouth gathers no foot). Secondly, we need to realize that just by reading a history of the philosophers and their great (and sometimes not so great) ideas that have gone before does not instantly make you a card-carrying philosopher yourself. Indeed, if the previous chapters have shown anything it is that history's great philosophers are just as human as the rest of us, they are by no means a special breed, like us they can be quite mad (*Diogenes of Sinope*), completely unreadable (*Kant*), misunderstood (*Nietzsche*), or even sometimes all of these at the same time (*George Hegel*).

Having persevered through the preceding pages there is also no expectation that it has all made perfect sense, and certainly there is no expectation that it has provided clarity on all (if any) of philosophies burning questions. Indeed, even such great and noble philosophers as *Lao Tzu* and *Emanuel Kant* admitted that there are some things for which we just have to accept that we (humans) just cannot expect to understand. Useful advice from such great sages, and even that well known twentieth century philosopher (and sometime actor/director), Clint Eastwood, stated it all quite succinctly when, speaking through his Magnum Force alto-ego Harry Callahan, he states that "a man's got to know his limitations".

We should thus also realize that there are still many things that will ultimately remain unfathomable or impenetrable to us, and sometimes there are arguments we just have to accept we can just never win. A wise man once said that there are two theories to arguing with women and neither of them work, and so it can be in philosophy as we argue against dogma and entrenched cultural difference, and the fact that at the moment, even the bods with watermelon-sized brains still just don't know enough about the universe and its mysteries to even come close to an understanding of it all. In the end though you should always remember that you and your ideas are wholly unique and just as valid as everyone else's, including those of *Aristotle, Descartes, Karl Marx,* your next-door neighbor, or your mother-in-law (even though the latter may well disagree).

It's also important to remember that at its very heart philosophy is really quite simple, it's just about asking questions and thinking, that's it, there's nothing more, no complex math to learn, no expensive equipment needed (even that optional pipe accessory I'm told is relatively cheap), no theories to be understood, no fancy qualifications to be first gained, no research grants to be found, and no special fashion, haircut, accent, or look is needed. Philosophy is thus something that even those of us whose IQ barely troubles the intelligence-needle can engage in, it's one of the things that distinguishes us from cats, dogs, amoeba, plankton in the sea, monkeys in the trees, rugby players, fans of bagpipe music, and all the rest of the animal kingdom. The only potential problem comes when those questions just end up creating more questions, which then needs more thinking, leading to more questions, and so on, and so all eventually just leading to a headache as big as the questions being asked.

But applying the techniques and approaches used by some of those who have clearly been quite successful (in most cases) at such questioning and thinking in the past, we can hopefully learn from their experience, apply it to our everyday lives, and so progress our own thinking without the future need for pain-relieving pharmaceuticals.

Understand each of the above points and you may well see that there is something positive that philosophy can offer you in terms of your own personal, working, and (if you're so inclined) spiritual life. You don't need to go out and buy a pipe and comfy chair, you don't need to grow a beard, wander around in open-toed sandals, fill your room with joss-sticks, you don't even need to find a seemingly welcoming tree to go and hug, you just need to apply the same simple principles that philosophers throughout history have applied, namely just question, think, challenge, listen, revise, and repeat.

And so having come to the end of what is admittedly a very brief and distinctly non-academic jaunt through a few thousand years worth of philosophical thought by some great, and some not so great thinkers, one thing seems now to be clear, and it's that for every philosopher (great or otherwise) there will always exist at least one other equal and wholly opposite thinking philosopher, and that even with all their reasoning and theories, at the end of the day both will still very likely be wrong. Philosophy often offers no definitive right or wrong answers, you can still be left feeling like your diagonally parked in a parallel universe, but it does offer ways of thinking and the opinions of others for consideration that will hopefully help you navigate your own way through life.

Nonetheless, we should all take heart, as although we can't all be *Aristotle*, and we may not all look good in a beard (some may not even be able to actually grow one), we can all still think, we can all learn from those thoughts, and at the end of the day that's really what philosophy is all about.

+++++++++++++++++++